BUDGETING

BUDGETING

Technology, Trends, Software Selection, and Implementation

NILS RASMUSSEN

CHRISTOPHER J. EICHORN

JOHN WILEY & SONS. INC.
New York • Chichester • Weinheim • Brisbane • Singapore • Toronto

Library of Congress Cataloging-in-Publication Data:
   Rasmussen, Nils, 1964-
      Budgeting : technology, trends, software selection, and implementation/by Nils Rasmussen, Christopher J. Eichorn.
         p. cm.
      Includes index.
      ISBN 0-471-39207-3 (cloth : alk. paper)
      1. Business planning. 2. Business planning—Data processing. 3. Industrial management. 4. Business enterprises—Finance. 5. Electronic data processing. I. Eichorn, Christopher J. II. Title.
   HD30.28 .R373 2000
   658.15′4—dc21
                                                                    00-039239
Printed in the United States of America.
10 9 8 7 6 5 4 3 2 1

Contents

Appendices

Preface

As the business world becomes increasingly more competitive and global in scope, the organizations that are better able to create future plans that are tightly linked to their corporate visions will move ahead of those that are not. Furthermore, the companies that are constantly assessing and analyzing past and present data and adjusting their future plans accordingly will be the ones that *stay* ahead of competition.

This book focuses on the management and technological aspects of corporate planning. The goal of this book is to provide you with a powerful set of tools that incorporate the most modern and proven budgeting and forecasting techniques and technologies with the trends we foresee for the future.

Accounting as a form of measuring the financial status of a company has been around for thousands of years, but ironically it is only during the last decade that most organizations have started to create professional financial plans. A large number of companies still use very static and unfocused budgets as their "financial roadmap" for the future. This has been a result of limited human resources in the accounting department, limited availability of powerful and user-friendly planning software, and a general lack of managerial focus on financial planning. Recently, however, the importance of planning and budgeting has received a lot of attention from consulting practices, as well as the media and educational institutions, and companies are rapidly upgrading their processes and routines to be able to create better, more detailed, and more frequent financial assessments of the future.

The author hopes to educate and inform the reader about the most frequently used budgeting methods available and how to utilize these in a modern planning process. Interviews with budgeting managers from leading companies in a number of industries give you valuable insight into common practices today. Furthermore, because modern technology will be the backbone of all future financial planning processes, the book goes into detail about budgeting software. It explains which functionality you need, how to select a new software solution, and most importantly, how to successfully implement it in your organization to excel in professional planning in the twenty-first century.

The book consists of five parts:

- Budgeting and Forecasting Overview
- Budgeting Software: Technology Trends and Functionality
- Software Evaluation and Selection
- Software Implementation
- Interviews

Part One: Budgeting and Forecasting Overview, introduces you to modern corporate budgeting and forecasting. You will read about the trends that today's financial managers need to be aware of in order to streamline their companies' planning processes for the future. The following topics are covered:

- Budgeting and forecasting trends
- Budgeting processes and approaches
- Popular budgeting methods
- Benchmarking
- Modern budget reports
- Popular financial ratios

Part Two: Budgeting Software: Technology Trends and Functionality, looks at the current trends in technology that are driving modern budgeting software. Any person planning to buy or build a new budgeting solution for their company needs to know the strengths and weaknesses of popular technologies such as Structured Query Language (SQL)-based systems and Online Analytical Processing (OLAP)-based systems. In addition to covering these technologies, Part Two looks at how the Web is quickly becoming a delivery vehicle and an important platform for most budgeting solutions. Furthermore, this section describes a number of key features found in many popular budgeting software products. We also take a look at important functionality that companies can expect to find in future versions of modern budgeting solutions. Also in Part Two, there is a separate chapter about spreadsheet-based budgeting. Last but not least, you will find a list of all significant budgeting software and vendor information which also contains important information such as product platforms.

Part Three: Software Evaluation and Selection, will help you to successfully evaluate and select the best budgeting software for your company's particular needs. You will find basic selection criteria that should be used by the selection team, as well as guidelines for how to set up a request for proposal (RFP) and how to get the most out of a product demonstration. Part Three also gives you tips on contract negotiations and using a software selection firm. A small but rapidly growing area in budgeting today is the use of application service providers (ASP). This section helps you analyze whether your company should use an ASP rather than attempt to manage a budgeting solution in-house.

Part Four: Software Implementation, discusses how to select the right people to put on the implementation team, with regard to both internal resources and external consultants. This part also covers project planning and gives you an example of a project plan for a budgeting software implementation.

Part Five: Interviews, shows how corporate officers across a number of industries have successfully created internal processes and implemented modern software solutions to help provide their companies with superior planning tools. We asked these experts to reveal some of the secrets behind their success —how they revamped their companies' budgeting processes, challenges they faced, and how they handled them. We also asked the managers what they foresee in the future regarding how they and other companies will prepare to meet the demands of long-term planning and budgeting.

This book also includes several Appendices which provide a number of value-added documents. You can use the documents as examples or templates for your own documentation needs in software selection and implementation, or you can tailor the provided information to your own needs. In particular, it is worth mentioning the comprehensive RFP sample, which lists most of the questions a company would ask a vendor in connection with a budgeting software selection. Utilizing questions from this list to create your own customized RFP can save you a lot of time and money, compared to doing it yourself or hiring a consulting company to write your RFP for you. The documents found in the appendices include:

- Sample non-disclosure agreement
- Request for proposal (RFP)
- Software and vendor list with addresses
- Sample implementation project plan
- Sample license agreement
- Sample support agreement
- Sample consulting agreement
- Dictionary of budgeting terms

In order to save you time and money in your software selection and implementation process, several useful documents from the Appendices are provided on the worldwide Web. Please visit http://wiley.com/rasmussen. The user password is Budgeting. These documents are in Word format and you will be able to download them and adjust them as necessary.

PART ONE

BUDGETING AND FORECASTING OVERVIEW

CHAPTER 1

BUDGETING TODAY: OVERVIEW AND TRENDS

For years, companies have viewed their budgets simply as a mandatory estimate of the upcoming year's revenues and expenses. However, this attitude is quickly changing as the marketplace becomes more competitive and organizations become more dynamic. Successful companies are constantly improving their ability to accurately predict their future operations and their related resource requirements. Not only does this heighten the importance of the budgeting and planning process, but it also changes the traditional roles of spreadsheets, legacy budget systems, and software created in-house.

A study by the Institute of Management and Administration shows how important budgeting and planning is becoming to corporations. (See Figure 1.1.) Controllers of large and small companies were asked to identify their most critical job functions, and nearly 59% rated budgeting as their key job function.

The same study showed that the budgeting process now involves more activities and individuals throughout the entire organization. In other words, the days where a few people at corporate headquarters created the budget in isolation are quickly disappearing: Budgeting has become an organizationwide activity. When asked how their role as controllers had expanded, the respondents ranked budgeting/control and strategic planning as the two leading activities. This further supports the notion that there is a strong trend toward a more complex budgeting and planning function.

	Number of employees		
	Combined	Less than 250	More than 250
Annual planning and budgeting	58.6%	56.6%	63.3%
Balance sheet management	52.2%	57.8%	48.0%
Monitoring spending	45.2%	50.6%	37.8%
Performance measurement	36.6%	32.5%	40.8%
Internal control	30.6%	26.5%	33.7%
Closing procedures	29.0%	30.1%	28.6%
Long range financial planning	29.0%	28.9%	28.6%
Other	8.1%	6.0%	10.2%

The Controllers Report #1, 1998, The Institute of Management and Administration

FIGURE 1.1   Critical job functions for controllers

Reprinted by permission. © 1998, Tim Harris, Editor, IOMA's Controller's Report. (212) 244-0360. http://www.ioma.com/.

RE-ENGINEERING THE BUDGETING AND FORECASTING PROCESS

Undoubtedly the expectations from corporate strategic planning have increased as a result of the changing competitive landscape and the availability of new technology. But even though companies are now spending more time than ever creating more detailed and more frequent budgets and forecasts, we are still in the early stages of advanced corporate planning. Most companies are still not happy with the planning processes they have in place and the results they see. Some often cited complaints and concerns are:

- Lack of employee motivation and initiative during the planning process
- Lack of clearly defined strategies to drive planning and forecasting efforts
- Minimal correlation between corporate strategy and operational plans
- Politics, rather than strategy, influencing the planning process

There is little doubt that every company has room for improvement. However, the improvements must start within the organizations themselves, with a re-engineering of the planning process. Unless the organizational issues are addressed, the planning and budgeting process will not be as effective nor as useful as it needs to be.

A great misconception is that new technology will take care of the current problems. Resolving problems with old, inflexible legacy budgeting software or out-of-control spreadsheet models often becomes management's focal point, rather than changing the company's planning process. As a result, a large number of companies go out and purchase one of the many new budgeting and planning software packages, thinking that it will completely solve their current challenges. However, in most cases, the problem is that although the new software usually replaces the old system and offers additional features and automation, the underlying organizational problems still remain. Thus the potential benefits to the company are smaller than if the whole planning process were revamped.

According to leading management consultants, certain key issues should be addressed in order to streamline the planning process:

- The amount of planning data should be limited.
- The type of planning data produced should be standardized.
- Data should be shared across the organization, in real time.
- Employee compensation should be tied to strategic plans.

Modern budgeting and forecasting software can help automate and improve many of these items, but the underlying weaknesses are usually not software related; they are organizational issues that must be addressed by top management. To fully realize the benefits of the software, all aspects of the budgeting process must be examined. When new software is implemented, maximum gains can be realized if everyone takes this as an opportunity to improve the entire budget cycle, not just the software used in the cycle. As an example, the inputs required, the flow of information, and the people involved should all be reviewed and questioned. (See Figure 1.2.)

Many resources, such as people within your organization, trade and professional organizations, and outside consultants are available to help re-engineer these processes.

As companies continue to redefine their budgeting and forecasting processes, several key trends have begun to emerge:

- Tighter integration of corporate strategy with budgeting
- Added detail in strategically important areas (such as revenue)
- More complex models
- Improved accuracy of budgets and forecasts
- Integration of available resources and tools
- More frequent revisions (re-forecasts and rolling forecasts)
- Increased employee participation and departmental involvement
- Streamlined budget reviews and approvals

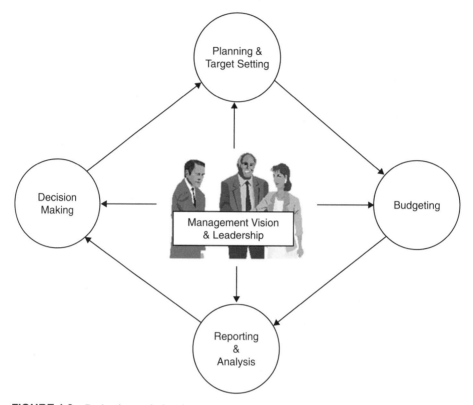

FIGURE 1.2   Budgeting and planning process

TIGHTER INTEGRATION OF CORPORATE STRATEGY WITH BUDGETING

Companies want to tie their budgets to their corporate strategy to make sure that the projected resource requirements are available to support the anticipated future of the company. In order to be profitable, a company cannot afford to have any shortfall between its anticipated revenues and expenses and its plans for the future. Furthermore, these future plans need to be effectively communicated so that all employees involved in the planning process know and understand the activities that will ultimately lead to better operating results.

In essence, what this means for the budgeting process is that headquarters must learn how to share strategy with the rest of the organization. For example, suppose a company has developed an operating plan to increase revenues by 10% and to decrease specific operating expenses by 5% over the next 24 months. After these targets have been set at the top level of the organization, they must be communicated effectively to all people affected by these targets. This information is vital so that managers can create budgets that reflect the corporate strategy.

Historically, linking corporate strategy with the budget process has not been successful in most companies. This is due partly to corporate structure and partly to the technology used within the corporation. Without efficient inter-departmental communication and technology, it is difficult to link the two. Using effective budgeting software can help close the gap between strategy and the budget. Implementing a budgeting software package where corporate targets are visible to the end user and all key budget figures are measured against specific targets at the point of data entry is one solution.

This break between strategy and budgeting may also be due to a general lack of focus on the budgeting process itself. Creating the local operating budget was often viewed as a completely separate activity from long-range planning. Today, however, it is becoming increasingly apparent that the two must overlap. Long-range budgets created at headquarters that do not agree with the current operating budgets used at the local level are completely useless. All plans and future projections at all levels of the organization must be geared toward the same goals and results.

ADDED DETAIL IN STRATEGICALLY IMPORTANT AREAS

As budgeting increases its importance to companies and accounting and budgeting tools become more integrated with increased functionality (including reporting capabilities), more, rather than less, detail has become the norm. However, the additional detail is manifested in the areas that drive the bulk of the business revenue and expenses. The resulting measurements are often referred to as key performance indicators (KPIs). Several reporting methodologies or performance measurement methods have been developed to assist companies in focusing on their key business drivers in both their planning processes and in their ongoing reporting. Some of the more recognizable ones are the balanced scorecard and activity-based budgeting. You can read more about these in Chapter 4.

Regardless of their reporting methods and level of detail, most companies today budget for all their profit and loss accounts, sometimes with a different level of detail for different financial items, and for key statistical items such as headcount or sales volume. Newer budgeting systems also allow for line item detail with text comments even at the most detailed level (many line managers do their line item detail calculations in a local spreadsheet). This simply means, for example, that an account such as 5670-Travel could be opened in a screen where the user can enter as many subentries as needed in order to come up with the total for the account. The strategic implications of this can be very important.

It is now possible for top management to focus on important business drivers and then drill down to the line item detail for any item. As a result, they can spend more of their time analyzing and taking action on the items that represent the most problems or opportunities (such as salary expense or revenue), and less time on items that are fairly static from year to year (such as rent).

Multi-dimensional Budgeting

In order to produce measurements for the key business drivers discussed above, companies now have to integrate multi-dimensional data from many of their business applications (such as the sales order entry system or human resource system) with their budgeting application. Bill Gates, former CEO of Microsoft Corporation, says "anyone who has participated in a budget review with the executive committee at Microsoft knows that we insist on having accurate numbers and insightful analysis of those numbers. Numbers give you the factual basis for the directions in which you take your products."[1] This means that with better integration between core accounting modules and with more focus on key performance indicators, line managers, as they sit down and attempt to enter their best vision of the future, will have access to much more historical transaction detail for these key items than ever before. (See Figure 1.3.)

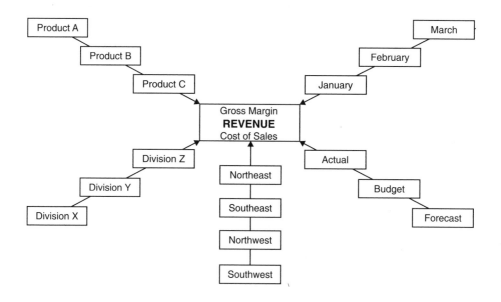

FIGURE 1.3   Information integration

---

[1]Bill Gates, *Business at the Speed of Thought* (New York: Warner Books, 1999), p. 214.

This also gives management a possibility to compare actual figures with budgets in the key operational areas of the business complete with important details, for example, sales per product per market per customer. Or it can mean that management can look at a profit and loss report for an entire department in one instance, and look at the profitability of all the projects undertaken by that department at the same time.

MORE COMPLEX MODELS

Another important trend in budgeting is the increasing complexity of budgeting and forecasting models. Although there is also a trend toward focusing on fewer budgeting items, those items that are closely examined are split into more detail than ever. New measurements of business performance are constantly being invented, and many of them demand source numbers that have not traditionally been part of the budgeting process, for example, revenue per square foot, customer satisfaction, and so on.

Frequent acquisitions and divestitures also represent challenges. It seems like corporations are getting ever more dynamic as they scramble for market share and positioning in a competitive marketplace. A majority of all organizations today are still using spreadsheets to distribute, collect, consolidate, and report budgets and forecasts. For small, stable companies with few departments and product lines or services, the spreadsheet is one of the best tools ever to support the budgeting process. However, mid-sized and larger companies face many challenges that make their spreadsheet budgeting models rather complex and hard to maintain. Some of these challenges are:

- Multiple acquisitions or divestitures per year

- Many products and services

- Large number of departments, divisions, subsidiaries

- Large number projects

- Large number of front-end systems to interface with the budgeting model

- Budgeting for subsidiaries and/or sales in foreign currencies and high-inflation countries

As companies are discovering the value of accurate, focused and detailed budgets as key strategic tools to their decision making, these business factors listed above represent challenges for their planning models. As a result, businesses now demand better budgeting and forecasting functionality from their software vendors (see Chapter 6 for more detail on budgeting software).

IMPROVED ACCURACY OF BUDGETS AND FORECASTS

If your budgets and forecasts are always far off the actual results for the period, there is an evident danger that:

- Bad decisions will be based on incorrect projections of the future.
- Management will pay less attention to budgets because they do not trust the numbers.
- The organization as a whole will suffer from lack of proper planning.

Poor accuracy of budgets has been and still is a problem for many companies. With the marketplace more competitive than ever, organizations are realizing the necessity of accurate numbers and forecasts.

Some budgets are not accurate because:

- They are derived from poor budgeting tools (e.g., spreadsheets with formula errors).
- Employees are allowed too little time to create good projections.
- Employees lack motivation (e.g., they ignore seasonal trends while budgeting revenues or expenses).
- Employees lack training (e.g., a new line manager might not know the business well enough to create an accurate budget).
- Key employees are not involved in the budget process (e.g., many companies have a very top-down oriented budgeting process where most or all budget figures are created by top management, with little involvement from line managers).

Improving the accuracy of budgets and forecasts will obviously make it easier for management to plan and execute a large number of operating activities in their company. Such activities include sustaining appropriate staffing levels, purchasing raw materials and supplies, maintaining inventory levels, properly adjusting employee incentive plans, and more. Just imagine the advantages over the competition if a company had accurate projections of how much they were going to earn and spend in the next year or two, which in turn would determine what cash flows they could expect, how many people they would need to hire, and in which markets they should focus their energy. Companies are now realizing how beneficial this information can be to them and are attempting to improve the accuracy of their budgets and forecasts by increasing employee involvement, investing in better budgeting tools, and so forth.

INTEGRATION OF AVAILABLE RESOURCES AND TOOLS

Larger and mid-sized companies, in particular, have many integration challenges in the budgeting process. On one side you have the integration of different planning processes that exist in different organizational entities, and on the other side you have the physical integration of different software.

Integration of the organization's planning processes

A natural result of different operational units being involved in different activities (e.g. manufacturing vs. sales) is that they employ unique planning processes. (See Figure 1.4.) In addition, many corporations are frequently acquiring new companies, with completely different budgeting cultures and processes. However, for top management to come up with a corporate strategy and set specific and intelligent targets for the future, there is a need for good communication both from the top down and from the bottom up. Thus, with the surge in interest in budgeting and planning, companies should be spending more time on improving their internal communication processes and streamlining their different planning processes and the integration between them.

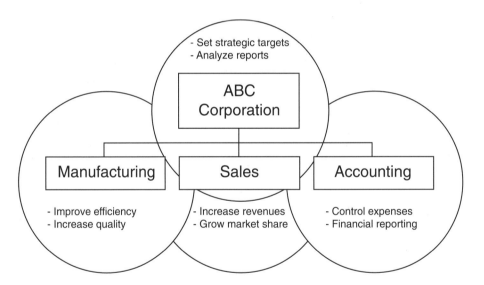

FIGURE 1.4 Planning integration

Integration of the organization's software

Typically, different planning processes also have meant the existence of local spreadsheet models that feed into a higher-level corporate budget model, or that companies have programmed their own budgeting software to handle their different divisions' planning. (See Figure 1.5.) Needless to say, this often results in delayed reporting, poor integration possibilities, double data entry, and lack of integrity in the overall budget.

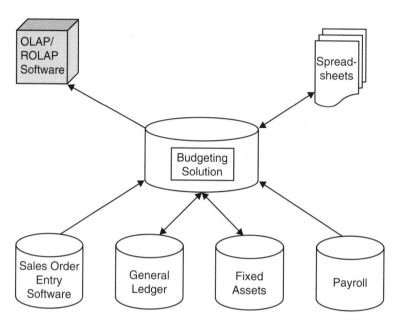

FIGURE 1. 5   Software integration

MORE FREQUENT REVISIONS

Nowadays, companies typically create an annual budget, and then revise this several times during the year (these revisions usually are called forecasts). Recently, a number of companies have dropped their extensive, annual budgeting process and instead have begun to rely on continuous forecasts, called rolling forecasts. Many companies prepare these forecasts on a quarterly basis, and they project for 12 to 24 months ahead.

Companies also distinguish between a short-term plan and a long-term plan. Due to a lack of reliable information and changing circumstances, the latter is always at a high level, and often it is completed solely by top management. The recent trend for short-term plans has been to revise them more frequently than the once-a-year budgeting ritual that was once the standard. Monthly or even bi-monthly revisions are becoming normal.

Also, it is important to distinguish between companies who simply revise their original budget until they reach the end of the year, and those that use the continuous rolling forecast discussed previously. The second is no doubt the best management tool, because it gives a continuously updated picture of a specific time in the future, which management can utilize in their decision making. However, because the planning becomes a monthly process, the people involved must be disciplined and the technology used should automate and simplify the data entry and reporting processes.

INCREASED EMPLOYEE PARTICIPATION AND DEPARTMENTAL INVOLVEMENT

Companies that have maintained a central budgeting process, essentially handled by the budgeting manager, usually have managed to avoid the many pains and delays that come with involving the whole organization in the planning process. However, these companies also have found that it can be hard to motivate employees to reduce expenses, increase revenues, and so on, when they have not had a say in allocating funds in the first place.

Another major disadvantage of a centralized budgeting process is that a tremendous amount of knowledge is hidden in the "trenches" of a company. Line managers know the day-to-day facts of their operational area, and most likely, they are the best people in the company to supply good budget numbers. For example, a sales manager is much closer to the action in the field than the corporate budget manager, and if there are some unexpected deals or trends on the horizon, these are not likely to be reflected in the budget or forecast unless the sales manager is involved.

Because of new technology, it is now easier than ever to involve employees at all levels in the budgeting process. Using modern web-enabled budgeting applications, you can easily communicate corporate strategy and financial targets to employees, and they can enter local budget figures with text comments that roll up to a corporate total. The employees only need access to a workstation that is linked to the Internet or Intranet and that has a web-browser such as Microsoft's Internet Explorer or Netscape (this is free software). (See Figure 1.6.)

The whole budgeting application and database resides on one central server, and there is no need to install or maintain the software in other places. Further on, a high level of security and simple budget screens allow a large number of employees at different levels in the organization to contribute their estimates with minimal need for training and supervision.

With the use of web technology it is also possible to involve people not directly connected to your organization, such as a reseller channel, in the budgeting process. With very simple instructions, they can log on to your web site with a password and provide you with their estimated sales for a specific future period. Because all the numbers go directly to a central server, they are available immediately for analysis by top management.

The ultimate goal for many companies that involve their whole organization in the planning process is to use their employees' knowledge to boost corporate performance. This will happen through improved accuracy of the

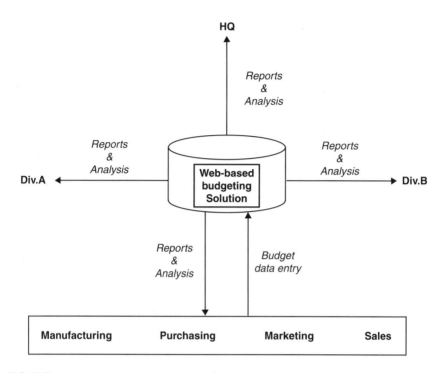

FIGURE 1.6   Web-based budgeting

company's numbers, increased employee understanding of why the budget figures are what they are, and by increasing each employee's motivation to
achieve those numbers.

STREAMLINED BUDGET REVIEWS AND APPROVALS

Who does not want to streamline their budgeting process? When can you sit
down and say that your budgeting process has reached an optimum level?
Probably not for a while, because modern budgeting and forecasting are still
being discovered, learned, and implemented in most organizations. That is why
budget managers everywhere say that one of their primary goals is to streamline their company's budgeting process.

There are many things to improve before the whole planning cycle is
fast, frequent, accurate, and smooth. Improvements are needed both on the
technology side and the human side:

- Existing operational data, competitive information, and economic data
  must be available to top management in an understandable format, so
  they can set realistic strategic targets for the organization.

- Strategies and strategic targets must be developed by senior management and told to managers so that they can create budgets that realistically support the corporate strategy (Figure 1.7(a)) rather than just having managers create budgets without any guidance (Figure 1.7(b)).

- The budgeting software must be flexible enough to support all key budgeting initiatives, such as communicating strategies and strategic targets down through the organization, as well as giving line managers local power to create their budgets and send them back again with supporting schedules and comments. It must also be able to give management consolidated and detailed reports as well as exception reports.

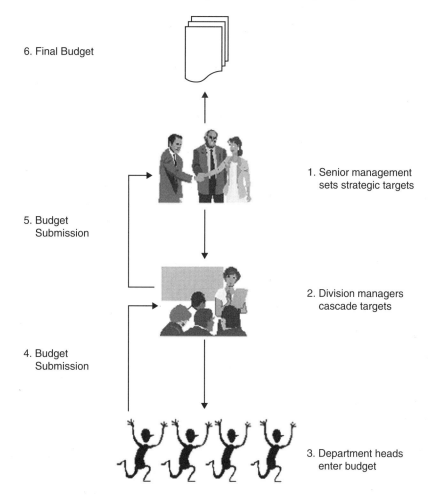

6. Final Budget

1. Senior management
   sets strategic targets

5. Budget
   Submission

2. Division managers
   cascade targets

4. Budget
   Submission

3. Department heads
   enter budget

FIGURE 1. 7A   Top-down bottom-up budgeting

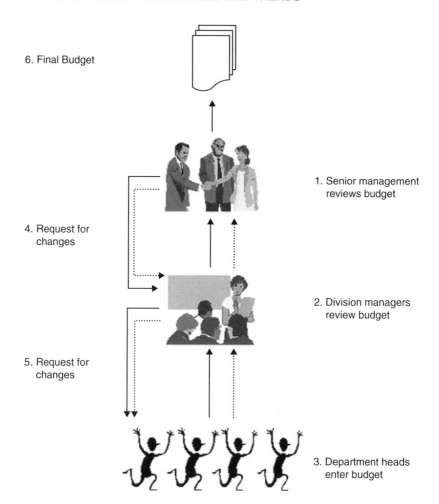

6. Final Budget

1. Senior management
   reviews budget

4. Request for
   changes

2. Division managers
   review budget

5. Request for
   changes

3. Department heads
   enter budget

FIGURE 1. 7B   Bottom-up budgeting process

- A full budgeting cycle should take a few weeks (not months!) to complete. Periodical revisions to a budget (forecasts) should take only a few
  days.

  Streamlining the budgeting process requires all the trends discussed in
  this chapter, and it can dramatically improve your company's long-term performance and competitiveness. A frequently updated budget that is the result of
  the collective knowledge and intelligence in your organization, and that utilizes modern technology and software to automate the reporting process
  should be your company's ultimate goal.

CHAPTER 2

BUDGETING PROCESSES AND APPROACHES

The budget is a formal statement of a company's expectations regarding sales, expenses, volume, and other relevant financial and statistical items for a future period of time. Historically, a comprehensive budget has typically been a statement covering a 12-month period. It is becoming normal to revise a budget during the year, and also to budget continuously (every month or quarter for the next 12 to 18 months). In addition, most companies operate with a high level, long-range plan that covers the next three to five years.

BASICS OF THE BUDGETING PROCESS

A budget generally consists of a pro forma income statement, pro forma balance sheet, and a cash flow statement. In addition, there are statistical reports covering projected head count, and so forth, as well as a number of underlying schedules with the details and assumptions necessary to calculate and document the financial statements. The budget has a life cycle with two major uses for management: a planning device and a control device.

Planning Device

After the budget is completed, but before the budget year itself has started, the budget serves as a planning tool for decisions that need to be made in order to take action today. For example, if the budgeted revenue in the first month of next year is a substantial increase from what it has been, marketing expenses may have to be substantially increased several months before the budget year in order to reach those numbers. The budget should tell you this so you can take action at the right time.

One of the most helpful features of modern budgeting software is to ease the work in preparing what-if scenarios and to help management quickly analyze multiple budget scenarios, before deciding upon a final budget. Multiple scenarios are also helpful to companies operating with so-called flexible budgets (geared toward a range of activities rather than a single activity level), where different budgets can be applied during the year based on the achieved activity levels of the company.

Control Device

Once the year budgeted has begun, the most important function of the budget is to serve as a control device. Actual results can be compared to budget amounts which allow management to quickly assess whether actual results are in line with expectations. If they are not, reasons for the variances can be investigated and corrective actions can be taken. Typical control devices are different versions of management reports which compare actual figures to budget figures, displaying the variances from budget in dollar amounts and/or percentages.

FORECASTING: HOW TO DERIVE THE BUDGET FIGURES

In order to create a good budget, you have to make certain predictions about the future. This is the hardest and often the most ignored activity in the budgeting process. Few people like to be held liable for their views of the future, particularly when there is a chance that they may be substantially wrong. Often this leads to budgets that are made to minimize personal risks, rather than budgets that are the best possible prediction of the future, and thus, the best possible planning tool for corporate decision-makers.

There are a number of forecasting techniques available, and they can be placed in two major categories: qualitative and quantitative.

Quantitative Analysis

This is the statistical approach to prediction of the future, and it typically involves different types of mathematical models such as regression analysis and time series analysis. This is a great forecasting tool if there are no major unexpected changes in the environment (such as an unexpected slump in the economy that leads to reduced sales). It derives forecast figures from historical data, and is unbiased by human opinion. The main disadvantage is that historical data is used to predict future results.

Qualitative Analysis

This is the subjective approach to predicting the future. Based on human judgment, you estimate future financial and statistical figures. The obvious advantage of this model is that you can incorporate future events such as the market entry of a major competitor, or other events that you believe will happen. The qualitative approach works best in business environments that are unpredictable and changing rapidly. Qualitative opinions are typically gathered from expert opinions, consumer surveys, and sales force polling.

Typically, a company's budget will be derived from a combination of quantitative and qualitative analyses. For example, the revenue figures might come from a combination of management targets and sales force opinions, while cost of sales and other items that directly relate to sales are calculated using various mathematical formulas.

BUDGETING PROCESSES

The specific methods employed by companies to create their budgets are extremely varied. However, the process used to create the budget generally falls into one of three major approaches:

1. Top-down
2. Bottom-up
3. Bottom-up/Top-down

Each approach has its advantages and disadvantages. What follows is a discussion of each process in more depth which should enable you to identify when the use of each process is most beneficial.

Top-Down

The top-down approach of budgeting means that upper management at the headquarters level completes the budgeting process with minimal involvement from the management of the individual operating units or departments. The levels beneath headquarters receive the budget amounts "from the top" and they are expected to adhere to these given amounts. Individual operating units have very little, if any, input into the determination of the budget amounts.

This approach usually has two variations, the first of which involves upper management completing and then distributing the entire budget. The lower levels in the organization receive a completed budget and have little or no input into the individual amounts and balances. The second variation, which is more common, involves upper management determining what the total budget should be for each department or operating unit and then distributing these targets or bogeys, leaving it up to middle management to create a budget that matches those targets. The underlying message of this approach can be perceived as "Here's the budget. Meet these numbers."

Advantages and disadvantages of the top-down approach

As with all methods, this approach has several advantages and disadvantages. First the advantages:

Administration   By completing the majority of the budget at a central level; the hassles associated with sending budgets back and forth are greatly reduced. Additionally, the troubles associated with consolidating budgets from various operating units and departments are eliminated. Redundant data entry can also be quickly identified and eliminated. Furthermore, involving fewer people reduces the amount of time required to complete the budget.

Incorporation of overall strategic goals   Creating the budget at a central level allows management to incorporate their overall strategic plans into the budget. For example, if management plans to restructure the company, or eliminate or consolidate certain operations, this can be reflected in the budget. If the budget were created at a lower level, these activities might not be known and therefore, not included. Management can assure that any corporate-wide initiatives are reflected in the budget.

Inclusion of corporate inter-dependencies   Budgets are not created in a vacuum. The effects of one department's activities upon another's are often hard to see or predict from the middle management level. However, at a corporate level, these relationships may be easier to recognize. If upper management is creating the budget, the relationships among the departments and operating units should be reflected in the budget. For example, if a new product is to be introduced, and the advertising department is not aware of this, the advertising department's budget will likely be understated unless an effective communication protocol for the budget process is established.

An event such as a new product introduction can have ramifications for the entire organization. In addition to increased advertising, a new product introduction will possibly require additional employees. Once again, if inter-company communication is not effective, or if the event is to be kept secret, the human resources department may be unaware of the event and fail to budget accordingly. Conversely, "double budgeting" may occur when individual departments or business units budget costs that are being budgeted by other departments. Creating a budget from a central location and then distributing the amounts eliminates this scenario.

And now, the disadvantages:

Employee motivation   By omitting lower and middle management from the budgeting process, it may be harder for everyone in the organization to embrace the budget and to actually strive to meet the targeted amounts. If employees begin to feel that their input is not valued and that they cannot contribute, employee motivation may become a problem. The success of any corporate-wide initiative depends upon the buy-in of all employees, especially at the middle-management level. At the extreme, if middle management feels that they have no control over the budget, they may begin to manipulate the actual results just to meet the budget, or they may completely ignore the budget.

Unable to access information at the source   Often lower and middle management have access to information that otherwise may be unobtainable by higher levels of management. By eliminating input from those closest to the actual operations, the opportunity to draw upon their knowledge and expertise is missed. Since these workers are often the ones that best know the key cost and revenue drivers, the most reliable and accurate information may not be included in the budget, causing the budget to be less accurate than it could be.

When should this method be used?

Taking into account the advantages and disadvantages of the top-down approach, when is the best time to use this method? A top-down approach is useful in very centralized organizations, in organizations having very homogeneous operations, or in small operations where there is little distinguishable difference between headquarters and the operating units. Additionally, this method should be used when middle management lacks the knowledge or expertise to develop a meaningful budget.

One aspect to look at is the variety and type of operations within an organization. Generally, to best utilize this method, local operations should be homogeneous, and it should be easy to factor in the variables for the individual locations, for example, amount of revenue, seasonality, etc. The local operations should exist as an extension of headquarters rather than as separate autonomous entities. Operating decisions should not be made at this level and management will probably not be privy to information that upper management is not aware of or that would greatly affect the budget amounts or process.

Furthermore, if management has all the information necessary to create an accurate budget, it may be just as efficient to develop the budget at a central level rather than create the budget at a lower level. Additionally, when time is a concern, the top-down approach is usually the most efficient method because fewer people are involved in the process. (However, remember that this can be considered a drawback—this lack of employee involvement can result in lack of support for and adherence to the budget.)

Finally, this method is also appropriate when the corporate infrastructure or budgeting software is not advanced enough to handle the collection and consolidation of budgets from multiple operating units or divisions. If headquarters is unable to effectively consolidate all the budgets from the business units into a corporate-wide budget, then a central top-down approach is favorable. Spending time reentering amounts and reworking budgets wastes valuable time that could better be spent modeling future outcomes. Furthermore, if resource restrictions prevent an adequate control and review process of individual budgets, then this method would be best.

To sum up, use the top-down approach when:

- middle management is new and does not know the operations well.

- middle management is not privy to all the anticipated changes and developments that will occur within the company.

- the company is very small and middle management has little additional information to contribute to the budgeting process.

- communication among departments is poor.

- lower and middle management do not have time to create a budget.

- the company does not possess the tools that would allow easy consolidation and review of budgets from multiple business units.

Bottom-Up

A bottom-up budget approach is, as its name implies, just the opposite of the top-down approach: the budget is established at the bottom levels of the organization—at the operating unit, departmental or cost/profit center level—and then brought up to the corporate level. When a company uses this approach, corporate management is primarily responsible for coordinating the budget process and approving the final budget. Guidelines and targets are set at the corporate level, but specific amounts and budgeted account balances are not passed down to the individual departments. Rather, these entities are given the freedom to create their own budgets at a local level. The size and management structure of the lower levels often determines the amount of autonomy allowed by headquarters.

This method can also be thought of as pushing the top-down approach down to the local level. Someone still has to develop initial targets and ensure that these targets are met. Although the individual departments have the ability to create their own budgets, they must still adhere to the parameters—these restrictions just happen to come from local management rather than corporate management.

Even though more of the budgeting is done at the local operating level, this approach requires strong centralized management. To create an effective, meaningful budget, management must clearly communicate corporate strategies, goals, and targets to everyone involved in the budget process. Upper management must explicitly identify who or what each department is budgeting—new employees, computer equipment, travel, and so on.

Additionally, the budget responsibility given to the lower levels has to be in line with what they have control over. Once the budgets are received at headquarters, they need to be reviewed and consolidated into one final budget. The process should be standardized as much as possible to minimize the amount of time spent consolidating the individual budgets.

Advantages and disadvantages of the bottom-up approach

As might be expected, many of the advantages of the bottom-up approach parallel the disadvantages of the top-down approach. Some of these advantages include:

Employee involvement and motivation   Including lower and middle managers in the budgeting process can enhance employee motivation by making these workers feel like they are an essential part of the organization. They are more likely to put serious thought into the process since they are not being told what to do, but instead, they are saying what they can accomplish for the year. Employees are more likely to achieve their goals when they are responsible for developing those goals. Furthermore, involving employees at the business unit or departmental level allows them to incorporate what they know about local operations and conditions into the budget—information that may not be available elsewhere. Involving lower and middle management helps dispel any beliefs or perceptions that the budget is created in a vacuum without any input from those that are affected by it.

Encourages communication among and within the various units/departments By giving the business units the responsibility of completing their own budgets, communication within and among the business units should increase. It is doubtful that one person will be able to develop their entire budget alone. They will need to contact the people that they work with to obtain all the necessary information. Additionally, since the activities of one business unit frequently impact other business units, the managers of these business units will need to communicate and plan together so that accurate budgets can be established.

Increased budget accuracy and more relevant variance analyses   Since the budgets have been developed by those closest to the activities being budgeted, the budgets should be more accurate than if they were designed by someone less involved. Furthermore, after the budgets have been finalized, those at the operational level are the most knowledgeable about the cause of variances from the budget. They should be in a better position to develop an action plan to identify and correct significant budget variances.

Some of the disadvantages of bottom-up budgeting are:

Time-consuming   One of the main disadvantages of involving more people is that the process becomes more time-consuming than if a few individuals had completed the budget. Therefore, whoever is in charge of the budget process needs to be able to effectively manage people and time. When the bottom-up approach is used, the budget schedule has to include time for review and approval by people at multiple levels in the organization. Naturally, the more people involved, the more time that will be needed.

Another time-intensive factor is the collection and consolidation of all the budgets. Depending upon the software used and the number of people involved, the amount of time required can vary considerably. For example, if a distributed spreadsheet model is used, controls must be put in place so that no changes can be made to the model. Otherwise, consolidating the individual budgets may become extremely difficult. Additionally, someone has to monitor the completion and submission of the individual budgets so that the final budget can be completed by the deadline. All efforts must be supervised so that the budgets are created using a common format and so that they can be consolidated and completed on time.

Inaccurate data   If a bottom-up approach is used, management at the local level must be capable of preparing a budget. Just because they are closest to the operations does not mean that they are uniquely qualified to complete the budget. If the budgeters are not aware of all relevant factors affecting the budget, if they do not have the resources to complete the budget, or if they have not been properly trained, the submitted budget will most likely be inaccurate and ineffective as a management tool.

When involving employees throughout the organization, corporate culture always plays a role. If lower managers are accustomed to routinely having their budgets slashed or if budgets are used to assess performance, it is possible that the managers will request more money than is actually needed or will set goals that are not very difficult to achieve. Top management needs to be able to verify that the budgets are a true reflection of what local management expects to happen. If the culture of the company is such that over- or underestimating budgets is standard procedure, then the budgets will likely lack accuracy and usefulness.

Weak communication among departments or business units will also lead to inaccurate budgets. When managers and employees do not communicate well during the budget process, the possibility that data has been omitted or double-counted increases substantially. Corporate management needs to make sure that explicit instructions are communicated clearly to all the parties involved in the budget process.

When should this method be used?

Taking these advantages and disadvantages into consideration, when should a bottom-up approach be used? The answer is, when local management is the most knowledgeable and most capable group that can create an accurate budget. Additionally, a bottom-up approach should be taken to help integrate lower levels of management with top management. Involving lower and middle managers in the budget process, and showing them that their input is valuable, is one way of creating a more cohesive and participatory corporate environment.

Also, when top management lacks the resources or knowledge of all operations, such as in a large conglomerate or a corporation having diverse operations or many divisions and departments, it is unlikely that these executives will possess the knowledge to develop accurate operating budgets for the entire company. In this case, lower management will probably be able to create a better budget than headquarters.

Furthermore, the bottom-up approach should be used when management has a high level of confidence and trust in lower management. The upper echelons will have to spend little time reviewing the accuracy and plausibility of the submitted amounts when they believe that lower management is capable of producing effective budgets. Another indicator for using the bottom-up approach is when communication among and within departments is strong. Everyone needs to know what they are responsible for budgeting. This is easier to coordinate when everyone communicates effectively.

The bottom-up approach is also useful when the budget infrastructure supports consolidating information from multiple sources. This is generally found in organizations that use software developed for multi-site entry, such as a web-based solution or a central database. If an organization does not have the proper software and budget process tools and tries this approach, extensive amounts of time will be wasted re-keying and verifying the accuracy of submitted amounts.

To recap, this approach is most effective when:

- lower management has the most knowledge about local operations.
- lower management can produce relevant and accurate budgets.
- corporate infrastructure supports communication among and within business units.
- departments are unlikely to have redundant or omitted data.
- budget inputs from multiple sources can be easily consolidated.

Top-Down/Bottom-Up: A Winning Combination

As illustrated, both the top-down and bottom-up approaches have their merits. The former approach may be too centralized whereas the latter may not be centralized enough. For most organizations, therefore, some type of hybrid approach makes the most sense.

A top-down/bottom-up approach combines and balances the best of the two approaches. This approach allows input from lower and upper management into the model. The budget process becomes a collaboration between lower and top management rather than a one-way exercise. In the combined approach, lower management submits the budget to upper management and then upper management modifies the submitted budget to reflect the operational knowledge that they have. This approach is almost always better than either an exclusive top-down or bottom-up approach.

One of the main challenges when using this approach is to determine everyone's role: too much direction from upper management, and the budget process may seem like it is dictated from above; too little direction, and the whole process may fall apart. Factors such as employee motivation, acceptance, control, and administration of the budget process must be considered for the budget process to be beneficial to all involved parties.

When deciding upon the level of authority and autonomy to assign each operating unit during the budget process, take into consideration:

- Who has profit and loss responsibility?
- Who can best influence operations to make sure that the budget is met?
- Who can best determine the causes of significant budget variances?
- Are there items that will affect the final budget that the local operations should not be aware of?
- Is local management sophisticated enough to create a meaningful budget that can be used as an operating plan?
- Does local management add any information that is not available at the corporate level?
- How independent are the local units?
- How centralized/de-centralized is the organization? Should this be changed?
- At what levels will the budget be reviewed?
- How much detail should be included in the budget?

SELECTING A BUDGETING APPROACH

A company's choice of budgeting approach is extremely important as it directly influences the success of the budget process. The entire budget cycle must be considered when selecting an approach: setting and communicating corporate budgetary guidelines, incorporating corporate strategy, distributing and collecting the budgets, and finally, consolidating and reviewing them. Also, the approach taken is dependent upon the length of the budget cycle, so the amount of time available for the budget cycle must be considered.

The preferred approach should also be dependent on the structure of the organization, the complexity of the desired budget, and the administrator's ability to handle the process. Regardless of the method, if the administrator is unable to manage it, completing an accurate budget on time will be very difficult. Available tools must also be considered. If the administrator can manage the process, but the software does not allow for a distributed budget model, the process will be dictated by the tools available to the administrator.

Generally, a hybrid top-down/bottom-up approach is the best method to use. However, as discussed in this chapter, many variables must be weighed when making that decision. The ramifications of each approach must be thoroughly considered. For example, although a top-down approach may be the fastest way to complete the budget, a negative message may be sent to middle and lower management, which in turn may affect other processes in the organization. Problems can be avoided by knowing your organization. Proper planning and analysis of the budget cycle will direct you toward the type of budget process that will be most beneficial to your company.

CHAPTER 3

BUDGETING METHODS

In order to determine future plans for the company, management must utilize a number of different budgeting methods and planning tools. Some are more popular than others. Several of the most common budgeting methods are:

- Prior year approach
- Zero-based budgeting
- Percentage of sales
- Rolling forecasts
- Balanced scorecard
- Benchmarking
- Activity-based budgeting

In this chapter, we will take a closer look at these methods and focus on those that are becoming most popular.

PRIOR YEAR (INCREMENTAL) APPROACH

When the prior year, or incremental, approach is used, the current year's budget is based on the prior year's actual financial results. The prior year budget amounts may also be used, but these are usually only sought when the actual amounts are not yet known.

Calculating the current budget can be a simple or a complex process. In the simplest case, a set percentage is applied to account categories. For example, if sales are planned to increase by 10% and expenses are expected to increase by 5%, the revenue accounts are increased by 10% from the prior year and expenses are increased by 5%. Although this quickly produces a budget, in all likelihood, the budget produced will not be very accurate. Applying fixed percentages to account classes cannot incorporate all anticipated operational changes from the prior year.

A more complex budget may be created using this method by determining the change from the prior year at the account level. Instead of applying the same percentage increase to all account categories, the anticipated changes in revenues and expenses are analyzed at the account level. For example, payroll expenses may be increased by 10% and marketing expenses may be increased by 15%. Of course, this implies that the person creating the budget is aware of the circumstances that led to the prior year's numbers. Using the prior year's results is an effective starting point, but only if the events that led to those results are known.

Unfortunately, that is the main disadvantage of this method. It is easy to apply a percentage or add an amount to a prior year figure, but if the drivers of that figure are not known, the budget amount will have little significance. If you do not know what a particular expense account is comprised of, how are you to know by how much that account will increase or decrease in the upcoming year? Simply increasing or decreasing the prior year amounts is using the past to predict the future. In order to predict effectively, the budgeter has to know what events were captured in the prior amounts and how those events will change. This is the main reason that the prior year approach is not widely used: it is too easy to apply percentages to bases without really knowing what that base is comprised of. However, for items where the increase from the prior year is easily available (such as rent), it is extremely useful.

Keep in mind that when using this method, percentage or amount changes are applied to either the prior year's budget or actual amounts. This method can be used to quickly create a budget that will provide a rough estimate of the upcoming year's results, though it is unlikely that it can provide the detail required by upper management. For items that remain relatively constant from year to year this method is appropriate, but for those items where a detailed build-up of the amount is required, another method should be used.

ZERO-BASED BUDGETING

Unlike the prior year approach, zero-based budgeting is a planning and budgeting method that requires managers to budget their activities as if the activities had no prior allocations or balances. In other words, the starting point is zero. Obviously, assessing costs this way can require a great deal of time. All costs and expenses involved in running a project or department must be analyzed so that an accurate budget can be produced. The main benefit of this, in an ideal situation, is that the person doing the budgeting will incorporate all known and expected costs into the budget. However, as this is quite labor intensive, what usually happens is that too little time is spent determining the budget. Therefore, the main benefit of this method is often lost.

When an organization decides to use a zero-based approach, it is expected that management will start from scratch and plan for all the activities that they know will occur during the year. For example, travel expenses would be budgeted by determining to which events people will travel, when those events will occur, who will be traveling, and then, finally, the costs of that travel: airfare, car rental, hotel, per diems, and so on. These amounts would then be entered into the budget for the months that they are expected to occur.

Revenue budgets are created using the same methodology. The manager must look at all potential customers, what they will be buying, how much they will be buying, and the sale prices of those items. This information then feeds into the cost of the sales budget. If different people are determining the sales and cost of sales budgets, they must work together since these items are so closely correlated. The budget will serve no purpose if revenues are projected at one level and cost of sales are projected at another level.

When zero-based budgeting is effectively used, it forces management to look at the upcoming operations and all the costs associated with those operations. Starting at zero forces managers to forecast their anticipated resource requirements. However, in doing so, many assumptions must be made. If insufficient time is spent with the assumptions, the budget will reflect this lack of planning. Therefore, if this method is used, everyone must realize that it is crucial to accurately assess future expenditures. If time does not permit this, then another method that requires less time, such as the prior year method, should be used.

PERCENTAGE OF SALES

When the percentage of sales method is used, all, or at least a majority, of the accounts are budgeted based on their relation to sales revenue. Frequently the percentages from a common-sized income statement, where each account shown is a percentage of revenue, are applied to budgeted sales revenue. The common-sized income statement is usually created using the prior year actuals, or if the year is not complete, the year-to-date actuals plus the remaining budget are used.

Since the amounts are driven by the sales revenue amount, the majority of the effort should be spent calculating an accurate sales budget. Once the sales amount is determined, the budget basically completes itself, because the remaining amounts are calculated using the sales amount. This method is often used with accounts that are closely related to sales, such as labor, material, advertising, and commissions.

Percentage of sales is a "quick and dirty" approach to creating a budget, which is the main advantage of this method. A budget can be quickly created using a spreadsheet as long as a common-sized income statement and a sales budget is available. However, it may also be used as a starting point to create a more complex budget. Once the initial amounts have been determined, they can be analyzed and changed to reflect any changes in operations from the prior year.

The main disadvantage of this method is that the calculated budget amounts are usually based on past activity. Time has to be spent analyzing the resulting amounts so that these amounts reflect projected results. If operations and/or activity levels are expected to change significantly, the prior year's percentages quite likely will not be applicable to the upcoming year. Knowledge of the current operating environment and anticipated organizational changes and items, such as anticipated cost-saving measures, need to be factored into the calculated amounts so that a precise budget can be created.

The percentage of sales method is most appropriate when:

- amounts and accounts are closely correlated with sales revenue.

- operations are not complex.

- little time is available to create a budget.

- the staff developing the budget is inexperienced.

Overall, the percentage of sales method is a quick and efficient method to create a rough budget that can be used as a starting point for a more detailed budget.

ROLLING FORECASTS

Rolling forecasts are not a set budget per se, but rather a continuous updating of the budget. Often a 12-month window is used, whereby each month the prior budget amounts are replaced with the actual amounts and budget figures are entered for the new month. Based on the actuals, the amounts in future periods may be updated to take into account information that was not available when the original amounts were budgeted.

Often a rolling forecast will be used in conjunction with a budget and not actually replace the budget. An annual budget may be created and held static, but during the year the original budget will also be updated to reflect the latest results. Any significant variances from the original budget can be highlighted and explained. Continuously updating the original budget allows management to determine how the assumptions used at the beginning of the year have changed.

For companies that are very young or that are in industries experiencing rapid growth, this can be very useful. Actual results often vary significantly from the original budgeted amounts. The original budget is still useful, as long as the assumptions under which the original budget was created are known. Metrics such as expense ratios, headcount, and so on can be compared to the original budget to increase the accuracy of the forecasted amounts.

The main benefit of incorporating rolling forecasts into the budgeting and planning process is that instead of being held to the original budget, management can use actual results to revise the original assumptions and then create a revised budget. The budget process becomes more frequent, but more meaningful. Also, by continuously forecasting 12 months into the future, the basis for the following year's budget is created automatically. When creating the forecasts, a relatively small number of people should be involved and amounts usually should be entered at a higher level than the budget.

By increasing the frequency of projections, everyone should know what is expected of them, the information they must provide, and to whom it should be provided. Also, the results of this process will be more meaningful because only a few periods (instead of an entire year) are being projected.

BALANCED SCORECARD

What Is a Balanced Scorecard?

A balanced scorecard is a tool that businesses can use to link the strategies of different business areas within a corporation, such as finance and customer support, to the overall corporate vision. David Norton and Harvard Business School professor Robert Kaplan introduced the balanced scorecard concept in 1992. They found that the typical financial measures most companies were using to assess performance and make strategic decisions did not provide management with enough information to effectively manage their companies.

Instead of merely generating the usual financial reports, Norton and Kaplan suggested that management focus on the financial and non-financial metrics that really indicate how well their businesses are performing. By looking beyond past financial performance and integrating other performance measures, companies can really concentrate on where their business is going.

Businesses can assess the values of these metrics and then gear their progress toward attaining these goals.

In recent years, the balanced scorecard methodology has become a widely accepted school of thought. A number of well-known management consulting companies offer implementation services, and software vendors are improving their applications to handle balanced scorecard reporting. The Gartner Group estimates that at least 40% of Fortune 1000 companies will have implemented the balanced scorecard by the end of the year 2000. Furthermore, the balanced scorecard concept doesn't just apply to large corporations: many mid-sized and smaller companies are also becoming interested in the methodology.

The idea behind the balanced scorecard is to focus only on that information that is relevant to decision making. By using less, but more relevant, data, the data is more readily accessible, more concise, and more time can be spent analyzing the data rather than collecting it.

It is important not to try to measure every activity of the business. For a balanced scorecard approach to work, the metrics must be limited to measuring only those items that are most important to the organization. If there are too many measures, too much time is spent collecting the data to create the measures, negating the benefits of the scorecard.

Determining what to measure is often the most difficult aspect of this concept. Management must clearly identify the goals of the company so that quantifiable measures can be developed. These measurements should cover not just one, but several functional areas. The most commonly used measurements generally fall into the following categories: financial results, customer satisfaction, process and/or quality related, and growth. An example of a financial metric may be Return on Equity (ROE), whereas a process-related one may be the number of orders delivered on time.

Once the measurements are determined, the company must communicate them to the entire organization. Because these measures are used to assess the achievement of long-term strategic goals, everyone must understand the purpose of these measurements and see how their day-to-day activities can affect these measurements. Often, the overall performance metrics can be broken down into smaller components so that individual performances toward these goals can be measured.

Furthermore, the results of these measurements must be readily accessible. Using technology, such as corporate intranets and the Web, ensures that people can access this data. It is essential that everyone involved be capable of seeing what type of progress they are making. Quick access to this information permits management to see what is working and what is not, allowing them to make any necessary corrections before it is too late to achieve the desired results.

Why Use Balanced Scorecards in the Planning and Budgeting Process?

The way we do business is changing

It used to be simpler to keep track of the performance of a business and create future plans. However, as key business conditions are changing, performance measurements and planning also need to change. The idea of the balanced scorecard is to focus on the financial and statistical metrics that are linked to the strategic goals of the company without spending valuable time and money planning and reporting every possible line item at every level in the business. The balanced scorecard approach also encourages management to include general industry comparisons as well as competitive comparisons in the planning and reporting process. (See Figure 3.1.)

Business Driver	Yesterday	Tomorrow
Competitors	Few/Big	Many/Small
Markets	National	Global
Manufacturing	Mass Production	Flexible
Products	Standardized	Innovative
Service	Standardized	Custom

FIGURE 3.1   Changing business drivers

The balanced scorecard is a better management tool than standard reports

The majority of companies use the general ledger as their primary information source, so as a result, reports to management are often held hostage by the monthly close of the accounting cycle. With the balanced scorecard, because financial as well as non-financial data is captured, the reliance upon the general ledger close decreases significantly. Also, only the relevant key data that is vital to the company's operation is reported, so the scorecard reports are concise and easy to read. Management is able to spend their time analyzing the real drivers of the business without being distracted by non-relevant information.

Maybe one of the most important aspects of the balanced scorecard approach is that it is a tool that is directly linked with the corporate strategy. Whereas most companies today have a budgeting and planning process that is not tightly integrated with their strategic objectives (and thus has much less value as a business management tool), the metrics in the balanced scorecard approach represent the organization's strategic targets and the related tactical plans.

Time and cost savings

On the average, financial budgets contain 230 line items and take 4.5 months to develop.[2] The balanced scorecard approach recommends that a business focus the budget on 40 or fewer line items. By using an 80/20 rule, meaning that the budget is focused on those items that drive 80% of the business, both the time and the cost of the budgeting process can be dramatically improved. Many corporations are not gaining full value from their costly and time-consuming strategic planning exercises because the annual operating plan is disconnected from the strategy. By linking the operating plan with overall corporate strategy, the relevance and effectiveness of the operating plan is increased.

Motivates and involves employees

Another benefit of the balanced scorecard is to link employee compensation to the performance metrics. After the scorecard measures have been established and the results measured, management may find that employee compensation and bonuses can be linked to performance. This increases the focus and effort spent on achieving the targets set forth in the balanced scorecard, and therefore, the achievement of corporate goals.

Potential problems with the balanced scorecard

The balanced scorecard is not without potential problems. First, it is much too easy to try to measure everything. It can be very difficult to identify the key drivers that lead to a company's success. Therefore, too many measures may be selected and the amount of time necessary to capture the data may outweigh the value of that information. Furthermore, if too much emphasis is placed on meeting the scorecard measurements, it can be detrimental to the achievement of the company's long-term goals. Also, if the wrong metrics are chosen, the appropriate actions will not be promoted. It is also important to make sure that non-financial metrics are included in the scorecard; otherwise, there is little difference between using and not using the scorecard approach.

---

[2]Cathy Lazere, "All Together Now," *CFO Magazine,* February 1998. (cfonet.com/html/Articles/CFO/1998/98 FEallt.html).

BENCHMARKING

Benchmarking can be used in the planning process by comparing your actuals not only with your own budgets and forecasts, but also with your key competitors and industry averages. Although benchmarking has been around for years, technology has changed the way in which companies use benchmarking. The amount of information available and the accessibility of that information has increased dramatically primarily as a result of the Internet and a raised awareness of benchmarking.

Companies no longer need to go through a lengthy process to determine to which companies to compare themselves and then to collect data on those companies. Instead, much of the information is now available on-line and can be obtained with little effort. This can speed up the benchmarking process, but there is a caveat: it may also produce fewer benefits than could be achieved from more thorough research.

Mark Czarnecki, president of The Benchmarking Network and author of *Managing by Measuring: How to Improve Your Organization's Performance through Effective Benchmarking*[3], recommends the following 12 steps for effective benchmarking:

1. Develop senior management commitment.

2. Develop a mission statement.

3. Plan.

4. Identify customers.

5. Perform research.

6. Identify partners.

7. Develop measures.

8. Develop and administer questionnaires.

9. Scrub and analyze data.

10. Isolate best practices.

11. Conduct site visits and interviews.

12. Present findings and monitor results.

Information for benchmarking does not always have to come from outside your own company. Those departments or divisions that are the best in the company should also be considered for benchmarking standards.

---

[3]Mark Czamecki, *Managing by Measuring: How to Improve Your Organization's Performance through Effective Benchmarking,* Amacom, 1999, p. 52.

Benchmarking is often used to measure process related items, such as number of defects, days sales outstanding, accounts receivable collections, and so on. It is critical to identify those measures that management believes will improve profitability and then learn as much about the drivers of those measures as possible. Once the appropriate measures have been determined, management can go about finding others against which to measure themselves. The deliverable for this whole process is a set of recommendations for change within the organization.

Due to rising expectations of faster and quicker results, benchmarking teams no longer have the luxury of time. Spending a year gathering data and then suggesting recommendations for change is no longer acceptable. Luckily, there are now many resources to help decrease the amount of time required to gather meaningful data. First, companies should look internally. If other benchmarking projects have already been performed, these prior studies may contain beneficial information. Also, trade associations have access to information that is very useful to a benchmarking project. Furthermore, industry networks, such as the American Productivity and Quality Center in Houston, and private consulting companies are just a few sources that can provide benchmarking information tailored to your company's specific needs.

Identifying the drivers of the processes that you wish to improve can aid the planning process by making everyone aware of company goals. Resources can be appropriately budgeted and allocated for the year once the appropriate measures have been determined.

ACTIVITY-BASED BUDGETING

Activity-based budgeting (ABB) is an innovative approach that can help organizations become more competitive by linking the budgeting process to organizational strategy. According to ABB advocates, part of the problem with the traditional budgeting process is that it pushes and extends spending levels based on existing spending rates rather than working backward from where the mix of products, service-lines, channels, and customers place workloads on the organization's cost structure. Management is using historical information rather than more relevant operating projections to make future decisions. Furthermore, traditional budgeting does not identify or quantify waste, root causes of costs, workload drivers, or value adders.

ABB allocates resources based on activity workloads rather than on individual general ledger line items. Although logical and feasible, correlating budget items to an organization's operations is not without obstacles. Overcoming these hurdles will allow organizations to plan their resource spending defensibly.

Some of the underlying principles of ABB are:

- Forecast workloads rather than basing the budget off of last year's numbers and adding a percentage.

- Recast the budgeted workload costs into budgeted departmental spending needs.

- Replace traditional fixed or variable cost thinking with the more robust flexible and multiple activity-volume budgeting.

- Apply budgeting principles to other cost forecasting decisions, such as outsourcing, trade-off analysis, capital investment justifications, and customer quotations.

- Budget and manage with a business process/financial statement view, not just with a hierarchical organizational view.

- Link the organization's boardroom vision and strategy to the spending resource levels for better alignment and reduction of non-value adding costs.

- Integrate activity-based planning and budgeting with balanced scoreboard leading indicator performance measures.

- Translate strategy into a process and activity framework by performing activities and cross-functional processes that support the strategy and assessing current performance against strategic goals.

ABB focuses on business activities and the cost drivers of those activities. Budgeting the costs of activities rather than just budgeting the cost of individual line items allows companies to more closely align their budgets with their anticipated operations, allowing the annual budget to become more of a strategic planning tool.

CHAPTER 4

POPULAR BUDGETING REPORTS AND RATIOS

Many types of reports may be created and used to assess how well a company, department, or other reporting entity is performing with respect to their budget. Because a budget is created to project the performance of a future event, budget amounts are almost always shown in relation to another number: current year budget amounts compared to current year actual amounts, prior year actual amounts, and prior year budget amounts are just a few of the comparisons that can be made.

POPULAR BUDGET REPORTS

Several variations of budget reports are located at the end of this chapter. These reports are:

- Actual/Budget Comparative Income Statement (Figure 4.1)
- Common-sized Income Statement—Actual and Budget (Figure 4.2)
- Exchange Rate Analysis (Figure 4.3)
- Exception Report (Figure 4.4)
- Balanced Scorecard—KPIs (Figure 4.5)
- Annual Estimate Using YTD Actuals (Figure 4.6)
- 12-Month Budget (Figure 4.7)

- Budget Version Comparison (Figure 4.8)
- Sales Budget by Product and Market (Figure 4.9)
- Quarterly Sales Budget by Product (Figure 4.10)
- Quarterly Gross Margin Budget by Product (Figure 4.11)
- Headcount (Figure 4.12)
- Five-Year Forecast (Figure 4.13)
- Quarterly Projection and Forecasts (Figure 4.14)

POPULAR RATIOS (PERFORMANCE MEASUREMENT)

Stand-alone numbers are meaningless unless they are compared to something. One way of comparing is to put an actual figure next to a budget figure and look at the difference between the two. Another way is to determine the relative difference by dividing one number by the other. The latter is done by using what is referred to as ratios.

Examples of Measures of Operating Performance Using Rates of Return

The following examples are measures of operating performance using rates of return:

Return on assets—calculated by dividing the year's operating income (before interest and taxes) by average total assets employed during the year.

- Sometimes called the "productive ratio."
- Useful for comparing your company to similar companies.
- The formula assists management in gauging the effectiveness of asset utilization.
- Formula: $\dfrac{\text{Operating Income}}{\text{Average Total Assets}}$

Rate of return on common stockholder's equity—calculated by dividing net income (less preferred dividends) by average common stockholder's equity.

- Measures the ultimate profitability of a firm from the standpoint of the common stockholders.
- Formula: $\dfrac{\text{Net Income} - \text{Preferred Dividends}}{\text{Average Common Stockholder's Equity}}$

Return on sales—calculated by dividing net income by net sales.

- This performance index is used solely when studying similar companies or when comparing the company's operations over different periods.
- Formula: $\dfrac{\text{Net Income}}{\text{Net Sales}}$

Analysis of Future Prospects of a Company

Because stock market prices are quoted on a per share basis, it is useful to relate earnings on the same basis. Four customary measures used by financial analysts in evaluating the future prospects of a firm include:

1. Earnings per share—calculated using net income (less preferred dividends) and dividing by the average number of common shares outstanding.
   - Formula: $$\frac{\text{Net Income} - \text{Preferred Dividends}}{\text{Average Number of Common Shares Outstanding}}$$

2. Price-earnings ratio—calculated by dividing the common stock's market price by the common stock's earnings per share.
   - Assuming some knowledge of the company and industry, the price-earnings ratio might indicate whether or not the stock is overvalued.
   - Formula: $$\frac{\text{Common Stock Market Price}}{\text{Earnings Per Share}}$$

3. Dividend yield—calculated by dividing the common dividends per share by the common stock's market price.
   - Dividends are considered a rate of return on investment.
   - Formula: $$\frac{\text{Common Dividends Per Share}}{\text{Common Stock's Market Price}}$$

4. Dividend payout ratio—calculated by dividing common stock dividends per share by the common stock earnings per share (expressed as a percentage).
   - Indicates whether a firm has a liberal or conservative dividend policy.
   - Formula: $$\frac{\text{Dividends Paid on Common Stock}}{\text{Earnings Per Share}}$$

Financial Strength

In assessing the financial strength of a firm, it is helpful to understand the concept of Trading on Equity. This term refers to the use of borrowed funds, particularly long-term debt, in the firm's capital structure. If borrowed funds can generate a higher rate of return than their costs, the Trading on Equity is profitable. The excess return on borrowed funds (over their cost) benefits the common stockholders because it increases their earnings. Use of borrowing to increase earnings is referred to as Leverage. It must be used judiciously because risk is involved and Leverage also can magnify losses. Ratios and Averages used to analyze financial strength include:

1. Equity ratio—calculated by dividing common stockholders' equity by total assets.
   - The equity ratio indicates the extent of the owner's investment in the firm.
   - Formula: $$\frac{\text{Common Stockholder's Equity}}{\text{Total Assets}}$$

2. Debt to Total Asset ratio—calculated by dividing total debt by total assets.

   • The Debt to Total Asset Ratio indicates the extent of a firm's borrowing.

   • Formula: $\dfrac{\text{Total Liabilities}}{\text{Total Assets}}$

3. Debt to Equity ratio—calculated by dividing total debt by stockholders' equity.

   • The debt to equity ratio indicates the relation of the owners' and creditors' position.

   • Formula: $\dfrac{\text{Total Liabilities}}{\text{Total Stockholders' Equity}}$

4. Bond interest coverage—calculated by dividing annual bond interest into operating income.

   • The result is often referred to as "times interest earned." It provides a measure of the protection afforded bondholders.

   • Formula: $\dfrac{\text{Annual Bond Interest Expense}}{\text{Operating Income}}$

5. Preferred dividend coverage—calculated by dividing annual bond interest plus preferred dividend requirement into operating income.

   • Provides indication of the safety to preferred stockholders.

   • Formula: $\dfrac{\text{Annual Bond Interest Expense} \; + \; \text{Preferred Dividends}}{\text{Operating Income}}$

Measuring Liquidity

In evaluating the liquidity of a firm we often refer to its Working Capital position. This can be called the short-term credit analysis. Working Capital is the excess of Current Assets over Current Liabilities. Other liquidity and efficiency ratios include:

1. Current ratio—establishes the relationship between current assets and current liabilities. It measures a firm's ability to meet its current obligations. It is sometimes called the banker's ratio.

   • Formula: $\dfrac{\text{Current Assets}}{\text{Current Liabilities}}$

2. Quick ratio—sometimes analysts calculate the ratio between the liquid (quick) assets and current liabilities. Quick current assets are cash, marketable securities, and receivables.

- It may provide a better reading on a firm's ability to meet current obligations than the current ratio.

- Formula: $\dfrac{\text{Current Assets} - \text{Inventory} - \text{Prepaid Assets}}{\text{Current Liabilities}}$

3. Inventory turnover—calculated by dividing average inventory into cost of goods sold.

   - This allows a measurement of any disproportionate amount of inventory.

   - Formula: $\dfrac{\text{Average Inventory}}{\text{Cost of Goods Sold}}$

4. Average collection period—calculated by dividing the year's sales into trade receivables and multiplying this number by 365.

   - This average collection period tends to measure if the recovery is adequate, slow, or past due.

   - Formula: $\dfrac{\text{Trade Receivables}}{\text{Sales}} \times 365 \text{ Days}$

Income Statement
Company: SPORTY Manufacturing
Currency: USD

	ACTUAL 9906	BUDGET 9906	BUD VAR	ACTUAL 9901 - 9906	BUDGET 9901 - 9906	BUD VAR
Operating Revenue	**$4,233,000**	**$4,622,515**	**($389,515)**	**$26,359,690**	**$27,649,913**	**($1,290,223)**
Cost of Goods Sold	$2,466,950	$2,480,000	$13,050	$13,903,949	$15,146,000	$1,242,051
Wages, Salaries, Social Expenses	$59,697	$173,453	$113,756	$358,180	$1,020,153	$661,972
Other Operating Expenses	$25,300	$46,640	$21,340	$150,318	$288,960	$138,642
Depreciation	$11,800	$10,000	($1,800)	$70,780	$60,000	($10,780)
Total Operating Expenses	**$2,563,747**	**$2,710,092**	**$146,346**	**$14,483,227**	**$16,515,112**	**$2,031,885**
Operating Profit	**$1,669,253**	**$1,912,423**	**($243,169)**	**$11,876,463**	**$11,134,800**	**$741,663**
Interest Income	$10,000	$11,000	($1,000)	$60,000	$75,000	($15,000)
Interest Expense	$6,800	$7,500	$700	$40,800	$45,000	$4,200
Total Financial Items	**$3,200**	**$3,500**	**($300)**	**$19,200**	**$30,000**	**($10,800)**
Inc. Bef. Taxes & Minority Int.	**$1,672,453**	**$1,915,923**	**($243,469)**	**$11,895,663**	**$11,164,800**	**$730,863**
Taxes	$85,000	$84,000	$1,000	$510,000	$518,000	($8,000)
Minority Interests	$7,000	$6,500	$500	$42,000	$39,000	$3,000
Net Income	**$1,594,453**	**$1,838,423**	**($243,969)**	**$11,427,663**	**$10,685,800**	**$741,863**

FIGURE 4.1   Actual/budget comparative income statement

Income Statement Company: SPORTY Manufacturing (US1) Currency: USD				
	ACTUAL 9901	% of Revenue	BUDGET 9901	% of Revenue
Revenue	**$4,295,000**	**100.00 %**	**$4,585,830**	**100.00 %**
Cost of Goods Sold	$2,399,999	55.88 %	$2,561,000	55.85 %
Wages & Salaries	$59,697	1.39 %	$169,265	3.69 %
Other Operating Expenses	$22,418	0.52 %	$67,375	1.47 %
Depreciation	$11,780	0.27 %	$10,000	0.22 %
Total Operating Expenses	**$2,493,894**	**58.07 %**	**$2,807,640**	**61.22 %**
Operating Profit	**$1,801,106**	**41.94 %**	**$1,778,190**	**38.78 %**
Interest Income	$10,000	0.23 %	$12,000	0.26 %
Interest Expenses	$6,800	0.16 %	$7,500	0.16 %
Total Financial Items	**$16,800**	**0.39 %**	**$19,500**	**0.43 %**
Inc. Bef. Taxes & Minority Int.	**$1,784,306**	**41.54 %**	**$1,758,690**	**38.35 %**
Taxes	$85,000	1.98 %	$89,000	1.94 %
Minority Interests	$7,000	0.16 %	$6,500	0.14 %
Net Income	**$1,706,306**	**39.73 %**	**$1,676,190**	**36.55 %**

FIGURE 4.2 Common-sized income statement—actual and budget

INCOME STATEMENT
Company: SPORTY UK Ltd. (UK1)
Currency: USD

	ACTUAL 9901	BUDGET 9901	Variance	BUDGET W/Actual Rate	"REAL" Variance
Operating Revenue	**$9,261,598**	**$9,673,817**	**($412,219)**	**$9,117,116**	**$144,482**
Cost of Goods Sold	$3,752,624	$3,832,324	$79,700	$3,611,785	($140,839)
Wages & Salaries	$348,277	$361,688	$13,411	$340,874	($7,403)
Other Operating Expenses	$65,827	$60,764	($5,063)	$57,267	($8,560)
Depreciation	$19,954	$19,408	($546)	$18,291	($1,663)
Total Operating Expenses	**$4,186,681**	**$4,274,184**	**$87,503**	**$4,028,216**	**($158,465)**
Operating Profit	**$5,074,917**	**$5,399,634**	**($324,716)**	**$5,088,900**	**($13,982)**
Interest Income	$21,450	$21,172	($278)	$19,954	($1,497)
Interest Expense	$13,136	$13,232	$96	$12,471	($665)
Total Financial Items	**$8,314**	**$7,939**	**($375)**	**$7,483**	**($831)**
Inc. Bef. Taxes & Minority Int.	**$4,194,995**	**$4,282,123**	**($87,128)**	**$4,035,699**	**$159,296**
Taxes	$164,449	$167,612	$3,162	$157,966	($6,483)
Minority Interests	$10,695	$11,468	($773)	$10,808	($113)
Net Income	**$4,041,241**	**$4,125,980**	**($84,739)**	**$3,888,541**	**$152,700**

FIGURE 4.3   Exchange rate analysis

Exception Report
Company: SPORTY Manufacturing

	ACTUAL Jun-99	BUDGET Jun-99	Variance in $	Variance in %
Intercompany Sales	$23,000	$20,000	$3,000	15 %
Outside Services	$1,800	$800	$1,000	125 %
On-line Services	$1,600	$1,200	$400	33 %
Equipment Rentals	$1,600	$500	($1,100)	−220 %
Depreciation	$11,800	$10,000	($1,800)	−18 %

FIGURE 4.4   Exception report

Balanced Scorecard−KPIs
Company: SPORTY Manufacturing
June 1999

	Actual Jun-99	Budget Jun-99	Variance in $	Variance In %	Industry Average	Competitor XYZ
Net Revenue	$1,300	$1,100	$200	18 %	$922	$875
Average Revenue per Employee	$260	$220	$40	18 %	$85	$80
Gross Margin	$400	$350	$50	14 %	$280	$200
Average Gross Margin per Product	$25	$20	$5	25 %	$22	$15
Online Sales as a % of Total Sales	$15	$20	($5)	−25 %	$5	$10
Cash Flow	$35	$30	$5	17 %	$28	$15
Sales Pipeline	$3,000	$4,000	($1,000)	−25 %	na	na

FIGURE 4.5   Balanced scorecard—KPIs

Income Statement
Company: SPORTY Manufacturing (US1)
Year: 9906
Currency: USD

	ACTUAL 9901-9906	BUDGET 9907-9912	ANNUAL ESTIMATE
Operating Revenue	**$26,359,690**	**$27,713,500**	**$54,073,190**
Cost of Goods Sold	$13,903,949	$15,712,000	$29,615,949
Wages & Salaries	$358,180	$1,081,548	$1,439,728
Other Operating Expenses	$150,318	$257,820	$408,138
Depreciation	$70,780	$60,000	$130,780
Total Operating Expenses	**$14,483,227**	**$17,111,368**	**$31,594,595**
Operating Profit	**$11,876,463**	**$10,602,132**	**$22,478,595**
Interest Income	$60,000	$64,000	$124,000
Interest Expense	$40,800	$45,000	$85,800
Total Financial Items	**$19,200**	**$19,000**	**$38,200**
Inc. Bef. Taxes & Minority Int.	**$11,895,663**	**$10,621,132**	**$22,516,795**
Taxes	$510,000	$553,000	$1,063,000
Minority Interests	$42,000	$39,000	$81,000
Net Income	**$11,427,663**	**$10,107,132**	**$21,534,795**

FIGURE 4.6   Annual estimate using YTD actuals

Income Statement–BUDGET
Company: SPORTY Manufacturing (US1)
Currency: USD

	Jan. 2000	Feb. 2000	Mar. 2000	Apr. 2000	May 2000	Jun. 2000	Jul. 2000	Aug. 2000	Sep. 2000	Oct. 2000	Nov. 2000	Dec. 2000	2000 TOTAL
Operating Revenue	$4,953,610	$4,961,260	$4,977,158	$4,990,440	$5,021,215	$5,021,055	$4,985,755	$4,988,690	$5,001,235	$5,010,850	$5,005,355	$5,020,615	$59,937,238
Cost of Goods Sold	$2,700,000	$2,600,000	$2,560,000	$2,600,000	$2,450,000	$2,600,000	$2,700,000	$2,600,000	$2,800,000	$2,430,000	$2,600,000	$2,670,000	$31,310,000
Wages & Salaries	$39,357	$41,357	$48,065	$48,105	$48,268	$48,268	$48,268	$48,535	$48,535	$48,535	$48,535	$48,535	$564,361
Other Operating Expenses	$76,242	$32,033	$34,520	$30,589	$44,894	$32,488	$32,054	$29,550	$29,243	$46,200	$29,341	$29,324	$446,474
Depreciation	$3,490	$3,500	$3,500	$3,500	$3,500	$3,500	$3,500	$3,500	$3,500	$3,500	$3,500	$3,500	$41,990
Total Operating Expenses	$2,819,089	$2,676,890	$2,646,085	$2,682,194	$2,546,662	$2,684,256	$2,783,822	$2,681,584	$2,881,277	$2,528,234	$2,681,375	$2,751,358	$32,362,825
Operating Profit	$2,134,521	$2,284,370	$2,331,072	$2,308,246	$2,474,553	$2,336,799	$2,201,933	$2,307,106	$2,119,958	$2,482,616	$2,323,980	$2,269,257	$27,574,412
Interest Income	$12,000	$13,900	$12,000	$12,000	$16,000	$12,000	$12,000	$12,000	$12,000	$12,000	$12,000	$12,000	$149,900
Interest Expenses	$7,500	$7,500	$7,500	$7,500	$7,500	$7,500	$7,500	$7,500	$7,500	$7,500	$7,500	$7,500	$90,000
Total Financial Items	$4,500	$6,400	$4,500	$4,500	$8,500	$4,500	$4,500	$4,500	$4,500	$4,500	$4,500	$4,500	$59,900
Inc. Bef. Taxes & Minority Int.	$2,139,021	$2,290,770	$2,335,572	$2,312,746	$2,483,053	$2,341,299	$2,206,433	$2,311,606	$2,124,458	$2,487,116	$2,328,480	$2,273,757	$27,634,312
Taxes	$90,000	$98,000	$90,000	$104,000	$90,000	$110,000	$90,000	$90,000	$90,000	$90,000	$90,000	$90,000	$1,122,000
Minority Interests	$6,500	$6,500	$6,500	$6,500	$6,500	$6,500	$6,500	$6,500	$6,500	$6,500	$6,500	$6,500	$78,000
Net Income	$2,055,521	$2,199,270	$2,252,072	$2,215,246	$2,399,553	$2,237,799	$2,122,933	$2,228,106	$2,040,958	$2,403,616	$2,244,980	$2,190,257	$26,590,312

FIGURE 4.7 12-month budget

Income Statement
Company: SPORTY Manufacturing (US1)
Currency: USD

	Budget Version 1 9901	Budget Version 2 9901	Budget Variance	Budget Version 1 Year-to-Date	Budget Version 2 Year-to-Date	Budget Variance
Operating Revenue	**$4,585,830**	**$4,375,000**	**($210,830)**	**$27,649,913**	**$26,323,750**	**($1,326,163)**
Cost of Goods Sold	$2,561,000	$2,345,887	($215,113)	$15,146,000	$14,075,322	($1,070,678)
Wages, Salaries, Social Expenses	$169,265	$173,354	$4,089	$1,020,153	$1,040,127	$19,974
Other Operating Expenses	$67,375	$48,787	($18,588)	$288,960	$272,957	($16,003)
Depreciation	$10,000	$11,991	$1,991	$60,000	$70,206	$10,206
Total Operating Expenses	**$2,807,640**	**$2,580,019**	**($227,621)**	**$16,515,112**	**$15,458,612**	**($1,056,501)**
Operating Profit	**$1,778,190**	**$1,794,981**	**$16,791**	**$11,134,800**	**$10,865,138**	**($269,662)**
Interest Income	$12,000	$10,977	($1,023)	$75,000	$65,977	($9,023)
Interest Expense	$7,500	$8,900	$1,400	$45,000	$53,400	$8,400
Total Financial Items	**$4,500**	**$2,077**	**($2,423)**	**$30,000**	**$12,577**	**($17,423)**
Inc. Bef. Taxes & Minority Int.	**$1,782,690**	**$1,797,058**	**$14,368**	**$11,164,800**	**$10,877,715**	**($287,085)**
Taxes	$89,000	$85,000	($4,000)	$518,000	$510,000	($8,000)
Minority Interests	$6,500	$6,700	$200	$39,000	$40,200	$1,200
Net Income	**$1,700,190**	**$1,718,758**	**$18,568**	**$10,685,800**	**$10,407,915**	**($277,885)**

FIGURE 4.8 Budget version comparison

Sales Report
Company: SPORTY Manufacturing (US1)
Year: 1999–Budget Version 1 Figures
Currency: USD

PRODUCT:	MARKET:		
	Sweden	Mexico	Japan
Telemark skis	$1,684,500	$1,692,000	$1,698,000
Cross country skis	$1,925,280	$1,794,240	$1,877,120
Telemark skiing pants	$975,600	$975,600	$975,600
Telemark skiing jackets	$1,015,680	$1,015,680	$1,015,680
Fleece sweaters	$550,800	$550,800	$550,800
Racing gloves	$259,200	$259,200	$259,200
Fleece headbands	$162,000	$162,000	$162,000
Earmuffs	$129,600	$129,600	$129,600
Telemark poles	$583,200	$583,200	$583,200
Cross country poles	$388,800	$388,800	$388,800
Telemark touring skis	$1,254,000	$1,254,000	$1,254,000
Telemark racing skis	$1,358,280	$1,358,280	$1,358,280
Cross country touring skis	$1,174,380	$1,174,380	$1,174,380
Cross country racing skis	$1,388,040	$1,388,040	$1,388,040
Men's pants	$583,200	$583,200	$583,200
Women's pants	$583,200	$583,200	$583,200
Men's anorak	$712,800	$712,800	$712,800
Women's anorak	$712,800	$712,800	$712,800
Telemark touring poles	$421,200	$421,200	$421,200
Total Sales	**$15,862,560**	**$15,739,020**	**$15,827,900**

FIGURE 4.9   Sales budget by product and market

Quarterly Sales Analysis by Product
Company: SPORTY Manufacturing
Year: 2000–Budget Version 1 Figures

	1st Quarter	2nd Quarter	3rd Quarter	4th Quarter	Total
Telemark skis	$1,301,648	$1,384,500	$1,348,750	$1,384,000	$5,418,898
Cross country skis	$1,460,480	$1,503,320	$1,470,000	$1,473,920	$5,907,720
Telemark touring skis	$986,100	$986,100	$986,100	$986,100	$3,944,400
Telemark racing skis	$1,152,270	$1,152,270	$1,152,270	$1,152,270	$4,609,080
Cross country touring skis	$954,785	$964,775	$961,815	$969,585	$3,850,960
Cross country racing skis	$1,127,460	$1,127,460	$1,127,460	$1,127,460	$4,509,840
Telemark skiing pants	$751,050	$751,050	$751,050	$751,050	$3,004,200
Telemark skiing jackets	$781,440	$781,440	$781,440	$781,440	$3,125,760
Fleece sweaters	$443,445	$443,445	$443,445	$443,445	$1,773,780
Racing gloves	$198,000	$198,000	$198,000	$198,000	$792,000
Fleece headbands	$123,750	$123,750	$123,750	$123,750	$495,000
Earmuffs	$100,800	$100,800	$100,800	$100,800	$403,200
Men's pants	$453,600	$453,600	$453,600	$453,600	$1,814,400
Women's pants	$453,600	$453,600	$453,600	$453,600	$1,814,400
Men's anorak	$554,400	$554,400	$554,400	$554,400	$2,217,600
Women's anorak	$554,400	$554,400	$554,400	$554,400	$2,217,600
Racing gloves	$252,000	$252,000	$252,000	$252,000	$1,008,000
Touring gloves	$201,600	$201,600	$201,600	$201,600	$806,400
Woolen gloves	$176,400	$176,400	$176,400	$176,400	$705,600
Design 1 headband	$126,000	$126,000	$126,000	$126,000	$504,000
Design 2 headband	$151,200	$151,200	$151,200	$151,200	$604,800
SPORTY earmuffs	$100,800	$100,800	$100,800	$100,800	$403,200
Telemark poles	$453,600	$453,600	$453,600	$453,600	$1,814,400
Cross country poles	$302,400	$302,400	$302,400	$302,400	$1,209,600
Telemark touring poles	$327,600	$327,600	$327,600	$327,600	$1,310,400
Telemark telescope poles	$403,200	$403,200	$403,200	$403,200	$1,612,800
Cross country touring poles	$277,200	$277,200	$277,200	$277,200	$1,108,800
Cross country racing poles	$352,800	$352,800	$352,800	$357,000	$1,415,400
Total	**$14,522,028**	**$14,657,710**	**$14,585,680**	**$14,636,820**	**$58,402,238**

FIGURE 4.10   Quarterly sales budget by product

Quarterly Sales Analysis By Product–Budget Version 1
Company: SPORTY Manufacturing
Year: 2000

	1st Quarter	2nd Quarter	3rd Quarter	4th Quarter	Total
Telemark skis	$1,301,648	$1,384,500	$1,348,750	$1,384,000	$5,418,898
COGS	$455,577	$429,195	$485,550	$442,880	$1,813,202
Gross Margin	$846,071	$955,305	$863,200	$941,120	$3,605,696
GM (%)	65 %	69 %	64 %	68 %	67 %
Cross country skis	$1,460,480	$1,503,320	$1,470,000	$1,473,920	$5,907,720
COGS	$511,168	$466,029	$529,200	$471,654	$1,978,052
Gross Margin	$949,312	$1,037,291	$940,800	$1,002,266	$3,929,668
GM (%)	65 %	69 %	64 %	68 %	67 %
Telemark touring skis	$986,100	$986,100	$986,100	$986,100	$3,944,400
COGS	$345,135	$305,691	$354,996	$315,552	$1,321,374
Gross Margin	$640,965	$680,409	$631,104	$670,548	$2,623,026
GM (%)	65 %	69 %	64 %	68 %	67 %
Telemark racing skis	$1,152,270	$1,152,270	$1,152,270	$1,152,270	$4,609,080
COGS	$403,295	$357,204	$414,817	$368,726	$1,544,042
Gross Margin	$748,976	$795,066	$737,453	$783,544	$3,065,038
GM (%)	65 %	69 %	64 %	68 %	67 %
Cross country touring skis	$954,785	$964,775	$961,815	$969,585	$3,850,960
COGS	$334,175	$299,080	$346,253	$310,267	$1,289,776
Gross Margin	$620,610	$665,695	$615,562	$659,318	$2,561,184
GM (%)	65 %	69 %	64 %	68 %	67 %
Cross country racing skis	$1,127,460	$1,127,460	$1,127,460	$1,127,460	$4,509,840
COGS	$394,611	$349,513	$405,886	$360,787	$1,510,796
Gross Margin	$732,849	$777,947	$721,574	$766,673	$2,999,044
GM (%)	65 %	69 %	64 %	68 %	67 %

FIGURE 4.11   Quarterly gross margin budget by product

	1st Quarter	2nd Quarter	3rd Quarter	4th Quarter	Total
Telemark skiing pants	$751,050	$751,050	$751,050	$751,050	$3,004,200
COGS	$262,868	$232,826	$270,378	$240,336	$1,006,407
Gross Margin	$488,183	$518,225	$480,672	$510,714	$1,997,793
GM (%)	65 %	69 %	64 %	68 %	67 %
Telemark skiing jackets	$781,440	$781,440	$781,440	$781,440	$3,125,760
COGS	$273,504	$242,246	$281,318	$250,061	$1,047,130
Gross Margin	$507,936	$539,194	$500,122	$531,379	$2,078,630
GM (%)	65 %	69 %	64 %	68 %	67 %
Fleece sweaters	$443,445	$443,445	$443,445	$443,445	$1,773,780
COGS	$155,206	$137,468	$159,640	$141,902	$594,216
Gross Margin	$288,239	$305,977	$283,805	$301,543	$1,179,564
GM (%)	65 %	69 %	64 %	68 %	67 %
Racing gloves	$198,000	$198,000	$198,000	$198,000	$792,000
COGS	$69,300	$61,380	$71,280	$63,360	$265,320
Gross Margin	$128,700	$136,620	$126,720	$134,640	$526,680
GM (%)	65 %	69 %	64 %	68 %	67 %
Total GM	**$5,951,840**	**$6,411,728**	**$5,901,011**	**$6,301,744**	**$24,566,324**

FIGURE 4.11   Quarterly gross margin budget by product—*Cont.*

SPORTY MANUFACTURING   HEADCOUNT SUMMARY REPORT
                                     YEAR 2000

DEP. CODE	DESCRIPTION	JAN.	FEB.	MAR.	APR.	MAY	JUN.	JUL.	AUG.	SEP.	OCT.	NOV.	DEC.	YEAR AVERAGE
101	Accounting	5	5	6	6	6	6	6	6	6	6	6	6	6
105	Marketing & Sales	3	2	2	2	3	3	3	3	3	4	4	4	3
107	Human Resources	2	2	2	2	2	2	2	2	2	2	2	2	2
109	Manufacturing	28	29	29	30	30	30	30	30	30	30	30	30	30
	Total	38	38	39	40	41	41	41	41	41	42	42	42	41
	Prior Year	35	35	35	35	35	35	35	36	36	36	37	38	36
	% Change	8.6%	8.6%	11.4%	14.3%	17.1%	17.1%	17.1%	13.9%	13.9%	16.7%	13.5%	10.5%	13.6%
	Monthly Turnover	0	0	−1	−1	−1	0	0	0	0	−1	0	0	0

FIGURE 4.12 Headcount

Income Statement
Company: SPORTY Manufacturing (US1)
Currency: USD

5-Year Forecast	1999	2000	2001	2002	2003
Operating Revenue	**$59,200,000**	**$63,000,000**	**$73,400,000**	**$75,300,000**	**$79,900,000**
Cost of Goods Sold	$34,500,000	$31,900,000	$38,000,000	$39,400,000	$42,500,000
Wages, Salaries, Social Expenses	$298,328	$4,215,780	$3,600,000	$3,120,000	$2,880,000
Other Operating Expenses	$435,280	$611,375	$223,100	$209,100	$225,790
Depreciations	$21,600	$133,200	$120,000	$136,800	$144,000
Total Operating Expenses	**$35,255,208**	**$36,860,355**	**$41,943,100**	**$42,865,900**	**$45,749,790**
Operating Profit	**$23,944,792**	**$26,139,645**	**$31,456,900**	**$32,434,100**	**$34,150,210**
Interest Income	$121,000	$115,500	$133,000	$114,000	$114,000
Interest Expenses	$97,400	$84,000	$84,000	$108,000	$132,000
Total Financial Items	**$23,600**	**$31,500**	**$49,000**	**$6,000**	**($18,000)**
Inc. Bef. Taxes & Minority Int.	**$23,968,392**	**$26,171,145**	**$31,505,900**	**$32,440,100**	**$34,132,210**
Taxes	$1,225,000	$1,500,000	$1,620,000	$1,500,000	$1,620,000
Minority Interests	$124,000	$115,000	$143,000	$151,000	$120,000
Net Income	**$22,867,392**	**$24,786,145**	**$30,028,900**	**$31,091,100**	**$32,632,210**

FIGURE 4.13 Five-year forecast

EXTERNAL INCOME STATEMENT
QUARTERLY SUMMARY & MARGIN ANALYSIS
Forecast version: F1

	Jan.	Feb.	Mar.	Q1	Q2	Q3	Q4	YTD
	Actual	Actual	Forecast	Projected	Forecast	Forecast	Forecast	Projected
REVENUES:								
External Sales	$4,150,000	$4,200,000	$3,200,000	$11,550,000	$13,100,000	$13,100,000	$13,100,000	$50,850,000
Intercompany Sales	$145,000	$110,000	$0	$255,000	$0	$0	$0	$255,000
Total Revenues	$4,295,000	$4,310,000	$3,200,000	$11,805,000	$13,100,000	$13,100,000	$13,100,000	$51,105,000
COST OF SERVICES:								
Cost of Goods Sold	$2,400,000	$2,175,000	$2,900,000	$7,475,000	$9,500,000	$9,500,000	$9,500,000	$35,975,000
Gross Profit	$1,895,001	$2,135,000	$300,000	$4,330,000	$3,600,000	$3,600,000	$3,600,000	$15,130,000
OPERATING EXPENSES:								
Wages & Salaries	$59,697	$59,697	$24,861	$144,254	$74,582	$74,582	$74,582	$368,000
Payroll Taxes	$1,800	$2,400	$2,688	$6,888	$8,076	$8,076	$8,076	$31,116
Group Medical and LTD	$840	$1,000	$1,121	$2,961	$3,090	$3,090	$3,090	$12,231
Workers Compensation	$600	$900	$900	$2,400	$2,700	$2,700	$2,700	$10,500
Outside Services	$2,400	$1,800	$1,800	$6,000	$5,400	$5,400	$5,400	$22,200
Other Operating Expenses	$900	$1,000	$1,178	$3,078	$3,149	$3,149	$3,149	$12,525
Contributions and Donations	$600	$600	$600	$1,800	$1,800	$1,800	$1,800	$7,200
Achievement Awards	$580	$1,800	$1,800	$4,180	$5,400	$5,400	$5,400	$20,380
Educ. & Training	$438	$600	$600	$1,638	$1,800	$1,800	$1,800	$7,038
Office Supplies	$600	$600	$2,289	$3,489	$6,867	$6,867	$6,867	$17,223

FIGURE 4.14　Quarterly projection and forecasts

	Jan. Actual	Feb. Actual	Mar. Forecast	Q1 Projected	Q2 Forecast	Q3 Forecast	Q4 Forecast	YTD Projected
Printing & Duplication	$1,200	$900	$900	$3,000	$2,700	$2,700	$2,700	$11,100
Postage and Express Mail	$660	$600	$600	$1,860	$1,800	$1,800	$1,800	$7,260
Dues & Memberships	$820	$800	$800	$2,420	$2,400	$2,400	$2,400	$7,220
Books & Journals	$400	$600	$2,289	$3,289	$6,867	$6,867	$6,867	$17,023
Online Services	$960	$1,600	$1,600	$4,160	$4,800	$4,800	$4,800	$13,760
Small Equip. & Soft.	$600	$600	$2,289	$3,489	$6,867	$6,867	$6,867	$17,223
Equipment Rentals	$600	$1,600	$1,600	$3,800	$4,800	$4,800	$4,800	$13,400
Repair & Maint.	$800	$600	$2,289	$3,689	$6,867	$6,867	$6,867	$17,423
Sales and Use Tax	$800	$800	$800	$2,400	$2,400	$2,400	$2,400	$7,200
Sponsored R&D	$800	$600	$2,289	$3,689	$6,867	$6,867	$6,867	$17,423
Contracted R&D	$600	$600	$2,289	$3,489	$6,867	$6,867	$6,867	$17,223
Licenses	$600	$600	$600	$1,800	$1,800	$1,800	$1,800	$5,400
Advisory Board	$620	$600	$600	$1,820	$1,800	$1,800	$1,800	$5,420
Consultants	$400	$900	$900	$2,200	$2,700	$2,700	$2,700	$10,300
Accounting & Audit	$840	$800	$800	$2,440	$2,400	$2,400	$2,400	$9,640
Support—MIS Services	$420	$400	$400	$1,220	$1,200	$1,200	$1,200	$4,820
Travel & Lodging	$1,200	$1,200	$1,200	$3,600	$3,600	$3,600	$3,600	$14,400
Meals & Entertainment	$1,340	$1,400	$1,400	$4,140	$4,200	$4,200	$4,200	$16,740
Depreciation	$11,780	$11,800	$1,800	$25,380	$5,400	$5,400	$5,400	$41,580
Total operating expenses	$93,895	$97,397	$63,282	$254,573	$189,199	$189,199	$189,199	$822,170
Income (loss) from operations	$1,801,106	$2,037,603	$236,718	$4,075,427	$3,410,801	$3,410,801	$3,410,801	$14,307,830

FIGURE 4.14 Quarterly projection and forecasts—*Cont.*

EXTERNAL INCOME STATEMENT
QUARTERLY SUMMARY & MARGIN ANALYSIS
Forecast version: F1

	Jan.	Feb.	Mar.	Q1	Q2	Q3	Q4	YTD
	Actual	Actual	Forecast	Projected	Forecast	Forecast	Forecast	Projected
OTHER INCOME (EXPENSE)								
Interest Income	$10,000	$10,000	$10,000	$30,000	$30,000	$30,000	$30,000	$120,000
Interest Expense	($6,800)	($6,800)	($6,000)	($19,600)	($24,000)	($24,000)	($24,000)	($91,600)
Pretax income (loss)	$1,804,305	$2,040,803	$240,718	$4,085,827	$3,416,801	$3,416,801	$3,416,801	$14,336,230
Provision for income taxes	$85,000	$85,000	$129,000	$299,000	$358,000	$358,000	$358,000	$1,373,000
Income (loss) before minority interest	$1,719,305	$1,955,803	$111,718	$3,786,827	$3,058,801	$3,058,801	$3,058,801	$12,963,230
Minority Interest	$7,000	$7,000	$12,000	$26,000	$33,000	$33,000	$33,000	$125,000
Net income (loss)	$1,726,305	$1,962,803	$123,718	$3,812,827	$3,091,801	$3,091,801	$3,091,801	$13,088,230

FIGURE 4.14   Quarterly projection and forecasts—*Cont.*

PART TWO

BUDGETING SOFTWARE: TECHNOLOGY TRENDS AND FUNCTIONALITY

CHAPTER 5

TECHNOLOGY TRENDS

Current technology offers budgeting system vendors a host of integration, customization, and communication tools that were not available only a few years ago. Most PC-based budgeting applications are utilizing much of this new technology, while many older mainframe and Unix-based applications are falling far behind and are subsequently being replaced by the more flexible and up-to-date PC-based and Web-based systems. Figure 5.1 shows the past and future trends in budgeting software technology and related implementation times.

WINDOWS PLATFORMS, SQL, AND OLAP DATABASES

Most modern budgeting software vendors have chosen one of two different database technologies for their budgeting systems. One group of vendors offers Structured Query Language (SQL) databases while the other camp offers Online Analytical Processing (OLAP) databases. SQL-based products include SRC, Helmsman, BudgetPlus and Enterprise Reporting, and OLAP-based products include Adaytum Planning, Hyperion Essbase, and Oracle Financial Analyzer (see Appendix H for more information on software vendors).

Traditionally, applications (such as accounting applications) running on SQL databases have been developed for transaction oriented processes, while applications running on OLAP databases have been developed for analysis oriented processes. The reason you can now find budgeting systems based on both

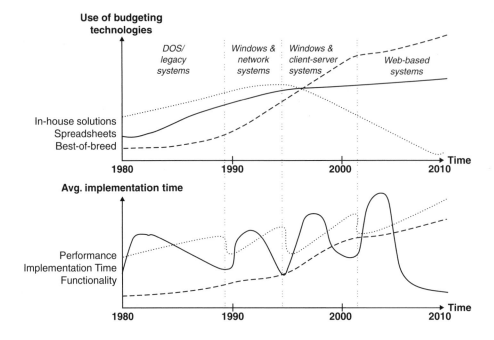

FIGURE 5.1 Budgeting technology—past and future.

technologies is that the field of budgeting and planning typically includes both a transaction oriented process combined with an analytical process. Figure 5.2 shows the typical steps included in a standard budgeting process.

STEP (for a simplified budgeting process)	Transaction Oriented	Analysis
Upload of actual transactions from the general ledger	X	
HQ input of different global assumptions	X	
Department input of budget figures	X	
HQ/department adjustments of budget figures	X	
HQ consolidation (incl. currency conversion) and report printing	X	
HQ analysis of budget (drill down, slice and dice, etc.)		X

FIGURE 5.2 Typical steps included in a standard budgeting process

Budgeting applications based on SQL databases often execute the last step (analysis) by linking to one or more OLAP applications. Software based on OLAP databases have typically accomplished the first steps listed in the table above by creating additional modules (such as currency conversion modules and adjustment modules) outside the central OLAP database. For many applications, both approaches will satisfy a company's key needs, albeit with varying amounts of flexibility.

In other words, because OLAP technology initially was intended for fast analysis of detailed and summarized data, transactions must be structured and summarized based on hierarchies in cubes, where each dimension (such as account, period, department, etc.) is part of the cube. For drill-down to be logical, all dimensions are organized into hierarchies, from lowest detail to totals. Once data has been entered, converted, pre-consolidated and indexed, the OLAP technology then allows for very fast and easy analysis and reporting. Applications based on SQL databases do not require hierarchies and very structured models. However, the weakness is that reports are not as fast as in OLAP systems, and you often need to re-execute a report to move down into a company hierarchy, rather than drilling down in a "live" report. The strengths of SQL-based systems are that you have complete freedom to design reports and budget input screens with a mix of data, whether it is based on a hierarchy or not, and you do not have to store pre-consolidated data or convert all data to one reporting currency. All of this can take place on the fly, as you run a report.

For companies that use multiple roll-up structures to consolidate departments/subsidiaries (e.g., legal structure, geographical structure, business area structure, etc.), there is a drawback with most OLAP-based systems: you must generate and store the same data in one data cube for each roll-up structure (because the structures define the drill-down paths). In SQL-based systems, data only need to be stored once because consolidation is done at the time of report execution and there is no drill-down to a lower level; instead there is a new report execution.

Another difference between the two technologies is that SQL databases usually are more open for integration with third party tools than proprietary OLAP databases. The implications for the user are that you can use standard query tools to read data from SQL databases and into a third party software (such as Microsoft Excel). With OLAP databases you often have to export the data to a file, or the vendor must program a link to your third-party software.

It is unclear which of the two technologies will dominate the budgeting applications market of the future. Many companies will opt for one or the other and thus experience both advantages and disadvantages. Other companies will use the combined approach where data entry, consolidation, and report printing are done in the SQL-based application and then the updated OLAP-based application is used for analysis.

For budgeting applications based on Microsoft SQL Server, there is a possibility of using technology built into the database. With the release of the SQL Server 7.0 database, Microsoft integrated an OLAP database (called Microsoft OLAP Services and formerly known as PLATO) into the SQL Server database. Several budgeting software vendors have already linked their applications to OLAP Services, and more are likely to follow.

BENEFITS OF OPEN DATABASE CONNECTIVITY SUPPORT

Another of the most important technologies introduced in budget systems in recent years is the use of the industry standard called Open Database Connectivity (ODBC) to allow easy access to data from different sources. Most modern database platforms now support ODBC and this makes it a lot easier to bring information into and out of the budget system. It also saves time and potential errors by eliminating the need for manual upload and download of information through text files (such as comma-separated ASCII files, fixed-space ASCII files, tab-separated ASCII files, etc.). A budget system that supports ODBC allows you to read or write different types of information from/to its database with relative ease, such as:

- Financial and statistical numbers
- Natural account numbers and descriptions
- Employee numbers, names, salary, and so forth
- Company and department codes and descriptions
- Product codes and descriptions
- Market codes and descriptions
- Project codes and descriptions

Note that although most vendors now tout ODBC compliance, beware that this is not a guarantee that you can "plug and play" your other ODBC compliant systems to the budgeting system and avoid manual intervention to move information back and forth. You will still face issues such as:

Duplicate records: The same information you are trying to upload already exists in the system you are attempting to upload to. Should the information be rejected or should it overwrite the record that already exists? Somebody must decide to handle this automatically or manually, and how errors and rejected items should be logged.

Conversion/filtering: If the budget system is reading actual figures from several different general ledger systems in the corporation, and the account number structures are different, most likely you will want to base your budget input screens and reports on a standard set of accounts. This means that you have to tell the budget system which account(s) in the general ledger(s) equals a corresponding account in the budget system. This information might be maintained in a conversion/mapping table built into the budget system, or it might be part of a separate integration product or module.

One of the first uses of the ODBC technology was to connect the budget system to spreadsheets. Microsoft Excel, for example, is probably the most popular reporting tool with which budget managers, controllers, and CFOs are familiar. Being able to read budget information directly into Excel means that the company's financial staff has a powerful report formatting and graphing tool at their disposal, independently of how good the report writer in the budget system is. It also allows the company to combine information from the budget system with sources that they might not otherwise have been able to access. Some budget software packages have gone as far as making Excel their sole report writer and input interface. This has both advantages and disadvantages, as discussed in the next section.

DECREASED RELIANCE ON SPREADSHEETS

Since their inception, spreadsheets have been very popular budgeting tools. They have been easy to use, familiar to budgeting managers, inexpensive, and very flexible in many ways. Historically, Lotus 1-2-3, Quattro Pro, and Excel have been some of the most popular spreadsheets. In recent years, Excel has completely dominated the market and has become the spreadsheet de facto standard. Even today, spreadsheets are by far the most common tool for budgeting and forecasting. However, as a result of corporate growth and organizational changes, almost all mid-sized and large organizations eventually find that that their spreadsheet models become too cumbersome to manage. Except for small organizations (typically with less than $20 million in revenue and less than 10 departments) that can easily manage their budgeting process in a spreadsheet, pre-packaged (sometimes called best-of-breed) budgeting software has become very popular.

Financial executives estimate that 80% of the total time required to develop a budget is spent on collecting and assembling the core data. There is a large cost associated with this effort, both in the time spent re-keying and validating numbers, and in the opportunity cost of not having enough time left to analyze the budget. By replacing a large spreadsheet-based budgeting model with specialized budgeting software, a significant resource drain can be turned into an automated planning process and a strategic advantage.

If you are experiencing one or more of the following issues related to your spreadsheet models, it might be a smart move to start looking for best-of-breed budgeting and planning software:

- You have a lack of software features to enable people at all levels in the organization to effectively collaborate and communicate.
- The person that created all the spreadsheets might leave the company and no one is left to maintain the model.
- Spreadsheets used across the corporation generally result in data and formats that require extensive integration at the corporate level.
- There are poor opportunities to consider a wide variety of scenarios. If the organization chooses to do more budget passes to improve the final results, the time and effort required can be enormous.
- Too much time spent maintaining spreadsheet links and macros
- Lack of audit trail when changes are made to the budget
- Lack of financial intelligence and functionality
- Time lost re-keying data
- Time consumed to write new reports
- Problems with users making changes to spreadsheet templates
- Problems with consolidations when there are organizational changes
- Lack of features to link corporate strategy to the budgeting process
- General lack of status reports and control of the budgeting and reporting process
- Lack of user security features to efficiently control read, write, and delete access

In addition, a spreadsheet-based budget model is often too rigid and complex to allow you to look at data from different points of view such as product line, customer type, business unit, and so forth. Because you can't view financial data from a variety of perspectives, essential business information and related decision making are not optimized. Because of difficulties in accessing and integrating data, executives can't get usable information fast enough or detailed enough to track shifts in the business. A modern budgeting tool should be able to address these problems and also give you additional benefits. For example, with dynamic variance reports and exception reports, as well as reports for benchmarking against competitors and industry averages, your budgeting and planning can go from being a headache to being one of your best strategic weapons.

How can a best-of-breed budgeting software application improve your budgeting and planning? Most modern budgeting software programs now offer many of the following benefits not common in spreadsheet software:

- A controlled input environment with business rules that ensure consistency

- Database storage with log files and recovery options
- Report writer optimized for financial consolidations and reporting
- Roll-up trees with drag and drop reorganizations
- Currency conversion
- Multi-dimensional analysis of your business

Potential downsides of budgeting packages in comparison to spreadsheets could be:

- Higher up-front investment in software and consulting than with a spreadsheet model
- Less end-user flexibility than with a spreadsheet model (where you can create formulas and enter numbers anywhere)
- Takes more time to learn than a familiar spreadsheet program

In many cases a company will roll out a budget software to the departmental level and have everyone use the same system. In other cases a consolidating parent company may only be interested in high level data and might continue collecting data in spreadsheets and let each subsidiary worry about their own detailed calculations and assumptions using local spreadsheets or other tools. The spreadsheet data from the subsidiary are then re-keyed (although this should be unnecessary) or uploaded into the parent's budgeting software for consolidation, adjustments, and reporting.

For parent companies that closely manage and monitor their subsidiaries, it will often make sense to do a full roll-out of a budgeting package. This will streamline the input and reporting process, and it allows the parent to drill down to detailed budgeting information anywhere at the departmental level in order to investigate and make adjustments and comments wherever applicable. Utilizing a centralized Web-based budgeting software throughout the entire organization is even easier because there is no need to install the application in every satellite office and data files do not have to be sent back and forth.

While it is fairly easy to pinpoint why spreadsheet budgeting and consolidations can cause headaches for mid-sized and large companies, it should also be made clear that buying a best-of-breed budgeting software package won't automatically solve all your problems. Before you can begin reaping the benefits, there will be database platforms to choose from, general ledger integration to take care of, new report writers to learn, and more. Be prepared to invest both time and money in software selection, implementation, and training before you are ready to launch your new application and to leave your old spreadsheets behind.

These issues, combined with the general trend toward more focus on planning with more complex and frequent budgeting and forecasting processes, are pushing an increasing number of companies toward the acquisition of best-of-breed budgeting software.

INCREASED USE OF BUDGETING SPECIFIC SOFTWARE

Also, as a result of spreadsheet difficulties in recent years, companies have started buying and implementing off-the-shelf budgeting software. This in turn has led software companies to develop a host of new applications. The prevalent technology is, for the most part, a Windows-based or Web-based front-end with an SQL or OLAP database. Most of the systems available today have less flexibility than spreadsheets in the layout of reports and input screens, but they are much better in areas such as:

- User security/access control
- Consolidation
- Currency conversion
- Budget version control
- Audit trail
- Pre-built budgeting and forecasting functionality
- Multi-user handling

LESS DEPENDENCY ON IS STAFF TO BUILD AND MAINTAIN BUDGET MODEL

As a result of the move toward pre-packaged budgeting software with databases residing on network servers, the financial staff is taking full responsibility for building and maintaining the budget model. The IS staff that have traditionally been involved in programming reports (especially in older Unix and mainframe systems) and writing complex spreadsheet macros, now has a different role. This new role consists of overseeing and maintaining the budget system's database and, in some cases, handling the uploads/downloads to linked systems.

Most people contend that this is a good trend, because the IS staff should not need to spend their time learning about account numbers and financial statements, but should instead be specialists supporting the necessary infrastructure required to run the budget system smoothly.

MORE AUTOMATION OF TYPICAL IS DEPARTMENT TASKS

As modern budgeting systems have found their place in more and more organizations, the quest for automation has begun. Companies have pushed software vendors to automate many backend tasks that used to be laborious, manual activities. As a result, new software versions incorporate functionality to handle many tasks with minimal human interaction (see Figure 5.3). For example:

- Backup of database/budget model
- Copying one budget version to a new version
- Uploading basic tables (such as accounts, descriptions, etc.)
- Uploading actual figures
- Downloading budget figures to the general ledger
- Transferring budget figures from remote sites to headquarters
- Replication of headquarters budget model to remote sites

As a result of this automation, the budgeting staff needs less IS Department assistance to maintain the budget system.

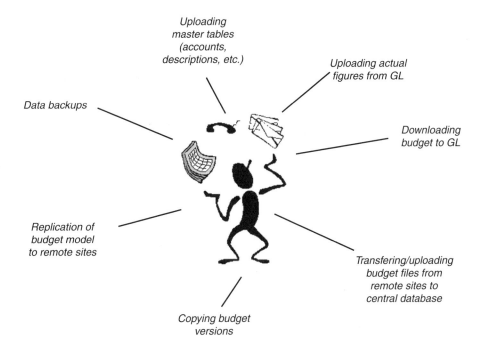

FIGURE 5.3   Traditional information systems tasks in the budgeting process

TIGHTER GENERAL LEDGER INTEGRATION

Budget managers are tired of all the manual labor traditionally involved with uploading information from the general ledger. Budget system vendors are responding with better integration functionality. Some processes support ODBC for direct loading of data. Others also offer mapping features (some sophisticated, some not) that allow the budget system to operate with the common chart of accounts that best supports the budgeting and forecasting process. In particular, this is important when the budget system spans multiple general ledgers in the corporation. All modern budgeting systems support uploading of information from ASCII files.

BETTER INTEGRATION WITH ANALYTICAL TOOLS

Corporate management gurus are preaching that management should focus on exception reporting and analysis of key trends, and software vendors have responded with a host of applications recently labeled "analytical software." A number of vendors (in particular those with systems based on the OLAP platform) have also started using this term to apply to their own budget applications. The word *analytical* simply refers to the fact that the software offers features such as drill down, exception highlighting, and graphing, that allows management to better analyze the company's situation. Many budgeting systems do not offer extensive drill down across multiple dimensions or graphing capabilities. Instead, these systems are creating tight links (typically ODBC based) to analytical applications such as Cognos Powerplay, Timeline, Knosys, Business Objects and Microsoft Excel (using features like Pivot tables and graphing).

LINKING TO PAYROLL, SALES ORDER ENTRY, AND OTHER SOFTWARE

The typical budgeting process is shifting from a focus on the whole chart of accounts toward more operational budgeting where the main focus is on creating detailed budget information for key business drivers (such as price/volume revenue generation, detailed payroll budgeting, P&L by project or business area, etc.). Accordingly, modern budgeting systems now support upload of information from payroll systems (employee information and salaries), sales order systems, and more. These links are often still ASCII file based with some conversion process involved, but they do save tedious (and potential error prone) manual re-entry of information into the budgeting software.

WEB-ENABLED APPLICATIONS SIMPLIFY CORPORATE-WIDE ROLLOUT

The Internet and the World Wide Web have also made a huge impact on budgeting software. A common trend is to involve corporate entities down to the departmental level in the budgeting process, even in large corporations with many subsidiaries. This presents the IS Department with several challenges. For example:

- Do all the departments have adequate hardware?
- Does everybody have LAN, WAN, or Internet access for transmission of files?
- How can a large number of typically non-financial users be trained adequately and at a low cost?
- If the budgeting application requires a local installation of a database, who maintains this and how costly is it to buy a large number of database licenses?
- When the budget manager at headquarters decides to make changes to the reporting model, how can all remote site installations be updated swiftly and without problems?

So far, budgeting application vendors have tried to solve many of these issues in several different ways. Some use spreadsheet templates that are e-mailed back and forth, others copy their whole application to the remote sites, while still others have integrated replication procedures that manage remote versions of databases and models. All of these solutions have drawbacks such as high cost, complexity, low security, and so on. Another solution has been to use a remote access software such as Citrix MetaFrame with Microsoft Terminal Server to access a central budgeting model through a wide area network or a dial-up connection. The drawbacks here are the telecommunications expenses incurred, cost of the remote access software, and the loss of speed due to the graphic-intensive screens that must be transmitted.

A very good solution seems to be to employ fully web-enabled budgeting software. Many vendors already have enabled their applications to allow web data entry and web report processing. Practically, this means that the whole budgeting database resides on a central server with a link to a web server that accesses the corporate intranet or the Internet. For the user, this means direct access to reports and data input screens, typically through a browser interface.

Having all users running reports and entering budgets directly on a common, central server can offer huge benefits for management.

Maintenance benefits:

- Little or no application maintenance on the client (end-user) side, meaning that management and users can spend most of their time on budgeting and analysis, rather than on system maintenance and troubleshooting problems with the IS Department.

- No need to send entered information by file to the head office, because data is entered directly into the central database, which saves time and avoids possible problems caused by communication errors.

- No application version conflicts. If you have worked with distributed applications before, you know that having a number of installations of a program at different locations demands strict control of new program versions. If somebody uses an old version, it can cause many headaches and delays before the site is upgraded and ready to go again. When the whole application resides on a server, this can be completely avoided. All it takes is one upgrade to the central server and all users everywhere can immediately benefit from the upgrade.

Information-flow benefits:

- Entered information is available to management immediately (because everybody works on the same database).

- End-users (e.g., sales departments) can run reports that, for example, compare them with other remote sales departments. With distributed applications, everybody must send their numbers to the head office which then creates summary and comparison reports and distributes these back out to all sales departments. Both time and labor can be saved by giving everyone access to a central database, both for data input and report generation. This is also more motivating for employees who can get virtually immediate feedback through the online reports.

- Employees on the road (e.g., a manager travelling to a subsidiary) have direct access to the central database, which is completely up to date, compared to copying files to a laptop and bringing them along. This allows for a mobile workforce that can stay in total synchronization with a company's central operations.

Figure 5.4 illustrates the use of a budgeting application running on a central database with remote users accessing it through the Internet or an intranet.

If the budgeting application is using an Internet connection, two key concerns are usually speed and secure transmission of sensitive budget data over the Web. Other issues are the somewhat limited graphical screen layout currently attainable with Web programming tools and the limitations of calculation possibilities. However, there is enormous interest in Web applications and these issues are being addressed by the software and hardware industries.

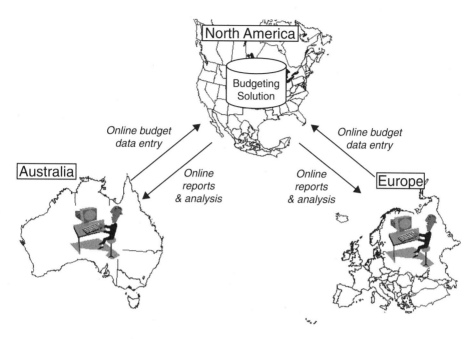

FIGURE 5.4   Central budgeting solution with online access

THE FUTURE: MORE FEATURES, BETTER INTEGRATION, MORE SPECIALIZATION

Apart from the few vendors who are still providing solutions based on older, proprietary file-based databases, modern budgeting systems are currently based on SQL databases or OLAP databases. Some experts predict that more systems will move to the OLAP platform in the future, because of its strong analytical capabilities, while others envision most systems based on an SQL database platform. Each technology provides different advantages, but the bottom line is, you should choose the type of database that meets your company's particular needs.

The fact is, Web technology is here to stay. Being able to use the communication protocol and infrastructure of the Internet (TCP/IP) or corporate intranets to allow for dynamic budgeting and reporting to and from remote sites will impact the planning process for most mid-sized and larger organizations. Modern budget systems will offer Web versions that allow for data input through a standard browser, and in the future some might also bypass the browser, creating a specialized budgeting interface that still uses Web technology for communication and presentation.

CHAPTER 6

FUNCTIONALITY OFFERED BY MODERN BUDGETING SOFTWARE

As described in Chapter 5, the world of budgeting is changing rapidly. Management is starting to understand how important it is to their organization today to have a proper plan for tomorrow, and new technology allows for a better budgeting process.

Although new systems automate many of the tasks that used to be time consuming, error-prone, and boring (such as entering data from other systems, e.g., the general ledger), you should not expect to spend a lot less time budgeting. Why? Because with the current focus on strategic planning, there will be many more questions to be answered (which translates into more reports and scenarios to produce), more information to collect, and more time spent analyzing and comparing numbers. This means that the better your budgeting routines and technology, the better equipped you are to support the planning process and the overall objectives of your company.

SUPPORTING YOUR PLANNING PROCESS WITH A MODERN BUDGETING SYSTEM: A STEP-BY-STEP EXAMPLE

It should be safe to assume that today, most people with budgeting responsibilities use some form of software application to aid them in their work. However, for many people this application is a homemade spreadsheet model, an older commercial application, or maybe even a mainframe application where most changes to the system must be performed by a programmer. In 1998, the PC-based budgeting software market really started to take off, with a number of new applications joining the few established brands. Organizations are rapidly changing over to professional budgeting applications, and if you have not yet used one or looked at one, the likelihood of having to do so in the near future is high. When you evaluate your next budgeting software, you should keep the budgeting process in mind and make sure that the software you consider supports and automates each step in the process. In order for you to get an understanding of the key workflow process in most newer systems, the following step-by-step example has been created (assuming that the strategic objectives have been set by management and that the budgeting model is tested and working). See Figure 6.1 for an illustration.

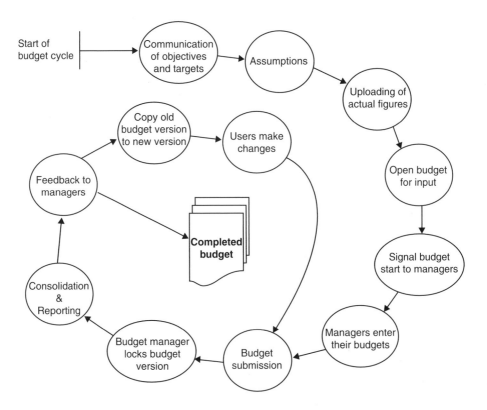

FIGURE 6.1   Example of a workflow with a modern budgeting system

1. Communication of objectives and targets to users with budgeting responsibilities.

2. The budget manager inputs any global assumptions/budget variables that have changed since the last budget was created.

3. The budget manager uploads actual figures for the prior year to be used for comparison purposes (and, in some cases, to calculate new budget figures).

4. Open up one budget version for input.

5. Send message to all users that the budget system now is ready and inform them of the completion deadline.

6. Budget users enter their budget numbers and comments. The system should have a number of tools to make this work as easy as possible. Most commonly used are allocation keys to spread annual totals across the months of the year, create budget figures as a percentage of actual figures for last year, and attach text comments to specific items they would like to explain.

7. Budget users submit their budget files (by electronic mail if they are not online with the same server as the central budgeting application) to the budget manager. If it is an organization with more than two levels of budgeting responsibilities, the budget goes to the next level up.

8. The budget manager locks the system for data entry (so that no one can change or enter data after this point in time).

9. The budget manager consolidates all the submitted budgets and runs a number of reports for review purposes. On some occasions, if management is happy with the figures they see, the budget is approved and frozen. If not, the process continues.

10. Based on the previous analysis, the budget manager sends comments to all the budget users, either by inputting comments directly into the budget system or by some other means of communication.

11. The budget users (or the budget manager) copy the prior budget version to a new one.

12. The budget users make the necessary entries/changes to the new budget and submit it again. This can be either a small adjustment or a whole new scenario.

13. The budget manager locks the system for data entry.

14. The budget manager consolidates all the submitted budgets and runs a number of reports for review purposes. On some occasions, if management is happy with the figures they see, the budget is approved and frozen. If not, the process continues (steps 10 through 14 are repeated).

Although sometimes forgotten by the people keying in budget figures at remote locations of an organization, a key purpose of the budgeting process is to provide management with educated projections about the future so that they can make better decisions today. While some items can be automatically calculated (e.g., cost of sales, rent, etc.) other items (such as sales and personnel expenses) must be carefully analyzed based on competitive factors, economic factors, strategies, and more. In other words, there are two major aspects to the creation of budget figures: One is mathematical (calculation based on a formula) and the other is psychological (your best guess of what the future will look like). If users are not doing their best to estimate figures, management may end up making poor decisions because the data they analyzed was too far from the real truth. Budgeting software can improve this psychological/human error problem by offering a user-friendly interface and eliminating unnecessary manual work. Of course, motivation, system training, and so forth are up to the budget manager.

There are a number of features you should be able to get in a modern budgeting system to allow you to improve your company's planning process. In this book, a *modern system* is defined as software that allows multiple users to simultaneously enter their budgets from anywhere, on a monthly (or weekly) basis (up to a five year forecast, for example). The input environment should be user friendly, with the ability to view details or summaries, and with features to allocate totals and to do calculations on the fly. The report writer should be powerful with enough flexibility to create all variations of reports demanded by management. Anything less would simply be what many accounting systems have offered for years, and would not add significant value to your organization's strategic planning process. In a modern budgeting software you should expect to see many of the following:

- Integration to get financial and statistical data into the system
- Integration to get transactional data out of the system and into other software packages
- Multiple, customizable dimensions
- Integration to maintain master tables
- Customizable input screens
- Data entry automation
- Linking the data entry activity to corporate strategic targets
- Data entry guidance (help, warnings)
- Online connection for remote sites
- Line item detail
- User defined calculations
- Workflow automation
- Powerful and user-friendly report writer

- Data Recovery
- Drill-down

INTEGRATION TO GET FINANCIAL AND STATISTICAL DATA INTO THE SYSTEM

As more and more general ledgers offer either built-in budgeting functionality or have partnered with a third party budgeting software, the hassle of importing financial and statistical numbers is slowly disappearing. However, the quickly growing selection of feature-rich budgeting software packages from independent companies, as well as the widespread use of spreadsheet models still makes integration a key issue for any company. Vendors are often touting ODBC links and automated data uploads (of historical figures) that should make the budgeting system a snap to keep up to date. However, the reality is very often different. In large organizations, where there is one central budgeting process, different entities often have completely different general ledger systems and/or account number structures. This immediately puts demands on the budgeting system to handle mapping of different account numbers to a common or consolidated chart of accounts for budgeting and reporting purposes (see Part Four for more information on mapping charts of accounts). Also, if data has to go through a mapping table before it can be loaded into the budgeting system, somebody has to maintain that mapping system, and at that point you are usually back to a user-driven, time-consuming uploading process.

In the new budgeting systems, integration will demand less work and awareness from the user, and will be automated with more sophisticated rules-based integration features.

INTEGRATION TO GET TRANSACTIONAL DATA OUT OF THE SYSTEM AND INTO OTHER SOFTWARE PACKAGES

Being able to extract data from the budgeting system is often just as important as being able to load data into the system. Most budgeting systems have good report writers, but are somewhat lacking in in-depth analytical functionality. This means that the budgeting package usually will give you a great interface for data entry of budgets and forecasts (both for distributed solutions and for central database solutions), and it will let you consolidate your entities based on different roll-up structures, and finally, it will give you all of your reports online or on paper. However, at that point, when the budget is collected, checked, and consolidated, it can be of great value to be able to easily drill down through the organizational hierarchy, rank entities based on a parameter such as sales figures, highlight exceptions, and create graphs.

This analysis sometimes built into the budget system, but often it comes as an integrated third-party software module or as a separate module from the same vendor.

Typically there are direct links to spreadsheet applications like Microsoft Excel. This gives the user simple analysis tools (like pivot tables) and great graphical possibilities. However, more advanced analysis demands OLAP technology. This technology creates "cubes" from the budget systems' data, and you can drill down through any dimension (such as organizational trees, product trees, and market trees), rank figures, show trends over a period of time, and do quick graphs by highlighting rows or columns.

Other integrations that extract data from the budget system offer links back to the general ledger package. This is often desirable if you want to compare actual figures with budget figures in the general ledger's report writer, especially if the general ledger has a report writer that is superior to that of the budgeting system.

Most often integration to extract data from the budget system comes in the form of either text files that are exported/imported, or ODBC links. Many budget system vendors are also going all out to create customized, tight links with specific general ledgers and analytical tools. The modern budget system trend is clearly toward less manual updates and more automated links, so your budget data should in no way be "stuck."

Figure 6.2 shows the most typical integrations between a modern budgeting application and other software applications.

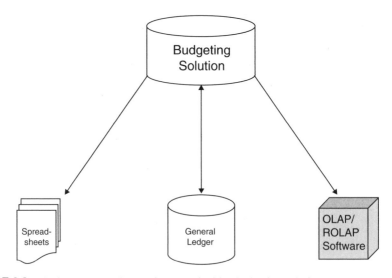

FIGURE 6.2   Typical systems that are integrated with a budgeting solution

MULTIPLE, CUSTOMIZABLE DIMENSIONS

Most modern budgeting systems allow you to split the different segments in the traditional chart of accounts (as found in the general ledger) into different dimensions. These dimensions can consist of different tables in an SQL database or different parts of an OLAP cube. Examples of dimensions are: company-department-natural account-currency-product-market-project.

Each dimension might have different properties. Take, for example, the "company" dimension. This dimension will usually have fields for: company code, company name, reporting currency, and so on. These are called customizable dimensions when the user can add, remove or change the different fields. Customizable dimensions give a company the flexibility to quickly streamline their budget process to best fit the software they have purchased. And more importantly, multiple dimensions allow for multi-dimensional reporting, which means that a company can go beyond simply budgeting by account and cost center. For strategically important accounts, such as sales, the budget system can allow for more detailed reporting, such as sales per cost center per product per market.

INTEGRATION TO MAINTAIN MASTER TABLES

A budget model normally uses the same "dimensions" as the general ledger. The word "dimensions" in this case refers to the different account segments in the chart of accounts. However, modern budgeting systems do not operate with one long account (or series of segments); they break the account segments into different dimensions called *master tables*. When the software uses all account segments from the general ledger, it should offer an integration that can upload all the segments with descriptions and populate the dimensions in the budget system.

Some examples of budgeting system master tables include:

- Account numbers and account descriptions
- Organizational entities (companies, divisions, departments, etc.) and codes and descriptions
- Currency codes and descriptions
- Product codes and descriptions
- Market codes and descriptions
- Project codes and descriptions

Other information that is often uploaded to the budgeting system includes:

- Exchange rates
- Tax rates
- Employee codes and names

CUSTOMIZABLE INPUT SCREENS

Most traditional budget systems had static data entry screens where the user chose an account number to work with, and then could select different options (such as different allocation formulas) from menus. However, because many companies have used spreadsheets as their primary budgeting tool, they have gotten used to highly customized input screens and calculations. Modern budgeting systems have responded to this demand by offering spreadsheet-based (or spreadsheet-like) user interfaces, where companies can customize the input screens to closely fit their particular industry needs.

DATA ENTRY AUTOMATION

Whereas traditional budgeting systems usually required manual data entry in most areas, modern solutions have built in a number of features that automate many of the previous manual tasks. You can now expect automatic:

- allocation of corporate overhead expenses to subsidiaries/departments.
- allocation of expenses from one department to other departments.
- assumptions—calculations of one item as a percentage of another (e.g., cost of goods sold as a percentage of revenue, or personnel taxes such as FICA, FUTA, SUTA).

LINKING THE DATA ENTRY ACTIVITY TO CORPORATE STRATEGIC TARGETS

Companies naturally want to clearly communicate their strategic plan to the line managers so they can keep these targets in mind as they create budgets and forecasts. For example, over the next 18 months, headquarters' goal might be to increase revenues by 10%, and to decrease operating expenses X, Y, and Z by 5%.

Some modern budget systems now offer screens where users can see instructions from HQ when entering figures into different accounts. Ideally, these instructions should reflect the corporate strategy. For example, when a user opens the account for Travel expenses to enter the forecast figures, she will see the text: "Travel expenses must be reduced by 10% next year." Therefore, a budgeting system that sends a warning or that prompts the user to check whether the entered forecast is less than 10% of last year's actual travel expenses can be very helpful. Regarding reports, the linking of forecasts to strategy can be accomplished with exception reports that show all items that are outside the parameters set in the strategy (e.g., Travel expense shows up if it is reduced by less than the targeted 10%).

Today's budgeting systems include screens where corporate headquarters can post the strategic targets (text comments and numbers) to the database at a high general level and for specific items (such as a group of operating expense accounts or a specific account), and the text and numbers link to the related input screens for the line managers who input the budgets and forecasts.

DATA ENTRY GUIDANCE (HELP, WARNINGS)

Many budget system users are managers at the department level that have few accounting or budgeting software skills so an advanced model might seem intimidating to them. However, modern budgeting systems have customizable field level instructions and business rules to reduce data entry errors. In some cases, entering budget figures consists of looking at last year's actual figures, and then entering the same numbers or similar ones into the budget model. This is often the case for relatively fixed expenses such as rent. For other budget items such as revenue, the data entry process is often based on human guesses. Usually, corporate goals (e.g., "increase revenues by 10% for next year") provide guidance for the entry of key budget items. As discussed, modern budgeting systems allow for data entry filters that warn a user if the entered number is outside a specified range. The data entry filter also can be a way to reduce input errors, as it will warn against entering a negative number in a field that only allows positive values.

ONLINE CONNECTION FOR REMOTE SITES

Remote sites have always provided a challenge for corporate headquarters in the budgeting process. Years ago, the remote sites would usually enter their budget on paper and then fax it to the corporate budget manager, who in turn would reenter the numbers into the budget system. Today, the majority of corporations have either a distributed budgeting solution where data is entered locally and then e-mailed as a file attachment to headquarters, or they let their remote offices connect to a central budgeting system through remote control software (such as that offered by Citrix Corporation). Though often slow compared to a local installation of a software, this solution avoids the problems related to installation/maintenance/updates of remote software installations.

Some budgeting systems provide good controls and features for maintenance of a budget model installation at remote sites, while other systems lack functionality for this purpose.

The newest and most revolutionary trend in the area of remote location budgeting is the use of web technology. Usually this means that the remote user can log on to a central budgeting application with a standard browser (such as Netscape Navigator or Microsoft Internet Explorer) and an Internet or intranet connection. Few budgeting systems currently offer web-based data entry modules with all the functionality of their client-server based systems, but almost all systems targeting mid-sized and large corporations will offer a powerful Web-solution in the near future. To a large extent, this will replace the hassle of maintaining remote budgeting applications and file transfers, and it will speed up the collection and dissemination of budget information. See Figure 6.3 for sample configurations of remote site budgeting.

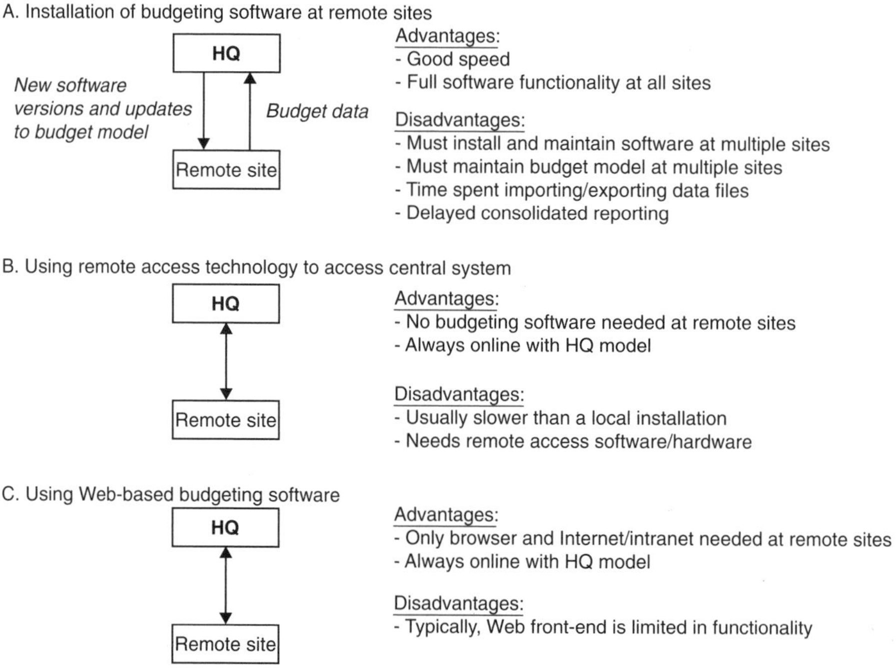

A. Installation of budgeting software at remote sites

New software
versions and updates
to budget model

```
        ┌──────────┐
        │    HQ    │
        └──────────┘
          ▲      │
          │      │  Budget data
          │      ▼
        ┌──────────────┐
        │ Remote site  │
        └──────────────┘
```

Advantages:
- Good speed
- Full software functionality at all sites

Disadvantages:
- Must install and maintain software at multiple sites
- Must maintain budget model at multiple sites
- Time spent importing/exporting data files
- Delayed consolidated reporting

B. Using remote access technology to access central system

```
        ┌──────────┐
        │    HQ    │
        └──────────┘
             ▲
             │
             ▼
        ┌──────────────┐
        │ Remote site  │
        └──────────────┘
```

Advantages:
- No budgeting software needed at remote sites
- Always online with HQ model

Disadvantages:
- Usually slower than a local installation
- Needs remote access software/hardware

C. Using Web-based budgeting software

```
        ┌──────────┐
        │    HQ    │
        └──────────┘
             ▲
             │
             ▼
        ┌──────────────┐
        │ Remote site  │
        └──────────────┘
```

Advantages:
- Only browser and Internet/intranet needed at remote sites
- Always online with HQ model

Disadvantages:
- Typically, Web front-end is limited in functionality

FIGURE 6.3   Alternative solutions for handling remote sites in the budget process

LINE ITEM DETAIL

As companies are moving beyond traditional budgeting where every account in the general ledger (or at least every profit and loss account) is assigned a monthly budget figure, modern budget systems are providing functionality that allows the user to enter specifications below the account number level. For example, to calculate travel expenses, an employee usually must estimate all the trips to be made next year and how much each trip will cost. Older budget systems have not offered possibilities for the user to enter their own text and numbers for items that roll up to an account number balance. Thus, people have often resorted to use of local spreadsheets for their own details and then entered the account total into the budgeting system. The result is that the detail has been unavailable to top management for analysis and comment. Also, if changes to the account total are required, the audit trail is often lost because the end users have not saved or provided the different versions of their own detailed spreadsheets. Modern budgeting tools offer line item detail capabilities, and thus, all or most assumptions and calculations behind each account number balance are contained within the budgeting database and are easily revisable.

USER-DEFINED CALCULATIONS

One of the most ignored features in both older and newer budgeting systems is the availability of user-defined calculations as part of the data entry process. For example, if the user is to budget the account called Office Equipment, he will probably want to calculate the number of chairs, printers, and so forth needed, multiplied by the average price per item. In other cases, the estimated amount at the account number level is calculated in different ways (e.g., by the use of Net present value [NPV], etc.). A number of budgeting systems provide Excel-based front-ends, allowing the user to allocate certain sections of the spreadsheet for their own calculations. The problem with this is that the user-defined calculations are not stored to the database (they remain only in the spreadsheet file) because they are outside the pre-defined cells that are stored to the database. Modern budgeting systems are getting better in this area and are starting to offer menu-based calculations that the user can select for different purposes, but in general, even newer systems have a way to go in this area.

WORKFLOW AUTOMATION

Workflow automation is another feature that many systems still do not offer. "Workflow" has become a buzzword in the world of accounting software, and it generally refers to functionality that defines a series of process-related tasks the user will go through. These tasks can either be defined and specified by the user (best option) or they might be pre-programmed into the system (see Figure 6.4). In relation to the budgeting process, a workflow process can consist of:

1. Input of corporate budget targets
2. Distribution of budget input templates (if there are remote locations not linked to HQ)

3. Input of budget

4. Collection and upload of budget files (if there are remote locations not linked to HQ)

5. Reconciliation

6. HQ adjustments

7. Report processing

Some budgeting packages have menus that reflect the workflow with graphical buttons (to go to a specific task) and arrows that point from one task to the next. Other systems are starting to implement task lists that can be programmed by the individual user to reorganize their particular workflow in the order they prefer. Completed tasks can be visually checked off to show where the process currently stands.

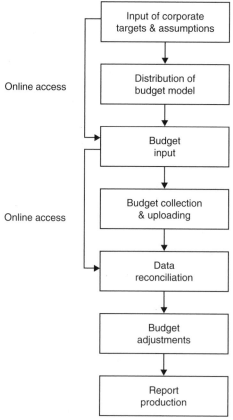

FIGURE. 6.4 Steps in the budgeting process that can be simplified with workflow features

POWERFUL AND USER-FRIENDLY REPORT WRITER

Older budgeting systems have, in general, offered rather poor report writing capabilities. More and more companies are now forecasting several times a year as part of their corporate planning process. Some are moving away from the annual budgeting process and have started forecasting on a rolling period basis, looking 12 or 15 months ahead with every new forecast. This has forced software vendors to add functionality to their report writers or, in some cases, to create entirely new technology. Because of the flexibility and familiarity that most people have with spreadsheet applications, many vendors have gone the route of making spreadsheet report writer interfaces to their applications. As modern budgeting systems develop increasingly more functionality in their report writers, the challenge is still to make it easy for the user to create new reports. To this end, we are now seeing report wizards and templates starting to appear, which guide the novice user step-by-step through the creation of a new report. Here also, many vendors still have a long way to go before companies are fully empowered to write most reports with ease.

FULL SECURITY

Historically, the security features in budgeting software have been of mixed depth and detail. Part of the reason for this is that the budgeting system was often installed and available to only one or a few people at the head office. Also, many sensitive details, such as payroll information, were handled outside the budgeting system with pen and paper or in separate spreadsheets. The totals were then plugged into budget system. Today, the overwhelming trend is toward enterprise-wide access to the budgeting application. Detailed employee payroll information, as well as sensitive product information (such as estimated prices and sales volumes), are some of the data entered or uploaded into modern budgeting systems. As a response to the new need for detailed security, application vendors are adding functionality. Most systems now offer read, write, change, and delete access based on a specific organizational entity (e.g., department, division, company). It is also normal to find security covering budget versions, time periods, and sometimes specific accounts or line items. The same detailed security should also apply to users who access the application through a web-based interface (in addition to firewalls and other external security features for web users).

DATA RECOVERY

One never knows when a database might become corrupt, or users might make mistakes, deleting entire sections of a budget. For years, it has been the practice to perform daily backups of network servers and databases. In addition to this, most budgeting systems that are based on industry-standard databases (such as Microsoft SQL Server, Oracle, and Sybase), have log files that register all users' actions and record all new data entered, updated, or deleted. If necessary, a skilled database technician can recover a database and put it back to the state it was in at specific moment in time.

DRILL-DOWN

Drill-down is another popular buzzword that most companies looking for a new budgeting system have on their check lists. Typically, this term refers to the ability to use the mouse to click on totals or sub-totals in rows or columns in a report/input screen to see the underlying detail (see Figure 6.5). For example, by clicking on Total Revenue, you will see all underlying revenue accounts. A user can also drill up and down the organizational structure/tree, and see the numbers on the screen change accordingly. Some modern budgeting system vendors offer drill-down directly in their core application, while others link the budgeting system to a dedicated OLAP tool that gives the user fast drill-down, analysis, and graphical capabilities.

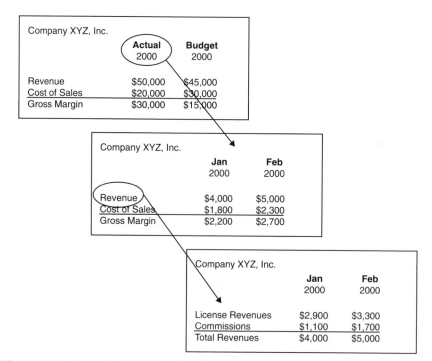

FIGURE. 6.5   Example of drill-down in a financial report

CHAPTER 7

WHAT WILL FUTURE BUDGETING SOFTWARE OFFER?

It can always be useful to try to predict the future (especially if your predictions come close to the fact). Whether you are planning to create an in-house budget system or are considering purchasing a best-of-breed solution, needs expressed by companies like yours are driving the development of future software functionality. Some of the features discussed in Figure 7.1 are already found in modern solutions, while others are planned for future releases. Often, a total solution from a vendor will encompass many of the listed features, but usually it will come through different modules with different underlying technology, interfaces, and solutions without a direct integration. As the popular budgeting packages evolve, more and more of these features will become the mature, advanced functionality that will empower your planning process. In order to make this information more accurate and useful, we'll focus on the next five years ahead. To make sound predictions, we need to look around the marketplace and attempt to see what type of budgeting functionality leading companies will be demanding. Furthermore, we must take a look at the direction of software technology, hardware technology, and communications to predict what type of systems most likely will be delivered.

Information and functionality needs:	What future budgeting systems will offer:	Comment
Comparison with key competitors or industry averages (benchmarking)	Functionality to quickly and easily set up dummy companies (competitors) in the budgeting system. Historical trends and comparisons for own company and competitors.	As companies are getting more specialized and even niche markets are becoming more competitive, it is important to look over your shoulder and compare yourself to competition.
Complete information	Must be an end-to-end solution that can present management with budgets, forecasts, and actual figures and statistics, and must be able to easily pull information from all key financial systems to the central database.	Needs a powerful report writer and flexible setup and integration features.
Fast delivery of information to decision makers	Automation of budget process. This starts with intelligent integration with front-end systems such as the general ledger. Using automated links, historical figures, account numbers, organizational tree structures, and so forth should flow through a filter and a rules-based syntax check and into the budgeting system. The rules should be user-defined, and automatically take care of most conflicts and updates. Only in certain cases should the user have to be prompted for questions regarding the upload. The budgeting system	Today, users and budget managers often spend more time entering and uploading information than they spend thinking about how to come up with good predictions of the future.

FIGURE 7.1   Future budgeting software functionality

Information and functionality needs:	What future budgeting systems will offer:	Comment
	should also offer allocation functionality, consolidation, adjustments, and comment handling.	
Accurate information	Validation controls and messages in connection with data entry and upload activities.	With lower level, previously uninvolved managers getting involved in the budgeting process, systems must provide maximum guidance and control to avoid entry of erroneous/inaccurate information.
Focus on key business drivers	Exception reports, key figures reports with built in drill-down, tight links to systems such as sales order entry/customer relationship management (CRM) software.	Companies are moving toward more budgeting detail in key areas, but they are focusing on the reporting items that drive their business performance. Exception reports and key figures keep management focused on what is important!
Exception alerts	Messages and information forwarded to the right person immediately if certain predefined parameters are violated. This proactive information delivery ensures quick responses. The message should contain or link to the numbers in question and to a responsible person. The message can be sent via e-mail, pager, or cell phone.	Today, it often takes weeks before a new budget reaches decision makers, and then there are so many reports and numbers that key deviations might be discovered late or never. In the future, new budgets (forecasts) could be produced as often as every month, so managers will not have time to look for exceptions, the exceptions must come to them!

FIGURE 7.1 Future budgeting software functionality–*Cont.*

Information and functionality needs:	What future budgeting systems will offer:	Comment
More employee information	This includes employee-level budgeting with tight links to the payroll system.	In an increasingly services driven economy, employees are becoming the company's most valuable asset, but also the most expensive one. Detailed employee budgeting helps plan for next years'/periods' resource needs, availability of manpower, and expenses.
Easy access to information	Many decisions made in order to enter good budget figures are based on having accurate information at the user's fingertips. For example, when entering travel expenses, the user needs to know how many trips will be made next year, and how much each trip will cost. Decision-makers also need easy, online access to reports. These should be "pushed" to them by e-mail or easily accessed ("pulled") from anywhere at any time.	Information such as typical travel expenses, exchange rates, and so forth should be linked or uploaded to the budget system to provide the user with timely and accessible information.
Analytical tools to investigate information and aid decision making	Many of today's systems offer drill-down capabilities, but they can be limited. For example, you can drill down on accounts but not necessarily on organizational hierarchies, or other dimensions such as products, projects, and markets. In the future, with increasing focus on key	Drill-down and analysis are only as good as the data you are investigating. It is therefore important to provide good and "clean" (adjusted, eliminated, currency converted, etc.) budget data to the analysis module/feature set.

FIGURE 7.1   Future budgeting software functionality–*Cont.*

Information and functionality needs:	What future budgeting systems will offer:	Comment
	business drivers, the budgeting system or linked module must be strong in this area.	
Analytical tools to aid data entry decisions	As companies are aiming to link corporate strategy and targets to the budgeting process, new systems will offer better budget input interfaces where new data are immediately measured against corporate targets. System will provide automatic comments and dialogue boxes to guide the users during the input process.	Much of the push to link strategy with the budgeting and reporting process can be seen in the Balanced Scorecard (BS) approach to performance measurement. Many budget software vendors are starting to include methodology from the balanced scorecard into the applications.
Useful and understandable information	Useful information means any text explanation or number that can assist in planning and making business decisions. This means that future budgeting systems must be able to integrate text and financial and statistical numbers into meaningful input screens and reports. The budgeting system should also offer multi-dimensional views of the data, so that each manager can view the information in the way it makes the most sense to them.	The systems will not be any better than the users feeding information into them. Again, this means that even when the software improves, the company must still be good at defining what is useful and what isn't, and must remember to include the proper instructions and screens to the end-user.

FIGURE 7.1 Future budgeting software functionality–*Cont.*

Information and functionality needs:	What future budgeting systems will offer:	Comment
Consistent information for dynamic organizations	Budgeting systems must be flexible and scalable to handle organizational change and growth, without major manual maintenance requirements in the budget model.	This will depend on the database the application is running on, as well as the functionality built into the software to handle changing organizations, e.g., features such as graphical roll-up trees, to handle acquisitions, reorganizations, and divestitures.
Systems that are easy to deploy, maintain, and learn	Here, one of the key drivers is Web technology. Using Internet communication protocols and Web-based interfaces, the time to deploy a budgeting application is virtually zero. Of course, there will still be a need for training. Much of this will be online help/training also deployed through a Web interface.	As corporations push the budget/input process down to at least the department level, sometimes to the individual level, the need to train large numbers of financially unskilled employees becomes a challenge. At the same time, costs must be kept down.
Systems prepared for application hosting services	Application service providers (ASPs) have been around for many years, but recently this market has heated up again because of the new and cheaper communication possibilities through the Internet, as well as new thin client technology. Future budgeting applications must be fully Web-enabled in order to offer a complete browser interface with access	In order for a customer to trust their budgeting application to an ASP host, not only must the application work well through remote access, but the customer must be ensured that the security of their data is intact. The benefits of utilizing hosting services will be most prevalent to companies with scarce technical resources.

FIGURE 7.1   Future budgeting software functionality–*Cont.*

Information and functionality needs:	What future budgeting systems will offer:	Comment
	to everything from input to reports, as well as access to model and security maintenance.	
Top security	Because most future budgeting systems will deploy web-based clients, either on a corporate intranet or the Internet, security is a top concern for management. Most budgeting applications will have to improve in this area. Read, write, update, and delete security needs to apply to all levels in the system's organizational hierarchy, as well as to individual budgeting accounts/items, different budget versions, different time periods, and other dimensions in the budget model.	It is the fear of all companies that competitors or other outsiders might get a hold of their future plans. They would rather use old technology than have their budgeting information stolen, so security must be top-of-the-line.
Functionality that recognizes different user roles	The software should have the functionality to automatically (based on setup) make different information available to the specific user to which it applies.	This will reduce training time and increase ease of use and efficiency. Today, most systems look the same (same menus, options, etc.) to all users; the restrictions are only in security access.

FIGURE 7.1   Future budgeting software functionality–*Cont.*

Information and functionality needs:	What future budgeting systems will offer:	Comment
Multi-dimensional information	Whereas the traditional budgeting system typically has been three-dimensional (period, business-unit, and account), modern budgeting systems should contain a large number of user-defined dimensions to allow decision makers to also analyze data by products, markets, projects, and so on.	Multi-dimensional budgets demand more scalability, security, automation, and analytical features from the software in order to manage the new data and to give the decision makers access to find and investigate the information. It is important that the different dimensions can handle accounting logic and user-defined relations in order to reduce the number of complex formulas (and maintenance of these) in input screens and reports.
Budget process tracking	As the budget process becomes an organization-wide exercise, budget software must offer adequate process tracking to give budget managers the necessary control.	Budget process tracking should show: • when strategic targets are set • when budgets are submitted • when budgets are reconciled • when budget reports are distributed/available
Multi-currency information	Traditional budget systems have had weak currency functionality. Modern solutions should provide managers with a complete set of features (such as currency conversion with unlimited number of rates per currency, cross-rate calculations, exchange rate effect reports, etc.)	The currency features should be easily accessible through menus, and not require budget managers to learn sophisticated business rules and formulas.

FIGURE 7.1   Future budgeting software functionality–*Cont.*

Information and functionality needs:	What future budgeting systems will offer:	Comment
Powerful input environment	Modern budgeting systems should provide easily customizable worksheets with powerful formulas and flexibility, as well as built-in validation and control features to take care of the budgeting needs for all levels in the organization.	Although many budget packages offer a functionality rich input environment that works well as a data collection tool for the head office, few have yet to also offer the reporting sites the flexibility they need to handle their detailed, local budget.
Smart report writing	Modern budgeting systems need to offer smart report writers that can convert common language expressions (such as "year to date") into formulas, or at least, offer most popular expressions from easy-to-use menus in the report writer.	Most powerful report writers are still only useful to highly trained financial staff or the IS department. Any decision-maker that needs to gather information in a nicely formatted report should be able to do so with minimal training and assistance.
Smart query tools	Whenever a user is looking for information but doesn't want to look for it in defined reports or drill-down from available views, he or she should be able to use a smart query function. For example, by asking for "Gross Margin, Canada, February," the budget system should call up a link to all reports and/or pre-defined views that correspond to the query, similar to a Web search engine.	The key for a smart budgeting query tool is that it be a natural part of the user interface and that it be extremely easy to use so decision-makers with minimal training will use it.

FIGURE 7.1 Future budgeting software functionality–*Cont.*

CHAPTER 8

BUDGETING SOFTWARE BUYER'S GUIDE

The market for professional budgeting software had very few players until about 1995 or 1996. At that time several new companies came out with their version 1.0 of brand new budgeting applications, and in the following years a number of new vendors have arrived. This is good news, because it stimulates competition and it offers more choices to all the companies out there who are ready to replace their own spreadsheet models or their old mainframe budgeting applications. Most vendors appeal to all industries, but several are also attempting (more marketing-wise than functionality-wise) to carve out specific industry niches for themselves.

According to International Data Corporation (IDC), the business analytics market is growing at a rate of 38% annually and is expected to top $7 billion by 2002. Business analytics is a software category consisting of budgeting/planning, financial consolidation, business performance management, and activity-based costing. This strong demand will continue to foster healthy competition among budgeting software vendors, and increasingly better functionality and user-interfaces can be expected.

For most companies, price is a relatively important issue, so Figure 8.1 organizes the products into three different price categories, from high to low. Note that the price does not necessarily reflect the number of budgeting features in the different products or the return on investment your company can expect.

High End ($60,000+)

Product/Vendor	Platform
Product: Hyperion Pillar Vendor: Hyperion Solutions Corporation Web: www.hyperion.com	Client: Windows-based, Apple OS Database: Proprietary
Product: Comshare BudgetPlus Vendor: Comshare Web: www.comshare.com	Client: Windows-based (Excel) Database: Essbase, Oracle, DB2, MS SQL Server
Product: Cognos Finance Company: Cognos Corporation Web: www.lex2000.com	Client: Windows-based Database: Cognos Finance OLAP
Product: Khalix Vendor: Longview Solutions, Inc. Web: www.longview.ca	Client: Windows-based Database: DB2, Informix, MS SQL Server, Oracle, Sybase

Middle Market ($15,000 to $59,999)

Product/Vendor	Platform
Product: SRC Advisor Series Vendor: SRC Software Web: www.srcsoftware.com	Client: Excel-based Database: MS SQL Server, Oracle
Product: Enterprise Reporting Vendor: Solver, Inc. Web: www.solverusa.com	Client: Windows-based Database: MS SQL Server, Sybase SQL Anywhere
Product: Helmsman Vendor: Helmsman Group, Inc. Web: www.helmsmangroup.com	Client: Windows-based Database: Oracle, Sybase, Microsoft SQL Server, Microsoft Access
Product: Best!Imperativ Planning & Analysis Vendor: The Sage Group Web: http://www.sage.com	Client: Windows-based Database: MS SQL Server

FIGURE 8.1 Budgeting software buyer's guide

Middle Market ($15,000 to $59,999)

Product/Vendor	Platform
Product: Adaytum Planning Company: Adaytum Software Web: www.adaytum.com	Client:Windows-based Database: OLAP database
Product: Control Company: KCI Computing, Inc. Web: http://www.kcicorp.com	Client: Windows-based Database: Oracle
Product: Powerplan Company: Powerplan Corp. Web: www.planningandlogic.com	Client: Windows-based Database: MS SQL Server, Oracle, 　　　　　Pervasive.SQL/Betrieve
Product: HORIZON Company: Walker Interactive Systems Web: www.walker.com	Client: Windows-based Database: DB2, Oracle, MS SQL Server
Product: Timeline Budgeting Company: Timeline, Inc. Web: www.timeline.com	Client: Excel front end Database: MS SQL Server
Product: Oracle Financial Analyzer Company: Oracle Web: www.oracle.com	Client: Windows-based Database: Oracle Express Server 　　　　　(OLAP)
Product: Budget2000 Vendor: EPS Software Web: www.epssoftware.com	Client: Windows-based Database: Pilot OLAP
Product: MIS Alea Vendor: MIS AG Web: www.mis-ag.com	Client: Windows-based Database: MS SQL Server, Oracle, 　　　　　Pervasive.SQL/Betrieve, DB2, 　　　　　Informix, Sybase

FIGURE 8.1　Budgeting software buyer's guide—*Cont.*

Low End ($1000 to $14,999)

Product/Vendor	Platform
Product: Budget Maestro Vendor: Planet Corporation Web: www.planetcorp.com	Windows-based software
Product: Personal Analyst Vendor: InAlysys, Inc. Web: www.inalysys.com	Windows-based software
Product: Super Budget Vendor: Super Budget, Inc. Web: www.superbudget.com	Client: Windows-based Database: Pervasive.SQL/Betrieve

FIGURE 8.1   Budgeting software buyer's guide—*Cont.*

WHAT CORE BUDGETING FUNCTIONALITY DO COMPANIES WANT?

As the focus on budgeting and planning processes have rapidly increased over the last few years, the need for more sophisticated budgeting software has become ever more apparent. The authors have interviewed a number of different companies seeking to acquire new budgeting systems, and Figure 8.2 is a list of their most sought after features. An "X" in the left column of this figure means that most modern budgeting systems offer the functionality, and whenever the column is empty it means that the functionality is still lacking in most systems. If any of the functionality listed is of key importance to you, pay particular attention to whether or not it is marked with an "X" as you evaluate different budgeting software packages for your company.

Common Feature	Functionality	Importance High/ Medium/Low
	Advanced allocation features (e.g., multi-tiered)	H
	Alerts triggered by pre-defined rules (actual/budget deviation, or gross margin less than 15%, etc.)	L
	Allocations—top/down, across the organization	H
X	Analysis—drill-down, drill-across, ranking, and so forth	H
	Automated maintenance of chart of accounts	H
	Automated maintenance of reporting hierarchies	H
	Automated upload of monthly balances from the general ledger (database link rather than file import)	H
	Batch report processing with timer	M
X	Budget process status tracking	M
X	Capital budgeting capabilities	H
	Cash flow analysis	M
X	Charting	M
X	Dynamic integration to MS Excel	H
X	Easy downloading of budget to the general ledger (with different file format options)	M
X	Electronic report distribution (or distribution of links to centrally stored reports)	M
X	Employee budgeting (salary expense, taxes, etc.)	H
X	Line item detail (data entry includes text comments)	H
X	Multi-currency features	M
X	Multiple dimensions (accounts, entities, products, markets, projects, employees, etc.)	H
X	Powerful report writer	H
	Programmable workflow (task lists, triggered events, etc.)	L
	Security specified down to lowest organizational level and account level	M
X	Uploading capability from other systems (such as payroll and sales systems)	H
X	User-definable calculations that link to corporate input model	M
X	User-friendly report writer (wizard-based or highly intuitive, such as a spreadsheet-based interface)	H
X	Web input and reporting	M
	Workflow automation	L

FIGURE 8.2   List of popular budgeting software functionality

CHAPTER 9

USING EXCEL AS A BUDGETING TOOL

Most people today are familiar with the spreadsheet as a financial reporting and budgeting tool. Research shows that spreadsheets are still by far the most used software for corporate budgeting and forecasting, the major reasons for this popularity being ease of use, flexibility, and low acquisition cost. Because Microsoft Excel now is the dominant spreadsheet on the market, we will focus on Excel throughout the rest of this chapter.

Also, when we refer to limitations and special features in Excel, we will be referring to the capabilities of Excel 2000. If you are using an older version of Excel, you should check with your Excel user documentation or Microsoft to verify whether a specific feature or limitation also applies to your version of the product.

WHEN TO USE EXCEL AND WHEN TO USE A BEST-OF-BREED BUDGETING TOOL

If you are faced with a "build versus buy" decision to solve your budgeting software needs, Excel will most likely be one of your alternatives. Most companies that purchase a new budgeting application do so after having grown out of their old home-built or commercial budgeting solution, or their spreadsheet model has become too large and unmanageable. Whatever decision you make, it is an important one because you will spend a lot of time and money either way, and you want to make sure you make the right choice from the start. In the following section we will go through a list of factors that will help you decide whether or not Excel is the right budgeting tool for you.

When You Should Use Excel

You should use Excel under the following circumstances:

- Many diverse budgeting entities that each require a customized budget model to handle their unique local needs.

- Very small company and/or simple enough budgeting needs that no database or special functionality is necessary.

- A suitable best-of-breed solution will be too expensive to justify the necessary investment in training, hardware, consulting, and software.

- No time to get a best-of-breed software fully operational because the budget process starts soon.

- Advanced reporting (such as variance reports, exception reports, etc.) can be handled by your accounting software report writer or a best-of-breed consolidation and reporting software.

When You Should NOT Use Excel

You should not use Excel under the following circumstances:

Control

Once a budget system is operational, there are many variables that can impact your level of control to ensure that the integrity of the model is always preserved. Some of the variables you need to be aware of are:

- Who has access to the budget model?
- When and how are backup files being created?
- If parts of the model are being distributed, is everyone using the same version of your spreadsheet model and of Excel?

Best-of-breed software generally has built-in features and routines to handle these issues with minimum user interaction and a high degree of control.

Security

If there are a number of users accessing your spreadsheet budget model, you will quickly find that the security of your data easily can be endangered. While best-of-breed budgeting software typically has built-in security that covers data entry, data viewing, data updates, deletion by the user, organizational entity, time period, etc., you need to retain control of all these aspects of your spreadsheet model. You can protect cells, worksheets, and workbooks from changes and viewing, and you can require passwords, but because there is no central user access control, security quickly becomes unmanageable with a large number of spreadsheets and users.

Performance

The speed of opening, recalculating, and saving a spreadsheet slows down as the model gets larger and more complex. For example, a spreadsheet model containing a hundred or more linked spreadsheets can often take ten minutes or more to recalculate (depending on computer hardware, network speed, etc.). If you make frequent changes, you will need to recalculate the model often. It will also demand more memory on your desktop computer. In general, a best-of-breed budgeting package will perform proportionally better than a spreadsheet model as the model grows larger. This is because the best-of-breed solutions use databases that perform most calculations on a powerful server in the network, and the databases themselves are designed to retrieve data as fast and efficiently as possible.

Sophistication

Best-of-breed budgeting software packages are designed to automate typical budgeting needs such as:

- Allocations between entities and budget items
- Complex consolidations
- Currency conversion
- Multi-year historical trends and forecasts
- Spreading of annual totals based on different business rules

All of these features can be manually built into your spreadsheet budget model, but the more you find yourself adding sophisticated formulas, the more maintenance work and security issues you will have to handle in the future.

Fast-growing company

If your company is in a period of rapid growth and new product lines or departments and divisions are frequently added or reorganized, a spreadsheet-based budget model will become very time-consuming to maintain. The problem is not the distribution of the model to new users, but rather the maintenance work required to insert rows and columns and spreadsheets into the existing model. Unless you exercise detailed control of all parts of the model, the integrity will likely be endangered, and you will begin to see incorrect calculations. Best-of-breed budgeting software programs are much better at organizing large volumes of data and can usually handle the addition of a new subsidiary or department in a few minutes, without compromising integrity.

Frequent organizational changes

Just as a fast growing company can cause problems, frequent organizational changes will also endanger a spreadsheet's integrity. For example, if employees move from one department to another, the spreadsheet with the payroll budget will not update (unless you have used sophisticated programming to handle this automatically). In a best-of-breed solution, such a change is normally handled by a central change in one location of the software, and then all input screens and reports will be updated automatically. Another example is when the company is reorganized and business units are moved from one division to another. A best-of-breed solution handles this change by allowing the user to drag and drop the business unit from one node in an organizational tree to another, while a spreadsheet model needs manual updates to all related formulas that consolidate or summarize data.

When a Combination of Best-of-Breed Software and Spreadsheets Works Best

Sometimes the central budget manager is mostly concerned with summarized (high level) data collection, consolidations, and reporting, while the company's divisions need flexible budget models that are uniquely designed to fit their local budgeting needs. In this case, the budget manager can employ a best-of-breed budgeting software at the central location, while each division can use a local spreadsheet model that they design to handle their own required level of detail and their specific business activity (such as a manufacturing plant versus a sales department). Once the local budgets are created they can be transferred to a general, high level spreadsheet template that is submitted to the budget manager, or sometimes, they can transfer their numbers directly to a Web front-end of the central budgeting software.

Another example of when a combination of a best-of-breed software and a spreadsheet model can be used is in autonomous organizations where there is little communication between divisions and there are large business differences. In this case, it will be almost impossible to construct a detailed enterprise-wide budget model. Usually, headquarters only requires divisions to submit a simple, summarized budget. In this case, the central office can employ a best-of-breed solution to collect, consolidate, and report the required budgets, while the divisions can employ local spreadsheet models customized to their own needs.

The cost of a best-of-breed budgeting software package can be a direct barrier to organization-wide use of it. As previously mentioned, it is increasingly popular to directly involve managers down to the departmental level in the budgeting process and in the use of a corporate budgeting model. In a midsized or large company with a hundred or maybe thousands of departments, this can add hundreds of thousands of dollars in licensing costs and maintenance fees to the budgeting software. Because of the prohibitive cost, management might decide to use spreadsheets to collect budgets from each department, and then upload these to a central budgeting software.

BUILDING AN EXCEL BUDGETING MODEL

Planning the Model Building

Once you have decided to build your budget model with Excel, you can save quite a few headaches by first doing some model planning. The larger and more complex your model, the more you should plan it before beginning your first spreadsheet. Here are some planning steps to consider:

1. Define the goal (expected end-result) of the budgeting model. This goal typically includes a budget report book with useful management reports and supporting detail, and access to analyze data and to produce multiple planning scenarios.

2. Based on your answer to number 1, define the type and lowest level of detail of the data you need to collect. For example, a model might consist of information by department by month, with certain revenues and expenses also entered by product, market, employee, project, and so forth.

3. Find out how frequently the budget needs to be updated, so you know how many versions of the budget model need to be saved and managed.

4. Define who the data entry users will be and who the report users will be and what type of access these people need to the model.

5. Make a master prototype of the model and verify with management that it provides what they expect.

6. Decide which spreadsheets will be the same for all business entities, and which spreadsheets need to be customized for particular entities.

7. Decide which parts of the budget model should be in the same spreadsheets and which should be in separate spreadsheets.

8. Create a flow-chart (see Figure 9.1) to help the administrator and users understand the workflow and the different pieces of the spreadsheet model.

9. Start with the highest level spreadsheets and work your way down to the most detailed ones.

10. Test each spreadsheet with real data as you go along, to make sure formulas and logic are intact and working properly.

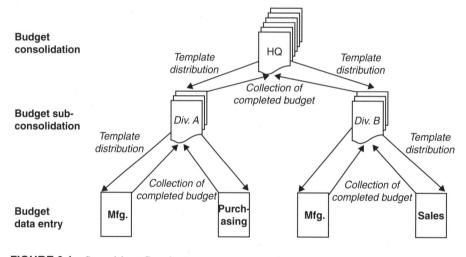

FIGURE 9.1   Spreadsheet flowchart

Structuring a Complex Model to Maintain Control and Integrity

Organizing the spreadsheets

One of the major differences between best-of-breed budgeting software and a spreadsheet model is that best-of-breed software uses database technology to store all data in a single database, whereas a typical spreadsheet-based model consists of a number of linked spreadsheets for each budget version and each year. As the years go by, you end up with an increasing number of spreadsheets, both because you might want to save historical figures, and because as your company grows, more business units need to be stored. Therefore, as the designer of a spreadsheet-based budgeting model, you should pay great attention to how you organize your model, so it will allow for change and growth without jeopardizing control and integrity. Some tips are:

- Create a directory structure on your server with a hierarchy for budget year, budget version, and division/department. This makes it much easier to organize and locate files as time goes by.

- Create a naming convention for all spreadsheets that makes it easy to distinguish year, budget version, business unit, spreadsheet type. For example: 01-B1-D101-P&L.XLS. This would mean: Year 2001, budget version 1, department 101, profit & loss.

- Unless you have a small budget model or other very good reasons for putting the whole model in a single worksheet or spreadsheet, try to design a logical set of linked spreadsheets. Very large spreadsheets can be a drag on both computer memory and performance, but even more important, they can be very confusing to anyone who is not working with the spreadsheet on a regular basis. It is better to break up a model into several worksheets and/or spreadsheets before you complete it, rather than wait until later, when you will have to redo all cell references and links.

Setting up security to prevent unauthorized access or changes

Microsoft Excel provides the following security and protection features:

- You can limit access to each individual worksheet or elements of it.
- You can limit changes to an entire workbook or elements of it.
- You can protect workbook sharing and the change history.
- You can limit access to a workbook by requiring a password to open it or save it, or you can recommend that others open the workbook as read-only.
- You can check for macros that might contain viruses whenever you open a workbook.

For detailed information, refer to your Excel online help file or your program manual.

Using macros to automate a model

One of the most powerful features of a spreadsheet is the macro functionality. A macro is a series of commands and functions that are stored in a Visual Basic module and can be run whenever you need to perform a particular task. Any repetitive task you need to perform, such as uploading files from the general ledger, printing, or automatically posting allocations, can be recorded to a macro and done for you at the push of a button (again, refer to your Excel manual for detailed information). Using a macro will also reduce the chances of human error.

Maintaining multiple budget versions

Most companies compile multiple budget iterations during the budget process. Whether this is to create several scenarios of the future, or it is an adjustment of the prior budget version to get closer to set targets, it is recommended that you save each budget version. Not only will this offer an audit trail to see what changes have been made, but it also allows you return to a previous version if need be. Unless you have a very small budget model, the best way to organize many budget versions is to keep each version in a separate spreadsheet and to store them in separate directories on the hard drive.

Employing a spreadsheet model in a multi-user environment

Depending on the size of a company, the level of budget detail to be entered, and the budgeting methodology used, there are several different ways to employ a spreadsheet model:

- Multiple users at the same location access the model on the local network or on their individual computers.
- Multiple users at remote locations receive the model by e-mail or other means, complete the budget, and send it back to the head office.
- Multiple users at remote locations access a centrally stored spreadsheet model through a Web interface or remote access software.

There is no right or wrong way to disseminate a spreadsheet-based budget model to multiple users. The most prevalent concerns for an administrator to consider are setting deadlines for budget completion and ensuring that files that have been used locally be returned to a specific network directory or e-mail address.

Protecting the model against unauthorized changes

Protect your model as follows:

- If several people are working on the same spreadsheet file, make sure that they do not overwrite each other's work. (This is achieved by issuing proper instructions as well as using password protection.)
- If remote users are going to access a central budget model, test speed and communication links prior to starting the budget process.

How to Maximize Performance

Nobody likes to wait for large spreadsheet models to open, recalculate, or save, especially when budget deadlines are drawing near. Many variables come into play to enhance spreadsheet performance. Some of the most typical ones are:

- Increase Random Access Memory (RAM) on your computer and/or server.
- Upgrade to a faster Central Processing Unit (CPU) on your computer and/or server.
- Improve connection speed for remote users.
- Break up large spreadsheets into smaller spreadsheets.
- Turn off automatic recalculation and let users control it (but make sure everyone is aware that recalculation is turned off).
- Check the logic in the model itself to ensure that only essential calculations are being used. (Overuse of calculations will slow down the process.)

Report Writing

After all budgets are collected, the next step is the consolidation of data and production of reports. The challenge is in making sure all cell and spreadsheet references are correct and are able to produce all the different reports required by management. The best way to speed up report writing is to create spreadsheets that summarize the budgets at the different levels, and then refer to the summaries as you write. In order to assure that reports contain the correct numbers, it is also important to create reconciliation calculations that serve as a control over the process.

ANALYZING THE NUMBERS

Excel offers very powerful analytical features. With little or no technical skills or training, a user can analyze budgets and variances, and visualize trends and other numerical scenarios using several built-in features. These include:

What-If Analysis

- Goal seek: When you know the desired result of a single formula but not the input value needed to determine the result, you can use the Goal Seek feature. When goal seeking, Microsoft Excel varies the value in one specific cell until a formula that is dependent on that cell returns the desired result.

- Solver: Use Solver to determine the value of a cell when you need to change the values in more than one cell and have multiple constraints for those values. To use Solver, the cells you want to work with must be related through formulas on the worksheet. (For more information about the Solver function, please refer to your Excel manual.)

- Scenarios: A scenario is a set of values used to forecast the outcome of a worksheet model. You can create and save different groups of values on a worksheet and then switch to any of these new scenarios to view different results. For example, if you want to create a budget but are uncertain of your revenue, you can define different values for the revenue and then switch between the scenarios to perform what-if analyses.

- Data Tables: A data table is a range of cells that show how changing certain values in your formulas affects the results of the formulas. Data tables provide a shortcut for calculating multiple versions in one operation and they allow you to view and compare the results of all of the different variations on one worksheet.

Pivot Tables

Larger amounts of data that can be organized in multiple dimensions, such as sales and cost of sales by product by month, can be sorted and analyzed using Excel's Pivot table feature.

Graphs

Excel contains a large number of two- and three-dimensional graphs that, if used properly, can extend the understanding of a budget and, ultimately, the value it offers management in decision making.

INTEGRATING TO THE GENERAL LEDGER

Almost all companies use actual figures from the general ledger(s) in the budget process. Sometimes actual figures are used to calculate budget allocations, and other times to generate budgets (for example, as a percentage of actual figures). Last but not least, actual figures are usually measured against budgets or forecasts on a monthly basis, in different types of variance reports, to demonstrate how the company is performing compared to the planned figures.

Few companies are satisfied with manually inputting actual figures into their spreadsheet-based budget models. As a result, most general ledger vendors have developed different methods of transferring monthly trail balances to Excel for use with the budget models. Sometimes it is a direct link, using a technology called ODBC (Online Database connectivity), and other times it consists of simple text file exports and imports. It is also common to find standard or specialized functionality to upload Excel budget figures back into the general ledger. In the latter case, the report writer in the general ledger is used for variance reporting.

The most common challenge of linking a spreadsheet-based budget model to a general ledger is the chart of accounts. Whereas a general ledger is completely based on an account number structure, a spreadsheet model is completely independent of account number references. A spreadsheet budget can be entered either at a higher level or a more detailed level than the chart of accounts. For example, by creating a spreadsheet that lists individual employees and their salaries or one that lists individual trips that roll up to a travel expense account, departmental managers can perform all the line item calculations necessary to arrive at an account number total. However, to simplify budget variance reporting, most companies use some sort of account number reference in all or part of their budget model.

USING EXCEL AS A FRONT-END TO A DATABASE

To avoid some of the pitfalls of spreadsheet budget models that are growing out of control, many companies decide to store their data in a database, and create Excel templates that store to and read from that database. This is similar to the way best-of-breed software works—a front-end user interface for budget input and report writing, and a back-end database for organized storage of large data volumes.

Some of the advantages of using a database with large Excel models are:

- Faster budget consolidations. In general, faster to open, update, and store individual spreadsheets (because fewer links and formulas are needed).

- Simpler and smaller spreadsheets, because the same spreadsheets can be reused for different departments, years, and so on.

Some potential disadvantages of using Excel with a database are:

- Requires more technical expertise to set up or change, especially in a multi-user environment.
- More complex to distribute the model to remote users.

Most companies that design their own spreadsheet budget models choose Microsoft Access as their database. The main reasons for this choice are tight integration with Excel, low cost, and ease of use.

BUDGETING WITH EXCEL ON THE WEB

One of the most powerful opportunities to simplify enterprise-wide budgeting with Excel is to employ it over the Web. You can use the following spreadsheet functionality on a Web page:

- Worksheets
- Pivot table reports
- External data ranges
- Ranges of cells
- Filtered lists
- Print areas

Keep in mind that you might lose some functionality and some formatting capabilities when publishing your spreadsheet model on the Web (consult your Excel user's manual or a Web expert for further details). If you are using Excel as a front-end to another data source (such as a Microsoft Access database), you should first check if the other data source has its own direct Web publishing functionality.

Following are the different ways you can post Excel data on the Web:

- Entire workbooks
- Noninteractive data or charts
- Interactive spreadsheets
- Interactive pivot table lists
- Interactive charts
- Combination Web pages (e.g., Excel data, a logo, some text)

Some advantages of putting your spreadsheet model on the Web include:

- Budget updates. If there are a large number of people using your budget spreadsheet model, it can be a major hassle to send out updates. If you put your Excel model on the Web, however, all you need to do is change your master spreadsheet and then repost it to the Web. All users will then have the updated version next time they open the Web page.

- Excel does not need to be installed on the users' computers. The budget users do not need anything other than a computer with access to the Internet or intranet (but certain plug-in components must be installed on their local computers. However, most required components can be downloaded from the Web).

Whether or not you choose to use Excel as your budgeting tool, you should now have a good idea of key functionality, as well as advantages and disadvantages. Before making a decision to go with Excel or a best-of-breed budgeting software, do a thorough analysis of your organization's budgeting process and needs, then pick the software that looks like it will give the best return on your time and money investment.

PART THREE

SOFTWARE EVALUATION AND SELECTION

CHAPTER 10

SELECTING A SYSTEM

STEPS IN THE SELECTION PROCESS

A budget system selection is similar to the purchasing process for other accounting and financial software packages. However, best-of-breed budgeting software is less complex than an accounting or enterprise resource planning (ERP) solution, so the whole selection process should be shorter and should require fewer people. Although the process need not be "scientific," many companies could definitely save time and frustration by taking an organized approach to their software acquisition process. This section discusses the key issues and items you should incorporate into your planning.

The first thing you should do is sit down and create a plan (see Figure 10.1). At the very least, this plan should:

1. Review the current situation.

   Review your current budgeting process, and research and document information needs that might surface over the next few years.

2. Choose the type of solution that best fits your needs.

   Based on number 1 above, you typically have three choices with regard to budgeting software:

   • Upgrade your current budgeting system (if possible).

   • Build a new system based on your organization's needs.

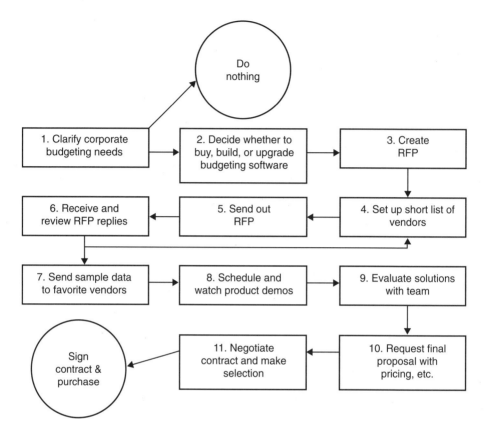

FIGURE 10.1   Example of a budgeting software selection process

- Purchase a commercial (pre-packaged) budgeting software.

   This chapter focuses on commercial budgeting solutions, and it assumes that you are moving in this direction.

3. Create a Request for Proposal (RFP).

   If you decide to look at a commercial budgeting solution, we strongly suggest that you approach potential vendors with an RFP (request for proposal) before you view any demonstrations or undertake any other steps in the selection process. Creating this document also serves as a very good learning exercise. It motivates key people and makes them think about what they are looking for in a product and a vendor. The RFP should describe thoroughly the type of functionality you are looking for, hardware and database requirements, vendor requirements, and so forth. There is a detailed

RFP example in the back of this book (see Appendix B) that you can use as a guide for your own RFP.

The following are suggested steps to follow when you create an RFP:

(1) Create a selection timetable.

(2) Create a list of all related parties in your organization.

(3) Write a short document outlining the scope of the project.

(4) Start with a sample RFP (see Appendix B), and modify it.

(5) Distribute your version of the RFP to key people and ask them to make additions and changes. Some people might only need parts of the RFP. For example, IS staff can focus on platforms, integration, infrastructure, and general technology issues. Accounting staff can focus on budgeting features.

(6) Review, clarify, clean up, and finish the RFP.

If you want to outsource the RFP and/or other parts of the selection process to a third party, see the next section, "Using a Software Selection Company."

4. Research vendors, create a short-list of vendors, and send out the RFP.

A few years ago, before budgeting and planning became a hot topic for businesses everywhere, less than a handful of budgeting software vendors existed. Today, however, you will find a number of vendors with solutions of different complexity, prices and technology platforms. Because you have more choices than ever before, you must thoroughly research the vendors and their solutions when you receive their replies to your RFP. Depending on the amount of time available, you should try to narrow the field down to about three to five vendors whom you invite to make a presentation to your organization.

The following is a list of resources you can use to gather information about vendors and their solutions (see Figure 10.2):

- RFP
- Buyer's guides (in accounting/financial and software publications)
- Product brochures
- Current users
- Company background brochures
- White papers
- Third party evaluations

- Vendor Web sites[4]

- Third party Web sites[5]

Keep in mind that many buyer's guides and other available third party information are not necessarily comprehensive and do not include all vendors. Also, product literature can be subject to vendor bias or the author's limited understanding of complex budgeting software. Therefore, your own evaluation of the software (see Getting the Most out of a Product Demonstration later in this chapter), as well as interviews with current customers, are the best gauge for software selection.

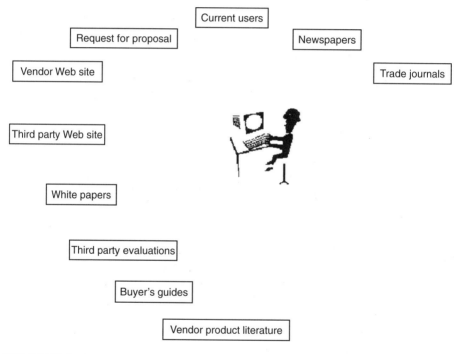

FIGURE 10.2   Sources of information for vendor and product research

---

[4]If you don't know the specific Web address, you can search the Web for key words such as "budgeting software," "budgeting and planning software," or "budgeting and consolidation." Be aware that you might not be able to get a comprehensive list of vendors with a Web search; it depends on which Web search engine you use, your key words, and indexing of vendors' Web sites on the particular search engine.

[5]See Note 4.

5. Some companies send out their RFP to all the vendors on their list and then let the vendors themselves decide (based on the content of the RFP) whether their software is qualified or not. This approach may still create a large number of replies with many pages of cumbersome information you will have to wade through in order to find the interesting candidates. A better idea is to do some vendor research in advance (check software prices, database platforms, vendor credentials, key features, etc.), and then send RFPs to a limited number of qualified vendors. Note: Do not forget to place a deadline on the RFPs you send out, so that your evaluation process does not lag because of slow vendor response time.

6. Review RFP replies.

After you have received all the information from the vendors, you and your team need to analyze and rank each reply. Normally, companies pick about three to five vendors to come on site and present their products, services, and solutions. If you choose too few, you may miss potentially good candidates (remember that a proposal is a written document and doesn't provide the full picture of a vendor and a solution). However, if you invite too many vendors, you and your team can easily end up spending weeks watching presentations. This is not only exhausting and costly, but it also can create biases toward vendors based on external factors such as where in the row of presentations they were, or how busy the evaluation team was on a particular day. It is therefore recommended that you choose a handful of vendors. If you are in doubt about certain vendors, give them a call and get more information.

When you study the vendors' replies to your RFP, you need to take them for what they are, biased answers to a list of questions. To make sure the vendors are as correct as possible with their answers, both your RFP and final software contract should stipulate that should you choose to purchase their product, the vendor is liable for the information they provide.

7. Send out demo material to the selected vendors (optional).

In order to get the most out of the upcoming product demonstrations, it can be a good idea to send out sample input screens, reports, roll-up structures, and a chart of accounts to the vendors. This will allow them to show you how your particular budgeting model will look and work with their budgeting package. During the demo, it will also be easier for your evaluation team to ask good questions because they will see a familiar model. However, if you plan to completely change your budgeting model, it might be a good idea to let the vendor show their own examples so you can get an impression of their range of capabilities without too much customization toward your old model.

8. Meet with vendors and review their company and product demonstrations.

Arrange for the presentations to be held and carefully evaluate each vendor and their solution. Try to have all the key people on your evaluation team present at all the demonstrations, so that everyone can get a complete picture before they choose their favorites (we will cover the evaluation process in more detail later in this chapter).

Getting the Most Out of a Product Demonstration

A product demonstration is your chance to get a firsthand look at the interface and features of a software package. If a skilled and experienced sales team is doing the presentation, you should be able to get a lot of valuable information from the demonstration. Normally, if you sent out an RFP, you already have information from the vendor about key features, but now is the time to see as much as possible with your own eyes. Also, if you have been unclear about anything until now, the demonstration is the perfect time to have your questions answered. Alternatively, you should request a workshop if you need to spend more time with the software package to verify if it is a good fit for your business needs. Some things to look for during the demonstration include:

- Vendor/reseller background
- Product history
- User interface
- Features
- Customization/flexibility
- Integration with other software
- Technology
- Documentation
- Implementation
- Pricing

Note: For detailed information in each area listed here, see the RFP example in Appendix B.

9. After the demonstrations, sit down and evaluate each one and select the favorite(s), or if more detail is needed or further questions arise, request a new demonstration. Use a Candidate Evaluation form to score each vendor. (See Appendix C, Software Candidate Evaluation and Rating Sheet.)

10. Request final proposal(s).

When you have found the vendor you feel fits your company's needs, request a final proposal with detailed maintenance, implementation, and support prices; implementation time estimates; sample project plan; and so forth. (See Appendix G for a sample project plan.) If there are several vendors that might fulfill your needs at a similar level, do not hesitate to ask all of them for this information so that you can make a final, detailed comparison between them. If two or more companies are in the running, this will give you some leverage in your negotiations.

11. Negotiate contracts/license agreements.

Once you have picked a favorite vendor and software solution, it is time to request a contract. This document will normally include the following:

- Exact software pricing based on your number of users, number of sites, modules needed, and so on
- Consulting and training rates and time estimates
- Software modules based on the functionality you have requested
- Project outline including activities that need to take place prior to model completion (see Appendix G for an example)
- Hardware and software requirements
- License agreement (see Appendix D for an example)
- Support plan (see Appendix E for an example)
- Other information that you have requested in writing (in your RFP)

12. Make final vendor selection.

Even after you receive the final proposal, you will usually need some further conversations to discuss or clarify certain items before you feel comfortable with the information. One of the negotiation points is often pricing (more about this later in the chapter). Once your company and the vendor have come to a final agreement, the last step is to sign a license agreement, and then to pay (based on payment terms). You'll then receive the software and documentation.

13. Sign contract and facilitate payment.

USING A SOFTWARE SELECTION COMPANY

Many companies solicit the services of third party firms to help them select the optimal budgeting solution. Sometimes these firms consist of single individuals with prior experience from the budgeting software industry who now work as consultants, helping their clients to pick the package that is right for them. Other times, companies engage the services of one of the Big Five consulting companies. Be aware that many of the Big Five have local, regional, or global strategic sales and/or consulting alliances with specific budgeting software vendors. Some have also produced their own budgeting software packages. In any case, do some research to be sure that their recommendations are not biased; the consultant's focus and loyalty should be to *you*.

In general, you should consider using a software selection company if one or more of the following are true:

- You don't have time to perform a thorough vendor/solution analysis yourself.

- You are considering technologies unfamiliar to you.

- Your corporate environment is very politically charged, so the internal selection process itself will cause unproductive conflict between different decision-makers.

- You want a third party to compile a needs analysis for your company which will match your needs with available budgeting products.

Before you hire a selection company, ask for a price quote. This will help prevent any costly surprises. Typically, fees range from $5,000 to $25,000, and can take from a few days to many weeks, depending on the time spent analyzing your needs and participating in demonstrations and evaluations.

CHAPTER 11

SOFTWARE EVALUATION: FACTORS TO CONSIDER

In general, the evaluation and purchase process for corporate budgeting software is similar to that of other niche software solutions, such as consolidation and reporting software. In other words, it should require much less time for evaluations and presentations than a typical accounting solution with a number of modules (general ledger, accounts receivable, accounts payable, payroll, etc.).

EXPECTED USE NOW AND IN THE FUTURE

One of the first questions you should ask yourself during the software evaluation phase is whether you are looking for a short-term or long-term solution. There are cases where a company needs to solve its budgeting issues immediately, without having time to perform an in-depth analysis of long-term organizational needs. Sometimes this is due to the fact that the in-house budgeting model no longer works properly or is too hard to maintain. Other times an immediate need arises out of organizational politics, when you cannot afford to wait any longer for the parties in various departments to provide their input to your budgeting software needs. However, in most cases, companies that invest in best-of-breed budgeting software are planning to stay with it for a long time, not only because it usually represents a significant investment in terms of money, consulting, and user training, but also because of the total time involved in writing all reports and setting up integrations with front-end systems. The selection process is not one you and your co-workers want to go through every year.

In other words, if you are going for a short-term solution, you should not be looking at the most expensive and most complex budgeting packages. However, if this is a long-term investment, you should spend plenty of time exploring your needs and product and vendor capabilities, and focus somewhat less on acquisition and implementation costs.

Another element to consider is the scope of usage in the near future versus what is expected in the long run. If your organization only needs a single location implementation and the budget model will be fairly simple with few planned changes, the software selection process should be fairly simple. If you are planning to expand the budgeting model and organizational usage down the road, you should spend more time looking into the functionality of software packages and their vendors. If you are acquiring a new software package today and you are investing in related training and implementation, you want to make sure that the software is scalable and can grow with you as the organization grows.

Database platforms are also an important consideration if you are hoping to make your new budgeting application a long-term investment. Many companies attempt to standardize on a single database platform, such as Microsoft SQL Server or Oracle, in order to reduce the need for human knowledge to manage the database (backups, troubleshooting, maintenance, etc.), and to simplify integrations and reduce the need for third party tools. Sometimes a current or future corporate database standardization can make your budgeting software selection harder, because the software you like the most might not be available on the required database platform. This conflict of interest will often force you to perform a cost-benefit analysis to figure out what is most important to your company, software features or database platform.

GETTING THE REST OF THE COMPANY TO BUY INTO THE PROCESS

If you have made up your mind that your company needs a new budgeting package, often you will still have to convince the rest of the people that will be affected by the new software. If you move ahead on your own without conferring with key users in the organization, chances are that few of them will support you if anything goes wrong during implementation, or if you have to suggest work-arounds and the like.

There is no sure formula for success in achieving company-wide consensus for a new software acquisition, but there are several things you can do to improve your chances. Today, most companies that decide to look for a new budgeting solution put together a project team. This team normally consists of representative end-users, information systems specialists, and key decision-makers. Ideally, each team member will bring special expertise and insight from their own area of the organization. The team will set up evaluation criteria (see RFP in Appendix B) to help screen the software packages and vendors, and they will participate in software demonstrations to see the different products first-hand. Through a point scoring system (see Appendix C) or other means of evaluation, the project team reaches a consensus and then makes the software acquisition. Whether the decision leads to the best possible solution or not, the support for the project will be much stronger than if one person alone had made the decision.

One of the most typical problems with an organizational roll-out of new budgeting software is most frequently found in larger, multi-site organizations. Remote offices often are not involved in headquarters' software evaluation and acquisition, but they are required to use the new software. This will often cause less than optimal use of a new software package at remote sites, and cooperation and goodwill to resolve ongoing budgeting software or reporting issues is not always ideal. Most companies that are successful in achieving organization-wide support do their own sales pitch to their divisions before a new budgeting software package is rolled out. By explaining the advantages of the new solution and by providing sufficient training and other assistance, top management can improve general understanding and promote goodwill toward the new solution.

COST/BENEFIT ANALYSIS

As a selection tool, a cost/benefit analysis helps to focus on the most suitable category of software, rather than trying to differentiate between similar budgeting solutions. For example, it can help you find out if your needs are better served by:

- SQL-based or OLAP-based software
- High-end or low-end software
- Web-based or standard client-server software

In addition to helping to distinguish between different software categories, a cost/benefit analysis can help you decide whether to stay with what you have or make a new software acquisition.

If you were to look at a range of companies using the different budgeting packages on the market, you would see that their levels of satisfaction range from highly satisfied to dissatisfied. Finding success with a particular solution is dependent on several factors:

- Software features
- Skills of implementation partner

- Skills and involvement of key employees
- Long term support and software upgrades from the vendor

In the software selection phase, matching organizational needs and constraints with software features is essential for success. One of the best ways to do this is to devise a list that weighs benefits against costs; for an example, see Figure 11.1.

A cost/benefit analysis table can become rather subjective because it is hard to assign a value to intangible items. However, because each item is weighted, it usually provides a better indication than simply drawing up a list of pros and cons with no assigned values.

Benefits	Score	Costs	Score
Saves X man-hours for end-users	6	$X in software and hardware required	-8
Improves control	7	X days of training/customization needed	-6
Offers better reports/analysis	9	Unfamiliar user interface	-7
Saves $X and time in report distribution	5	Need GL integration	-2
$X less than in-house programming	7	Takes time away from other projects	-4
Comes with good documentation	4	Might be replaced by new technology in a few years, thus requiring new investment	-4
Total Score	+38	Total Score	-28

Note: Scoring is from 10 to -10 for each item, where 10 is the highest score and -10 is the lowest score. A total score above 0 shows that the company most likely will achieve an overall benefit by purchasing the new software package.

FIGURE 11.1   Example of cost/benefit analysis for a new software acquisition

FEATURES AND FLEXIBILITY

Companies spend most of their time evaluating features and flexibility during the software evaluation phase. The key, of course, is to try to identify the functionality that your company needs and then try to match it against the different packages software vendors have to offer. Seldom will you find a perfect match, because most of the budgeting solutions on the market are built to fulfill the needs of a broad range of companies in the marketplace rather than your individual requirements. However, you should find that the lack of some features are balanced out by other functionality offered by a particular software package.

At the core of a feature study is the creation of an RFP document that specifies all the key features and requirements the company is seeking. Rather than going into detail on specific features (see Chapter 3's Prior Year (Incremental) Approach and Appendix B for detailed information on RFPs), see the next sections for some general advice on evaluating software functionality.

COMPATIBILITY WITH EXISTING SOFTWARE

It would make software evaluation a whole lot simpler if we could just ignore all current systems in place and focus on the features and functionality of the new budgeting package. However, the new budgeting software package usually must be integrated with several existing software packages (see Figure 11.2). For example:

- General ledger(s)
- Current spreadsheet models
- Payroll/human resource system(s)

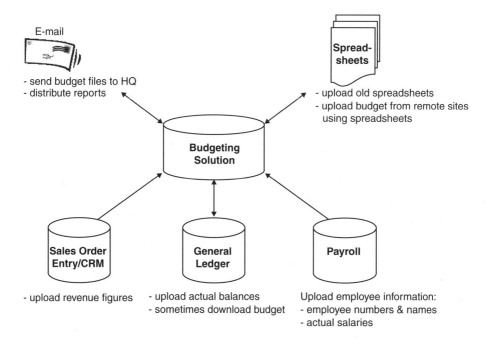

FIGURE 11.2   Compatibility issues to consider with a new budgeting solution

- Sales order entry system(s)
- Database software
- E-mail program(s)

Traditionally, exporting and importing text files have been the means of exchanging data between different applications. Some downsides to this are the extra manual work (with resulting human errors and mistakes), and slow data transfer speeds. This is beginning to change as budget and accounting applications as well as database vendors build custom interfaces to each other's applications and databases. When you are evaluating a new budgeting package, you first need to identify with which of your own current and planned applications it should integrate, and then ask the vendor to explain how this will be handled.

EASE OF USE

As with all other software out there, the most powerful budgeting applications on the market are not necessarily the easiest ones to use. Similarly, a simple application with just a few screens and menus can probably be mastered in a few hours, but it will not have the same features and level of flexibility as more complex budgeting software. In particular, you will find this to be true in the area of report writing. The more you want to customize reports and input screens to fit your company's particular business model, the more powerful the report writer you will need and the more time you'll need to spend learning it. While most high-end budgeting applications offer customization of menus, labels, reports, and so on, lower end software usually has limited functionality in these areas.

All modern budgeting applications have graphical user interfaces where you can use a pointing device, or copy/paste between windows, and screens offer a variety of different fonts and colors. Online help files and context sensitive help have also become common features to improve user friendliness. Each vendor has come up with its own unique screen layouts and user-related functions. The best way to get a good feel for a particular package is to watch an in-depth demonstration or, even better, to request demo copy or a workshop where you can get some hands-on experience to test the ease of use of the application. The goal is to find out if power-users as well as end-users will be comfortable with the application to the degree where they adopt it and learn all the features. The last thing a company wants is an application that is completely consultant dependent or that nobody knows how to use. Often, a company will find that they need the power of an advanced budgeting solution, and they accept that there is a ramp-up period to get users up to speed. In this case, the key is to provide good training and to motivate employees to learn the software in detail.

SOFTWARE STABILITY

This is often an overlooked item during software evaluation. Often, the decision to purchase one software over another can come down to small differences in features or how well the vendors presented themselves and their product. However, the closest a company usually comes to checking out the stability of the current version of the software is when they poll current users as to their opinions about the package. The same software can run better on one database or hardware platform than on another, but this is often ignored during a reference check. Also, different customers using the same application on the same database and hardware platform rarely use all of the same features. Certain features might cause crashes, memory leaks, or other stability problems, and this might only be a problem for a handful of customers.

To get the best possible understanding of different stability issues, you should ask for references with similar hardware/software and budget model configurations as the one your company plans to use. You should also check if the vendor has a reputation of producing reasonably stable software, and find out how the vendor will handle it if you experience a stability problem after you have purchased the software.

VENDOR-RELATED ITEMS

Sometimes it is easy to get buried in the small details of a product and forget that more important than the product itself are the company and people behind it. A number of times in the past, excellent software products have disappeared from the market within a few years because the companies behind them ran into problems, such as:

- Financial mismanagement
- Human resource issues (such as poor retention of key employees)
- Poor strategic vision and business execution skills
- Lawsuits or legal problems

  Some of the qualities to look for in a vendor are:

- A good reputation in the marketplace
- Happy users for the past several years
- Availability of high quality training and support in different regions and time zones
- A strong distribution channel and/or strong direct sales and service force
- Use of up-to-date technology in development, products, implementation, and support

- Online customer access to support-history database
- Professional development and testing methodologies
- Strong sales and good profitability
- Good future direction and strategies
- Well-developed list of third party products that work with their software (such as analysis tools, general ledgers, spreadsheet add-ins, etc.)
- Hosting services offered either through the vendor itself or through application service providers

WORKING WITH AN IMPLEMENTATION PARTNER

Whether you utilize implementation services from the product vendor, a reseller, or other partner, make sure that you will be working with a person(s) that is not only trained on the product, but that has prior implementation experience. In other words, before engaging a consultant, ask about his or her experience with the product, and how many other implementations of this particular product the person has done. Some companies even ask for references from the assigned consultant. Other things to look for are:

- Type of implementation methodology used (project plans, prototyping, testing, etc.)
- Average implementation time for similar projects
- Knowledge of database platform
- Knowledge of integration tools to link to your other applications

HOW TO SELECT: A SUMMARY

The process of selecting new budgeting software is handled in a wide variety of ways at different companies, from a single person doing a quick evaluation to large teams doing in-depth analyses of products, vendors, consultants, and existing customers. Some tips before you start your software evaluation process are:

- Consider whether your company has the skills to handle the evaluation, or if you should engage a software selection company (see Chapter 10).
- Do a thorough analysis of your current and future budgeting needs before you start looking at vendors.
- Create an RFP document (see Chapter 10 and Appendix B) to communicate your company's needs to vendors.

- Have all key people present at the product demonstrations.
- If needed, call vendors back for repeat demos, or specifically focused demos.
- If you believe your budget model and process is unique in any way, provide the vendors with specific information and request a customized demonstration.
- If you are in doubt about important features and how your users will handle them, request a hands-on workshop.

CHAPTER 12

THE NEW ALTERNATIVE: OUTSOURCING

Today, an increasing number of businesses seek to focus on their core functions instead of on their software, creating a seismic shift toward outsourcing that is leading businesses to application service providers (ASPs) for their information technology needs.

OUTSOURCING

One of the fastest growing trends in the software marketplace is application outsourcing, or "hosting services" as it is called. What hosting means is that instead of installing and servicing your new software application in-house, you contract with an application service provider to host the application for you. Having a third party host an application for you is by no means a new concept. For more than a decade, there have been ASPs that have worked as if they were your own IS department, except that they are not on your payroll and the application usually does not reside on site, or on your own hardware either. During the time when mainframes were the primary platform for most business applications, many companies chose to let an ASP host their application. One of the biggest drawbacks was high communication cost (usually dedicated phone lines) to link the user's computer/terminal to the application. Today, that has become less of an issue with the use of the Internet, corporate wide area networks (WAN), and much lower telecommunications rates.

HOW IT WORKS

Utilizing the Internet or other means of telecommunication (such as dial-up links, private virtual networks, dedicated lines, and a number of other options), you connect to the software application residing at the ASP's site (see Figure 12.1). Everything else you do inside the software program works just as if you had the software on one of your own servers in your office. More and more budgeting applications come with Web interfaces, which means that the user only needs a Web browser (such as MS Explorer or Netscape) and Internet/ intranet access to work with the application. Backups, application upgrades, and server hardware maintenance are handled by the ASP. For this service you normally pay a fixed or variable (or combination of the two) subscription fee. In this new era of application outsourcing, vendors and ASPs are still scrambling to best position themselves in terms of pricing and software-related services offered. In some cases you might purchase the application, and then let the ASP host it. In other cases, you might never own the application, but pay per usage instead. For example, you might be charged for the length of time logged in, amount of processing power used (typically measured by CPU time used), number of transactions entered/processed, or number of registered users.

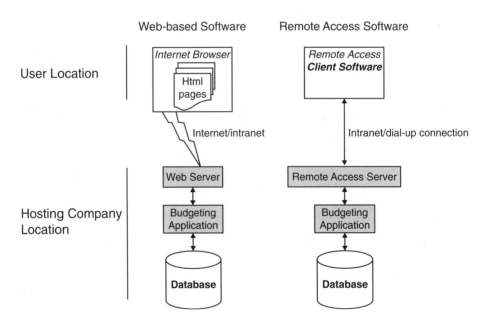

FIGURE 12.1   Example of configurations used with application hosting

At this time, most of the hosting services are focused on accounting applications, and less attention is paid to budgeting software. However, this will probably change as ASPs look for more applications to host and improvements in Web technology make it virtually irrelevant where the application resides.

WHEN YOU SHOULD CONSIDER AN ASP

Before you make the decision to install your budgeting application in-house or to outsource it to an application service provider, you need to analyze your organization's needs and capabilities. If the bottom line is that the company will reduce costs or increase revenue by outsourcing the application, then outsourcing may be the right decision. Of course, there are also other deciding factors, such as security concerns and user satisfaction, that will impact the decision. Some indicators that application outsourcing might be beneficial include:

Internal Factors

- Lack of in-house technical support and skills. Recruiting and retaining skilled IT professionals is often difficult and expensive. Your current IT staff might not have enough time to support an additional in-house application.

- No in-house power users. Most advanced budgeting applications are not learned overnight. A company needs power users that can write reports and input screens, as well as maintain the budget model when the chart of accounts, organizational structures, and information requirements change. If you don't have any people with the skills or time to become power users, you will need frequent visits from consultants or your budget model will quickly become obsolete.

- No budget for necessary infrastructure. An in-house budgeting application usually requires a powerful database server, so if you have remote offices, you'll need to install a Web server and proper security hardware/software. In addition, the cost of the budgeting application itself can sometimes be higher than outsourcing it.

- Rapid organizational change can outdate software. Most ASPs offer arrangements where you don't have to buy the application, but instead lease it and/or pay per usage. This means that if your company's needs outgrow the capabilities of the budgeting application, it might be quicker and less costly to move to a new software if you are leasing it.

External Factors

• New budget application technology. Until recently, budget software packages have been unable to allow for dynamic Internet/intranet access through, for example, a browser. Today, however, this is rapidly changing and remote access to a central server is becoming part of the standard capabilities. This means that an ASP can host the whole application, while all users access it remotely.

• Lower telecommunications costs. Many years ago when data centers where hosting mainframe applications for corporations, telecommunications were one of the major expenses. Today, however, with increased competition among telecom companies as well as the emergence of the Internet as an inexpensive information highway, linking up with an application residing at the ASP is no longer a major expense.

• Better support. If the ASP offers full support services (including budget model support), their support staff can look at your problem immediately, because the application resides in their location. This should translate into better and faster support. If you receive support from a third party, such as the software vendor or a reseller, your ASP can also let their support people get access to your model from any location (but obviously only with the proper security precautions).

• Lower consulting costs. Just as your infrastructure when using an ASP can let remote support people gain direct access to your application, consultants can do the same. This can translate into cost savings in reduced travel, hotel, and per-diem expenses, as well as quicker response from consultants because of zero travel time.

SELECTION CRITERIA FOR AN ASP

Because the application outsourcing trend is relatively new and there is little history as far as customer satisfaction rates, cost, and service offerings, it is wise to carefully study your potential ASPs before signing a contract. The players in this market consist of:

• Firms that have traditionally (in the mainframe era) provided outsourcing services

• Software vendors and resellers of software

• Hardware vendors

• Internet service providers (ISPs)

- Telecommunications companies
- Business process consultants

If you have decided to outsource your application, you need to select an ASP. The following is a list of items to consider when evaluating an application service provider.

- Experience. The prospective ASP should have some experience with the application. Are they trained to understand the software package and the technology platform it is based on? Some ASPs will only take responsibility for backups and making sure the application runs satisfactorily. In this case, you will also deal with the software vendor or reseller for software consulting and support services. Other ASPs are full service providers, and they will offer you implementation and support from consultants who are trained on your application.

- Knowledge. The ASP should have basic knowledge of the budgeting process and related procedures so they can be prepared to handle heavy usage time periods (such as the end of the budget cycle).

- Up-to-date Technology. Does the ASP have a modern technology infrastructure? For example, the Web is emerging as the optimum delivery mechanism for accessing remote applications. The outsourcing vendor you consider should offer the hardware, software, and knowledge to satisfy your requirements in this area.

- Vendor Experience. Because application outsourcing is a relatively new field, few ASPs have had long experience with the technology and services involved. However, this does not mean that most vendors offer the same level of quality. Find out who the vendor has hosted applications for and for how long, and check references.

- ASP Flexibility. Does the ASP have a business strategy that is aligned with your own company's goals for future growth and change? Try to discern the most likely software and organizational changes that your company will go through down the road, and then get a feel for how the ASP will cope with these changes.

- Customer Service. As with all your other business partners, you want to deal with people who are friendly and service minded. If you run into problems with the application, you do not want increased aggravation by having to deal with people who are unfriendly, ill-mannered, or inadequately trained. The ASP staff should be on their toes and able to help solve the problem quickly and put you back on track.

ENSURING CONTINUOUS SUCCESS

When you have found an application service provider that fits your requirements, the next step is to structure a contractual agreement that protects the interests of both parties and helps ensure mutual understanding and long-term success.

Make sure the contract properly covers such key areas as minimum acceptable processing speeds, data access security, back-ups, and disaster recovery planning. Because your own company's sensitive data will reside in the database at the ASP's site, it is important to include a non-disclosure agreement (in case the ASP needs to get access to your data). If the ASP is also going to provide you with application consulting and support services, specify these details in the contract.

Work to achieve a partnership with your ASP. Hosting a budgeting and planning application has traditionally been an in-house arrangement, and by outsourcing it, you are looking to achieve additional benefits. To realize these long-term benefits, it is important to nurture the relationship with the ASP by having regular status meetings and by keeping an open line of communication.

PART FOUR

SOFTWARE
IMPLEMENTATION

CHAPTER 13

SYSTEMS IMPLEMENTATION: PROJECT PLANNING

The importance of systems implementation cannot be overstated. No matter how much time is spent during the software selection and evaluation stage, if the implementation is not properly planned and executed, it is extremely unlikely that the project will meet either the cost or the time constraints. More important, it is highly unlikely that the software will deliver the expected benefits and produce the anticipated return on investment.

For a successful implementation, the software reseller and the customer must jointly develop an implementation plan and communicate often. This ensures that the client is aware of the progress and that any surprises can be quickly adjusted so that the project can continue as planned. Although it may seem that the bulk of the work is done during the selection and purchase stages, it is vital that adequate attention also be focused on implementation.

IMPLEMENTATION PHASES

A typical project involves the following phases (see Figure 13.1):

Phase I—Implementation Team Selection

Phase II—Planning

Phase III—Installation

Phase IV—Training

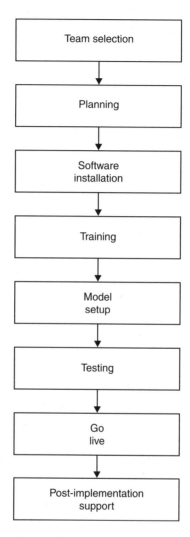

FIGURE 13.1   Example of implementation activities

Phase V—Model setup

Phase VI—Testing

Phase VII—Going live

Phase VIII—Post-implementation support

Implementation Team Selection

Selecting the proper implementation team is crucial to the project's success. A well-chosen team is comprised of the proper individuals from the client and from the implementer. Do not assume that the software implementation has to be completed by the same people from whom you purchased the software. Assuming that the software purchase did not also include the implementation, you are free to solicit bids from a variety of vendors.

You may contact other value-added resellers (VARs), other software vendors, firms that specialize in implementation, consulting firms, or independent contractors. Since the implementation approach can vary significantly, the bids can also differ quite a bit. It is important to learn why one bid is much more expensive or cheaper than another; the cheapest bid is not always the most economical choice.

When determining who to have on the team, the people from the client side must have project management experience and be able to make quick executive decisions. Additionally, they should have support from top management for the project. Ideally, the project manager will be able to make final decisions and will have implied executive support for the decisions that are made.

The project manager working for the implementation vendor should have experience with several implementations. Ask for references from other clients. Find out how well the implementation team met the projected deadlines and how well the final installation met initial expectations. It is also important to learn how well the implementer transfers knowledge to their clients and how well they handle post-implementation support.

Because so much time is spent on getting the system up and running, post-implementation support is often overlooked. Specify from the start who is responsible for what once users start accessing the system. This will prevent many headaches. It is also extremely important to know who is responsible for the costs incurred to resolve problems once the installation has been completed. What you think the implementer is responsible for can be significantly different than what the vendor believes they are responsible for. Pre-determining responsibilities up front can avoid confrontations once the system has gone live.

The number of people on the implementation team will be decided by the size of the project and the number of tasks to be completed. Having a large number of people on the team does not necessarily mean that the project will be completed in a shorter amount of time. Often, the bulk of the work can only be accomplished by a few people. Involve only people who can perform a specific function; adding more people than necessary may actually increase the duration of the project.

Planning

Once you have selected your implementation team and before any work is started, you should make sure you have a sound project plan in place. If you have been involved in software implementation in the past, you probably know why it is important to have a structured plan, and for both client and consultant to be involved in the creation and execution of the plan. For some helpful hints, see the sample project plan found in Appendix G.

Surprisingly enough, many companies go out and purchase expensive software without first asking for a summary level project plan and implementation expense estimate. This could help avoid cost overruns and surprises that often occur due to poor planning. For obvious cost control and planning reasons you should ask to get these services spelled out in a contract at the time you purchase the software.

A project plan also helps limit the scope of an implementation. Potentially, a consultant could remain on site long after the initial implementation should have been finished, because the scope of his or her work was never clearly defined. This sometimes happens because the company doesn't have sufficient internal resources available and they fail to develop project plans, do not clearly state the goals of the project, and do not assign responsibilities before the implementation starts.

Installation

Prior to having the consultant install the software, the hardware and personnel requirements must be known. Do not assume that the installation of the software is a minor task. Even though software can run on a wide variety of hardware, the hardware will directly impact the software's performance. Make sure you know what type of performance you expect from the software and find out what optimal installation parameters are needed to meet your expectations.

Normally the reseller will inform you what resources are needed prior to installation. Additionally, find out which personnel are needed from your staff to assist with the installation. Make sure the appropriate staff are available so that the software can be installed quickly and efficiently.

Training

Usually you will have a minimum of two classes of users: super-users or administrators, and end-users. The administrators will be responsible for knowing the nuts and bolts of the system and how the application has been customized to meet your needs. The end-users will be concerned with the routine use of the system and therefore, will not require the same level of training as the super-users.

Before finalizing the consulting agreement, find out how the reseller handles training; specifically, find out if everyone is trained as one class of user or if several types of training are offered. Unless everyone is going to be either a super-user or an end-user, different levels of training should be offered. Training is an important matter to discuss with the reseller. Make sure that your key personnel are not over- or undertrained on the system.

Model Design and Set-up

The model design phase is one of the most important phases in the implementation process. This is the time when either your existing budget models are replicated in the new system or your budget process and models are completely overhauled. Either way, without clearly communicating your needs and expectations to the consultants, you will end up with a model that does not suit your needs.

During this phase, make sure the people that have final authority over the budget process have signed off on the model. Often, what seems like a minor change can result in complicated modifications to a model that is in the middle of the design phase. To avoid these problems, make sure that you communicate to the implementation team exactly what you want from the system. Also, make sure that the consultant keeps you actively involved during this stage. You do not want any surprises or misunderstandings to occur during this process. The best time to get everything on the table is at the beginning of the process when specifications can be easily changed.

Testing

To ensure the success of the software implementation, the software must be thoroughly tested before rolling it out to all the end users. The software should be tested using a reference group of users. The timing of the test and selection of the reference groups are extremely important. Feedback needs to be received during the process to make sure that the system will be accepted by the end-users, but testing before the system is ready may give people a bad impression of the system. One alternative is to use people closely involved in the process who know the system is not complete. However, the drawback to doing this is that the feedback may be (favorably) biased since these are probably the people that selected the software in the first place.

The best approach is to select a core group of people that are open to change and that can effectively review the system. Once the system is close to completion, involve a group of end-users to test the system. The system must be tested for all possible scenarios before being put into production because whatever is not tested will surely appear once the system is in use. It is much easier to solve problems during the design phase than once the system has gone live.

Going live

After the testing has been completed, it is time to go live. By this time, there should be no surprises. All system kinks should be worked out, all performance issues should be addressed, and all end-user training should be completed. If all the prior steps have been performed correctly, going live should be the easiest step in the entire process.

Post-implementation support

That said, only in an ideal world will there be no problems once the installation has gone live. Ask your consultant the most important question with respect to post-implementation: does the implementer consider the implementation complete as soon as the first user starts using the system or after they are sure that all kinks have been worked out of the system? Most of the problems will appear during the first week of use. You should make sure that the implementer is available during that first week to assist in problem resolution.

Furthermore, when these problems initially appear, it is important to isolate the causes. Problems generally fall into one of several categories: a minor problem that can be quickly resolved and will not appear again; a flaw in the budgeting model that can be fixed without affecting the rest of the model; a flaw in the budgeting model that can be fixed but only by modifying the entire, or at least a significant portion, of the model; or a technical problem inherent in either the software or hardware that will affect performance until it is resolved.

Flaws in the budget model are generally caused by not involving the appropriate people in the implementation process and overlooking desired functionality. If all users are not considered when designing and testing the model, it is almost impossible to develop a model that is acceptable to everyone. Depending upon the severity of the flaw, it can be extremely costly and time consuming to correct. Interviewing all anticipated users, creating a checklist of desired functionality, and properly testing the system will decrease the possibility of these types of errors.

Technical problems with either the software and/or hardware should not appear if the system has been properly tested. However, the environment in which the system was tested is not likely to remain static. Therefore, it is important to know who to contact for support. Also, the implementer generally will provide very limited support if the problem is hardware and not software related. Determining upfront who should be contacted for different types of problems can decrease the amount of time required to resolve the problem.

Having enumerated the components necessary for a successful software implementation, Chapter 14 will give more in-depth coverage to each of the phases.

CHAPTER 14

DETAILED IMPLEMENTATION

The following Project Checklists should be helpful in planning and managing your implementation.

GENERAL PROJECT CHECKLISTS

Phase I—Implementation team selection

- Identify the project leader from your organization.
- Identify who will have final approval of the budget model.
- Check availability for those that will be involved in the implementation.

Phase II—Planning

- Interview management to identify the project's scope and budget.
- Create a project plan.
- Arrange travel and lodging for the consultant(s), if necessary.
- Obtain information to be given to the consultant prior to on-site work, including samples of current reports, input screens, and roll-up structures, as well as facts about the general ledger(s) including product name and platform, chart of accounts with segment description, integration options, and possible file formats.
- Verify that the software has been received from the vendor.
- Verify that the proper hardware is available and ready for installation.

- Make sure that the proper workspace and equipment is available for the consultant.

- Find out what type of support is offered from the implementer—how long and for how much?

Phase III—Installation

- Verify that the proper IT support is available when the software is to be installed.

- Determine on what workstations the software is to be installed.

- Make sure that the software will not conflict with any existing applications.

Phase IV—Training

- Determine which people are to be trained and the level of training that they will need.

- Find out what is needed for training—projectors, flipcharts, PCs, network connections, etc.

- Have all workstations prepared prior to training (not right before it starts).

- Check that all workstations run as expected.

- Have copies of all training materials available.

- Learn the software and model well enough so that you are not always dependent upon the consultant.

Phase V—Model Design

- Know the objectives of the model.

- How do you want to use the information once it is input into the system?

- Do you want to use an existing budget model or create a new one?

- At what level do you want to budget?

- How long is the budget process? Is it long enough to review and analyze the amount of data requested?

- Identify who has the final authority to approve the budget model.

- Make sure that the model satisfactorily meets everyone's needs.

- Verify that the model is not overly complex.

- Determine where the budget data is to be used once the budget is complete. Will the data continue to reside in the budget system or will it be imported into the general ledger (G/L) system?

- Learn what is required to maintain the budget model and system.

Phase VI—Testing

- Determine who will comprise your reference group.
- Allow plenty of time to test the model for all possible scenarios.
- Test for adding and deleting users in the system.
- Make sure that accounts can be added and deleted.
- Make sure that when data is added, deleted, or modified, the model functions as expected.
- Test user security. Make sure that users can only access the data that they are supposed to.
- Incorporate feedback into the model.
- Delete all test data prior to going live with the system.

Phase VII—Going live

- Make sure that all test data has been deleted.
- Verify that the system is prepared to handle all users.
- Incorporate routine back-up procedures.
- Appoint a contact person for support questions.
- Notify all users of the budget submission deadline.

Phase VIII—Post-implementation support

- Plan for the next budget.
- Track users' satisfaction with the model and solicit recommendations for improvements.
- Identify requested modifications and learn the implications of making those modifications.

PROJECT PLANS

A key management tool for smooth software implementation is a good project plan. What is a "good" project plan? There is no definitive answer to this, but as a rule of thumb, you should have a plan that describes milestone activities, lists the parties involved, and gives discrete start and end dates. On the one hand, a project plan that is too detailed often ends up scrapped because it is too cumbersome to maintain, but on the other hand, a project plan that is not detailed enough can also end up unused because of insufficient information. Generally, project plans that fall somewhere in the middle will work the best. (See Figure 14.1.)

Activity	Hour Estimate	Involved Parties	Start Date	End Date
Installation				
Training				
Model Planning				
Implementation Activity A				
Implementation Activity B				
Implementation Activity C				
Model testing				
Organization-wide roll-out				
Model approval				

FIGURE 14.1   Typical items listed in a project plan

Project Duration and Costs

Regarding payment for services, companies sometimes ask their implementation partner to sign a statement that specifies a low (minimum) amount and a high (not-to-exceed) amount, based on a project plan with time estimates. In addition to cost estimates for contracted work, it is also common for a company to ask the contractor to agree to maximum travel costs, as well as hotel expenses, and any other expenses related to the software implementation. The idea, of course, is for the company to make sure that the total cost of installation is understood before the purchase takes place. This not only allows them to compare the total cost of the product with similar products on the market, but also helps ensure that the total cost is within their budget.

Model Design

The model building process will work in different ways, depending on which vendor and product you choose. Some general tips (do's and don'ts) before you start are:

Don'ts

- Don't blindly copy your old budget model; look for ways to improve it.
- Don't try to build the most advanced budgeting model in the industry the first time. You will know more about needs and capabilities after using the model for a while.
- Don't start your budgeting process with a new model that has not been thoroughly tested.
- Don't automatically let your general ledger/chart of accounts drive your budgeting model.

Do's

- Roll up your sleeves and get involved in the project.
- "Sell" the project and its purpose to all key people involved. Have at least two people thoroughly trained in the details—in case one quits.
- Take advantage of features in your new budgeting software.
- Create a quick prototype early on to visualize how the initial model will work.
- Create input screens that allow you to collect data of high value for decision makers (e.g., more information about revenues, less on expenses that are not relevant to the bottom line).
- Write reports that drive decision-making and control first; less significant reports can be added later.

LARGE PROJECTS VERSUS SMALL PROJECTS

Although most of the same formulas for success are true for both larger and smaller projects, there are still some differences to keep in mind. First of all, what is a *large* project? There is no clear answer to this, but if we compare the implementation of an enterprise resource planning (ERP) system to that of a best-of-breed budgeting solution, the ratio in implementation time would probably be 1 to 10 or 1 to 20. This means that if it takes one or two years to implement an ERP solution, it will normally take not more than one or two months to implement a budgeting solution.

However, to focus on the latter, you will certainly find some successful projects that lasted as little as two weeks and others that lasted as long as six or nine months. The duration of these projects are dependent upon factors such as:

- Model size and complexity
- Available internal and external key human resources during the implementation
- Quality of project planning and execution
- Stability of business environment during implementation (such as mergers, acquisitions, loss of key employees, etc.)

There are many variables that can affect the outcome of an implementation, and it is therefore important to scale the project plan to the size of the project. If an implementation needs no budget process re-engineering, no major integrations, and requires only a few reports, the level of detail required in the project plan is naturally less than with a complex implementation. Activities not pertaining to the actual construction of the budgeting model would likely be excluded from the project plan.

However, if the implementation is for a global corporation with multiple charts of accounts, a large number of remote sites, a large number of users, and many assumptions and other underlying parameters, then the project obviously demands much more attention and time. You will have to put considerable effort into creating a good project plan and assembling the right implementation team.

PEOPLE TO INVOLVE IN YOUR PROJECT

Your project is defined and executed by a team of people, some from your own organization and some from your implementation partner's organization. If you do not carefully select your implementation team, even the best software packages on the market can end up worthless to your company.

Putting together a good budgeting project team is not an easy task because most organizations have a very limited number of people from whom to choose. You will have some choices when putting together the team though, so here is a list of qualities that you should look for in the candidates from your own organization:

- Model administrators: Pick people that you believe will stay in their positions for a long period of time.
- MIS: Try to find a person that does not have his or her own agenda unrelated to the goals of your project, and one that will support your project whenever there is a need for MIS help (e.g., installation, integration, communication links, etc.)
- Decision-maker: If not yourself, make sure to put a person in charge that is capable and willing to make decisions and make things happen. In

other words, you don't want a person in charge that can seriously delay the project because of indecisiveness or fear of risk.

When working with outside consultants, normally you will have a choice of consultant(s), although sometimes you may have to wait for the right one to be freed from other ongoing projects. Consultants with years of experience might cost more than other consultants, so you must discern if your project is complicated enough to demand senior consultants.

Request consultants that have experience and ask to see their résumés with prior implementations—you don't want your project to serve as a training ground. If you think there might be a personality conflict between any of your external and internal team members, consider this when forming the group. You should also consider personalities when putting together a group of people who have never worked together before. In short projects this is less crucial, but in longer projects it can be very important to the final outcome of the budgeting and consolidation model.

All in all, a software implementation project is only as good as you and your implementation partner make it, so be sure you have a working plan and build the best possible project team to execute that plan.

Using a Big Five Implementation Firm

All of the Big Five consulting firms can, in one way or another, play a role in the implementation of your new budgeting software. Depending on which company you look at and the particular offices within each of the global companies, you will find that they can assist in:

- Software selection services (writing RFPs, market research, recommendations)
- Project management
- Software programming (creating/customizing software)
- Implementation

Whether you use a Big Five firm is generally dependent on the size of the project; obviously, the larger the project, the more resources and experience that are required. A Big Five firm may be able to assist when the vendor or other consultants do not have the necessary experience and resources to complete the project. However, do not hire a Big Five firm just for the sake of having a large consulting firm. Be extremely diligent during the selection process: make sure that the company possesses the skills you are seeking, that they will get along with the other consultants involved in the project, and most importantly, meet and interview the individual consultants that will be working on your project.

MODEL MAINTENANCE AND SUPPORT (WHO AND HOW)

After the implementation is complete and the model has gone live, the work is still not finished. There will almost always be items that don't function as planned, users that require changes, items that were overlooked, and flaws in the system that weren't previously apparent.

Any problems with the model need to be prioritized according to their severity. Obviously, critical flaws or bugs in the system will need to be fixed immediately. During the planning stage, you should have specified what types of problems the implementation team would be responsible for fixing. If not, you may spend valuable time just trying to determine who is responsible for resolving the problem instead of getting the system back up and running.

As far as the other items that were either overlooked or that the users have now decided they would like to have, they will have to be assessed to determine what type of impact they will have on the rest of the model. If the requested changes will significantly affect the model, you should probably hold off on these items until a major revision is planned. Additionally, changes that seem minor may have unforeseen consequences that will affect other portions of the model. Therefore, prior to making any changes to the model, assess how the entire model and other users will be affected by these changes.

In addition, sometime during the year your organization will most likely add new G/L accounts and may possibly acquire or divest other subsidiaries or operations. Learn the types of organizational changes that will impact your model, how the model can handle these types of changes, and who will be responsible for updating the model. Make sure that your budget model can handle the types of changes that you anticipate, otherwise you will have to spend time and money either drastically modifying your existing model or creating a new one.

TIPS TO ENSURE FASTER AND BETTER IMPLEMENTATION

Because implementation expenses usually make up a large percentage of the total cost of a new budgeting solution, a rapid implementation can be a great way of ensuring that you finish your project on time and within your budget. As you will see in the following paragraphs, a quick implementation is more dependent on cultural, organizational, and project management issues than on the software tools provided by your software vendor.

Using Templates

In connection with budgeting models, the word template typically refers to standard data entry screens and reports that can be used as is or can be easily modified to work with different models. Most vendors and third party consultants have a database of templates as part of their tool kit. These templates usually come from demonstration and training models, as well as prior budgeting models built for other customers in the same industry. If there are many other installations of the software in your industry, there are probably also templates available that reflect the unique needs of your company.

Templates can save many implementation hours because they give you pre-defined formulas and formatting, and often provide smart solutions to advanced issues that are not part of a particular software's standard functionality. Always ask your consultant what types of templates he or she has available, and then compare them to your own needs to see if you can take advantage of them.

Quick Decision Making

One of the major factors that delay a project is slow decision making by the internal steering committee. Whether it consists of only a handful of people or many key people (such as CFO, controller, or budget manager), the internal steering committee should have the flexibility during the implementation period to meet as frequently as necessary in order to make decisions and resolve problems that arise during the project. It is critical that committee members communicate well with each other and be able to reach relatively quick consensus on the issues that arise. This will avoid mixed feedback to the implementation team and minimize costly delays due to the reconfiguration or rebuilding of models.

Delegate Less Important Decisions to the Project Team

A large number of non-critical decisions, such as the background color, or fonts, or the use of alternative formulas that all produce the same result should be delegated to the full-time project team. Delegation speeds up decisions and moves the project along at a healthy pace. High-level decision-makers should only be brought in when important business issues arise. The project team should be staffed with people who have the expertise to make 80% to 90% of all decisions so that the implementation is continuously moving forward.

Find the Right People for the Project

Although a stand-alone budget software implementation is not close to the complexity and duration of an ERP project, it is still of high enough importance to warrant looking around the company for the best people possible. A poorly staffed project will result in a mediocre budget model and it might possibly lead to a failed implementation and a software investment with zero return. To the extent possible, exert your influence on the selection of the consultant(s) who work with your team, so that you get people with solid experience and a good reputation.

The size of the project team for a budgeting software implementation will vary with the size of the company, the complexity of the project, and the deadline. For example, an implementation for a $20 million single company, where the software is to replace a fairly simple spreadsheet model, will demand much less time and human resources than that of a large multinational corporation with multiple sites. The project at the smaller company will typically require one external consultant and one skilled financial staff member on the project team. At the large company, there will usually be several consultants and several corporate team members (both from finance/accounting and from the IS department) involved in the project.

In the larger projects, it is important to assign leadership responsibility to one person, so there is never any doubt to whom team members report and where the ultimate responsibility lies. When possible, it will also be of great benefit to avoid putting people with clashing personalities on the project team, thereby avoiding potential conflicts during the implementation.

Focusing the Implementation on Core Budgeting Needs

There is no prescribed time for how long a project should last. Some implementations might take only two weeks, while very large projects might have a duration from six to nine months. The good news is that a proper needs analysis and project plan should take most of the guesswork out of the scope of a project. When one of your goals is to make implementation fast and effective, it also means that you need to focus on your company's core budgeting needs. You must sort out important business needs from "nice-to-have" features, and take a phased approach to the project.

Essential needs should of course be part of the initial implementation, and many of the other needs can be addressed half a year or a year later, depending on your budgeting and forecasting cycles. Sacrificing a full-blown budgeting system implementation in favor of a key-needs implementation can have many benefits:

- Faster implementation

- Lower cost

- Less drain on organizational resources

- Easier to make changes if requirements change during the project/year

- Easier for new employees to learn (because model is less complex)
- Faster to make core model changes
- Gives users a chance to learn the model before deciding on further additions to it

Train the Right People at the Right Time

The specific approach used to train the project team can make or break the implementation and/or the long-term success of the budgeting software organization wide. There are probably more approaches to training than there are budget software packages on the market. Different vendors have their own home-grown training courses, resellers often have their own training approaches, and third party consulting companies seldom create their own training programs. How do you know which is the best way to train your project team? Unfortunately, there is no "right" answer, but experience certainly shows that certain approaches to training work better than others. Some general recommendations include:

- Starting a project with basic training will give the team members an overall understanding of the budgeting tool and its structure and limitations. This training should not be too detailed (details are quickly forgotten) and not oriented toward end-users. The focus should be on model architecture, design options, capabilities, and limitations.

- After conducting a needs analysis and defining your integration issues (such as linking to the general ledger(s) and payroll system), it is time for detailed training. Now the team members should either be trained according to detailed standard training plans, or the trainer should customize the training based on the needs of the client. Although the customized approach usually will cost more, it will pay for itself because the training will be much more relevant and to the point.

- Detailed training on modules, such as a Web interface, that are to be implemented in a later phase of the project should be delayed until just before implementation starts. This will ensure that team members have a fresh memory of the module's features and functionality when they roll up their sleeves and start working with it.

Assuring That the Related Hardware and Software Infrastructure Is in Place

One of the project team's first activities after basic training should be to investigate the different features of the budgeting package, and to prototype important parts of the new model. Therefore, it is essential that the new solution can be installed and configured immediately before or after basic training. The last thing you want is to have weeks of delays because you are waiting for a new server or other critical hardware to arrive.

Long delays always result in more expensive and less effective implementations. Delays can also render the initial basic training useless if the team members cannot remember what they have just been taught. To be on the safe side, you should ensure that all necessary hardware and software are in place before the start of basic training.

Getting Ready for Uploading Actual Figures and Last Year's Budget

Almost all budgeting models use actual figures in both reports and in input screens. They are used for actual-to-budget comparisons and in formulas used to derive budget figures. This means that the historical actuals are needed to test the budget model during the project. Also, when the system goes live, all the historical data must have been uploaded and reconciled.

The best test environment for a new budgeting system is to upload last year's budget and check that the new software model arrives at the same results. Entering fictitious figures here and there to test formulas usually is not sufficient, as you will not get the in-depth results needed before the new budgeting tool goes live. In order to get the data upload done in a timely manner, it should be done after the basic structure of the new model is in place, but before you have completed all reports and input screens.

Communication, Communication, Communication

The fastest road to failure in any project is poor communication between top management, the project team, consultants, and future users of the system. If a project is to be implemented in a quick and efficient manner, this point cannot be stressed enough. Before, during, and after the project, concerns must be heard and evaluated, and goals and expectations must be set at realistic levels and then communicated to the people affected by the new system.

It takes leadership from top management to support the project team and "sell" the project to the rest of the organization. This will help gain important support during the implementation and also motivate users to accept the system change after the solution goes live.

Strong Project Leadership

Every project needs a leader who can keep the team together, coordinate efforts, and communicate with top management. Preferably, the project leader should be a key manager that has the respect of the team and top management. A fast implementation demands fast and good decisions, and the project leader is the catalyst for this process. He or she needs to understand the budgeting process as well as the new technology to be implemented. If the project team makes a decision that must be defended and sold to the steering committee or other people in the organization, this responsibility falls to the project leader. He or she should have the personal skills and strength to push the issues through.

Whereas a fast budgeting software implementation is desirable because it will save money and time, it is not for every organization. If you feel that several of the items discussed in this section are not attainable, it would probably be a safer bet to give your project more time.

A NOTE ON INTEGRATION ISSUES

Normally, it is not a big task to upload the actual figures from a general ledger (GL) into a budgeting software application. However, depending on the size and structure of an organization, GL integration may or may not be a snap. The amount of work that goes into an integration is either very little (see Scenario 1) or it can be more significant (see Scenario 2).

Scenario 1: Budgeting with a Single Chart of Accounts

In a simple situation, a company has a single GL database with a single chart of accounts. These are the accounts that will be used by every department when the budget amounts are entered. This typically is the scenario for small and mid-sized companies that do not have any subsidiaries. In this case, the GL integration should be simple, both in regard to uploading account balances and in transferring the budget figures back to the GL once the budget process is completed. The latter is often not done, because many modern budget software packages also function as the company's report writer, and thus, there is no need to load the budgets back to the GL.

Scenario 2: Budgeting with Multiple Charts of Accounts

For many mid-sized and large companies, the budget process may involve consolidating information from subsidiaries that have different charts of accounts. The account structures may vary significantly among companies and the accounting software that is used may come from different vendors, making it difficult to create a single budget model that can be used by all companies.

Until you acquire new budgeting software, you are probably handling your planning process using a spreadsheet model, an in-house application, or an older commercial package. In any case, most companies manage multiple charts of accounts by creating a new consolidated account structure (or these items are simply rows in a spreadsheet) for use in corporate budgeting and reporting. However, some companies set up a chart of accounts in their budget package using all the accounts from the subsidiaries' GL's. This might look like the easiest solution up front, but it may not be so in the long run. Here are some thoughts about the two ways to set up your budget system's chart of accounts:

Creating all subsidiary accounts in the budget system chart of accounts

For an example of a non-uniform corporate budgeting system chart of accounts, see Figure 14.2.

Subsidiary A	Subsidiary B	Subsidiary C	Corporate Budgeting system
3010 Sales	30000 Net Revenue	3099-10 Revenue	3010 Sales
4000 Cost of Sales	41000 Cost of Goods Sold	4080-10 Cost of Sales	30000 Net Revenue
			3099-10 Revenue
			4000 Cost of Sales
			41000 Cost of Goods Sold
			4080-10 Cost of Sales

FIGURE 14.2   Non-uniform corporate budgeting system chart of accounts

Advantages:

- Fast to handle uploading of actual figures because all accounts are the same as in the GL's.
- Subsidiaries can work with accounts with which they are familiar.

Disadvantages:

- Budget screens must be set up to handle the correct account, depending on which subsidiary is entering their budgets.
- Reports must be set up to handle different accounts, depending on which subsidiary you select.

- Consolidated report formulas get complex because they need to refer to all the subsidiary accounts.
- Because of more complex formulas in many reports, they are harder to maintain.
- Reports might need to be updated every time a subsidiary has created a new account in their local general ledger.
- Some subsidiaries might have the same account number but with different descriptions, which can be confusing.

Creating a consolidated chart of accounts in the budget system (see Figure 14.3)

Advantages:

- It is easy to maintain reports.
- It is easy to maintain budget screens.
- It is easy to maintain the chart of accounts because it is normally independent of changes in the subsidiary chart of accounts. This, in particular, is important as web based budgeting is gaining popularity and a central database and budgeting model often is administrated by a few people at the corporate office.

Disadvantages:

- Consolidated accounts are unfamiliar to subsidiaries.
- Mapping of accounts is required for uploading of actual figures from subsidiaries.
- Maintenance of account mapping is required when subsidiaries add new accounts.

Subsidiary A	Subsidiary B	Subsidiary C	Corporate Budgeting system
3010 Sales	30000 Net Revenue	3099-10 Revenue	3000 Sales
4000 Cost of Sales	41000 Cost of Goods Sold	4080-10 Cost of Sales	4000 Cost of Sales

FIGURE 14.3   Uniform corporate budgeting system chart of accounts

In general, it is recommended that companies with multiple subsidiaries and multiple charts of accounts create a consolidated chart of accounts (Scenario 2) in their budgeting system. Of course you should first make sure your new budgeting software has the functionality to manage diverse charts of accounts. Then, analyze all potential advantages and disadvantages (such as those previously mentioned). Experience shows that the most efficient and easy to maintain budget systems operate with a consolidated chart of accounts. It allows for more time to analyze data and less time spent on budget model maintenance.

PART FIVE

INTERVIEWS

CHAPTER 15

INTERVIEWS

In this chapter you will find interviews with managers at nine companies of different sizes and in various industries. The following companies are profiled:

American Furniture Company

American Pharmaceutical Association

Blue Cross of Northeastern Pennsylvania

Bonneville Power Administration (BPA)

Car Wash Partners, Inc.

E! Entertainment Television Networks

Infiltrator Systems, Inc.

Morningstar, Inc.

SalesLogix Corporation

AMERICAN FURNITURE COMPANY

E. R. (Ed) Haskin, Jr.

Personal Background:

Work history (most recent job first):

Company:	Title:
American Furniture	Assistant Controller
E. R. Haskin, Jr., CPA	Owner
Haskin Technologies, Inc.	President
Sandia Detroit Diesel	Financial Manager
Sandia National Laboratories	Computer Auditor
Arthur Anderson & Co.	Senior Consultant
General Accounting Office	Supervisory Auditor

Current Responsibilities:

Support for accounting and management systems. Emphasis on implementing company-wide budgeting at present.

Company Background:

Industry: Retail Furniture

Product(s)/Service(s): sell furniture and home products

Organizational structure: Privately held company with 8 stores and two distribution centers

Size:

Number of employees: 950

Revenue: $100,000,000

Interview

The budgeting process

1. How long does your budget process typically last (from the time that people can create a budget to the time that it is finalized)? *4 months*
2. How long do you plan for it to last? *4 months*

3. How does your budgeting process begin? *Personnel budget listings are prepared using Human Resources current data on positions as the base.*

4. How many people are involved in the process? *30–35 managers are responsible for the preparation and review. One of the accounting staff spends about half of the year on budget and other accounting staff spend less time.*

5. What are some of the biggest obstacles you face during the budgeting process? *The large amount of data to be handled is the largest obstacle.*

6. What have you done to address these obstacles? *Software is used to reduce the data handling load.*

7. How would you like your budgeting process to change in the future, e.g., more/less employee involvement, shorter/longer duration, more/less approval and review, new software, abandon budgeting, and so forth? *We have just implemented budgeting. It will become more routine and faster as we adjust to it as a company. We expect more software aid will make the process easier. Managers will also assume more of the budget preparation job.*

8. How do you use or plan to use the Internet/intranet in your budgeting process? *We don't use it at present. We may use it in the future for data entry and review by managers.*

9. What impact do you expect technology to have on your budget process in the future? *It will make the mechanical part of the process quicker, easier, and cheaper.*

Budget reporting and usage

1. What type of reports do you use to communicate the budget? *Computer generated reports. Each responsible manager is provided a complete printout of his/her part of the year's budget by month. The monthly financials include the budget figures along with the actual figures.*

2. What are the most beneficial key metrics (performance indicators) in your industry? *Percent of sales data such as gross margins and salaries as a percent of sales are the most common measures. Such figures as sales per square foot and sales by employee are also very relevant, but are only produced periodically for the company.*

3. How do you incorporate these metrics into your budget reports? *Percent of sales figures are incorporated in both budget and actual reporting.*

4. How do you define significant budget variance? *We do not use a standard definition. The reviewer uses his/her judgment. For example, a 1% variance would be significant for gross profit but not for the travel expenses of a department. Executives also look at relatively large dollar changes in some areas.*

5. How do you address significant budget variances? *The reason for the variance is identified and discussed with relevant parties.*

6. How are your budgets used (to assess financial results, reward performance, etc.)? *They are used to plan and set goals for the year and also to reward good performance.*

7. How do you foresee your budget being used in the future? *Budgets will help the company to plan better and to devise more sophisticated financial incentives.*

Budgeting software, selection, and implementation

Software usage

1. What type of software do you use for your budget process, (Excel, specific budget software, etc.)? *We use a best-of-breed financial reporting, consolidation, and budgeting package.*

2. How has the use of technology helped or hindered your budgeting process? *Software has made it possible to budget at a detailed level with input from all relevant management personnel.*

3. What type of time savings have you realized as a result of your software usage? *n/a. So far we have used the same software.*

4. How is your budget integrated with your actuals to calculate variances (e.g., import of budget amounts into G/L, export of G/L amounts to budget software, etc.)? *Our budget software is also our financial reporting software and has its own database. We import the G/L data into the database.*

Software implementation

1. Would you consider your software implementation successful or unsuccessful? Why? *We consider it successful. It has greatly aided our budgeting process.*

2. What factor had the most influence on the outcome of the software implementation? *The flexibility and reporting capabilities of the software.*

3. What were the biggest obstacles in the implementation of your software? *Availability of the appropriate hardware.*

4. How were either you or someone from your company involved in the software implementation? *The software was implemented with company personnel including myself.*

5. What advice would you give to other companies to ensure success with their budgeting software implementation? *Make sure that senior management supports the effort.*

6. If you have recently implemented or purchased budgeting software, how has your budgeting process changed? *n/a*

7. If you could redo the implementation, what would you change? *We would start earlier in the year.*

AMERICAN PHARMACEUTICAL ASSOCIATION

Mark Delcoco

Personal Background:

Work history (most recent job first):

Company:	Title:
American Pharmaceutical Association	Controller
American Bankers Association	Assistant Controller

Current Responsibilities:

Manage staff of five in all accounting functions; analyze monthly financial statements; oversee annual budgeting process; manage annual audit and tax return preparation.

Company Background:

Industry: Professional Association

Product(s)/Service(s): Membership

Organizational structure: n/a

Size:

Number of employees: 85

Revenue: $18,000,000

Interview

The budgeting process

1. How long does your budget process typically last (from the time that people can create a budget to the time that it is finalized)? *3 months*

2. How long do you plan for it to last? *3 months*

3. How does your budgeting process begin? *With an all staff meeting to kick off the process and answer questions.*

4. How many people are involved in the process? *Almost 40 people are involved at some time during the process.*

5. What are some of the biggest obstacles you face during the budgeting process? *Since our budgeting process takes place in the summer, the biggest obstacle is working around staff vacations.*

6. What have you done to address these obstacles? *This year we are starting the process one month earlier to allow more time for budget input.*

7. How would you like your budgeting process to change in the future, e.g., more/less employee involvement, shorter/longer duration, more/less approval and review, new software, abandon budgeting, and so forth? *As mentioned previously, longer duration for budgeting process is desired in addition to less employee involvement.*

8. How do you use or plan to use the Internet/intranet in your budgeting process? *At this time, we do not have any plans to use the Internet for budgeting purposes.*

9. What impact do you expect technology to have on your budget process in the future? *Technology has, and will continue to have, a major impact on the budget process.*

Budget reporting and usage

1. What type of reports do you use to communicate the budget? *Overall company, divisional, and departmental reports.*

2. What are the most beneficial key metrics (performance indicators) in your industry? *n/a*

3. How do you incorporate these metrics into your budget reports? *n/a*

4. How do you define significant budget variance? *10% and at least $5,000*

5. How do you address significant budget variances? *Significant budget*

variances are addressed at the senior management level. If appropriate, alternative plans are implemented.

6. How are your budgets used (to assess financial results, reward performance, etc.)? *The budget is used to assess financial results.*

7. How do you foresee your budget being used in the future? *No different than the way it is being used now.*

Budgeting software, selection, and implementation

Software usage

1. What type of software do you use for your budget process (Excel, specific budget software, etc.)? *Best-of-breed budgeting software.*

2. How has the use of technology helped or hindered your budgeting process? *This technology has helped our budgeting process significantly by facilitating and streamlining the process.*

3. What type of time savings have you realized as a result of your software usage? *The budgeting system is now owned by our general ledger vendor. The integration feature has saved considerable time.*

4. How is your budget integrated with your actuals to calculate variances (import of budget amounts into G/L, export of G/L amounts to budget software, etc.)? *At the beginning of the process, the G/L amounts are exported to the budget software; at the end of the process, the budget amounts are imported into the G/L.*

Software purchase and selection

1. How did you organize your software selection process? *We were looking for a system that was compatible with Great Plains accounting software.*

2. What challenges did you encounter during the software selection process? *Our situation was to build a system in-house, or purchase an off-the-shelf system. However, we only found one existing system that was compatible with Great Plains.*

3. What were the top factors you used to compare the different budgeting solutions? *Compatibility with accounting software, ease of use, price, time to design and implement.*

4. What features (in general) did you overlook that you wish you hadn't? *n/a*

Software implementation

1. Would you consider your software implementation successful or unsuccessful? Why? *Successful. The system was up and running by our budget kickoff meeting. User response was positive.*

2. What factor had the most influence on the outcome of the software implementation? *The people directly involved in the implementation had the most influence.*

3. What were the biggest obstacles in the implementation of your software? *Time.*

4. How were either you or someone from your company involved in the software implementation? *I managed the implementation, and with the assistance of a consultant, designed the forms and reports to be used in the budget process.*

5. What advice would you give to other companies to be successful with their budgeting software implementation? *Make sure you have a definitive plan, and the support of upper management, before implementing the software.*

6. If you have recently implemented or purchased budgeting software, how has your budgeting process changed? *Prior to the implementation of the budgeting software, we used an antiquated spreadsheet system. Programming on the old system was very time-consuming and expensive. The process now is definitely less stressful, and the system is easier to use. Also, reporting capabilities are much greater on the new system.*

7. If you could redo the implementation, what would you change? *I wouldn't change anything.*

BLUE CROSS OF NORTHEASTERN PENNSYLVANIA

Kevin Hogan

Personal Background:

Work history (most recent job first):

Company:	Title:
Blue Cross	Manager, Budget & Analysis

Current Responsibilities:

Responsible for managing the corporate budget process related to operating expenses. Responsible for the monthly reporting of Budget versus Actual Operating to management and the Board of Directors (BOD).

Company Background:

Industry: Health Insurance

Product(s)/Service(s): Health coverage

Organizational structure: Non-Profit

Size:

  Number of employees: 1,100

  Revenue: n/a

Interview

The budgeting process

1. How long does your budget process typically last (from the time that people can create a budget to the time that it is finalized)? *1 month for budget preparers; 2–3 months from start to presentation to BOD*

2. How long do you plan for it to last? *2–3 months*

3. How does your budgeting process begin? *Roll out of Business Plan; Marketing Projections; Roll out to departmental management to begin budgeting operating expenses for coming year.*

4. How many people are involved in the process? *Four members on my staff; about 150 departmental management staff preparing budgets*

5. What are some of the biggest obstacles you face during the budgeting process? *Getting people to understand costs charged to their departments*

6. What have you done to address these obstacles? *Meeting one-on-one with management to help them understand their costs.*

7. How would you like your budgeting process to change in the future, e.g., more/less employee involvement, shorter/longer duration, more/less approval and review, new software, abandon budgeting, and so forth? *Management to review their departmental costs on a monthly basis instead of reviewing when preparing budget in the middle to late part of the year.*

8. How do you use or plan to use the Internet/intranet in your budgeting process? *Currently no intention to use, except for two or three people outside of our main office.*

9. What impact do you expect technology to have on your budget process in the future? *Purchased the budgeting software in 1999. Look to expand use in 2000 by developing new reports and analysis.*

Budget reporting and usage

1. What are the most beneficial key metrics (performance indicators) in your industry? *Cost per Contract; Contract per Member.*

2. How do you incorporate these metrics into your budget reports? *Show comparisons from Budget to Actual; benchmark against surveys from other Commercial insurers and Blue Cross/Blue Shield Plans.*

3. How do you define significant budget variance? *Usually 5% change, but review significant dollar changes.*

4. How do you address significant budget variances? *Seek explanation from management to determine reason for significant change.*

5. How are your budgets used (assess financial results, reward performance, etc.)? *Financial Results*

6. How do you foresee your budget being used in the future? *Reward performance for controlling operating expenses.*

Budgeting software, selection, and implementation

Software usage

1. What type of software do you use for your budget process, e.g., Excel, specific budget software, etc.? *Best-of-breed budgeting and reporting software.*

2. How has the use of technology helped or hindered your budgeting process? *Increased analysis capabilities; eliminated distribution of paper reports by budget department.*

3. What type of time savings have you realized as a result of your software usage? *Report writing capabilities without aid of IT programmers. Elimination of hard copy reports.*

4. How is your budget integrated with your actuals to calculate variances, e.g., import of budget amounts into G/L, export of G/L amounts to budget software, etc.? *Import actual data from our GL system to the budgeting package.*

Software purchase and selection

1. How did you organize (key activities) your software selection process? *Attend software show, then prepared RFP, then send to software company's from list obtained at software show.*

2. Which challenges did you encounter during the software selection process? *Difficulty in assessing one system versus another by only having a demo from company for a few hours.*

3. What were the top factors you used to compare the different budgeting solutions? *Ease of developing forms and reports by finance staff, and not IT staff. Integration with current financial systems.*

4. What features (in general) did you overlook that you wish you hadn't? *Did not overlook. But wish system had capability of drilling down to actual data in our GL through the budgeting and reporting software.*

Software implementation

1. Would you consider your software implementation successful or unsuccessful? Why? *Successful. Implemented software in about two months once consultant started. Our main goal was to replace current mainframe system.*

2. What factor had the most influence on the outcome of the software implementation? *Ability to understand programming language of system by finance staff.*

3. What were the biggest obstacles in the implementation of your software? *Due to all of the company's management working on the system, there are a majority of non-financial management working on system. Basically, people getting familiar with system.*

4. How were either you or someone from your company involved in the software implementation? *My staff and I worked with consultant on entire budget package.*

5. What advice would you give to other companies to be successful with their budgeting software implementation? *Lay out all of your needs in a systematic and orderly fashion. Try to think of every possible scenario. Learn the system intimately without relying on IT staff.*

6. If you have recently implemented or purchased budgeting software, how has your budgeting process changed? *Minimally. Looking at options for the second year of using system.*

7. If you could redo the implementation, what would you change? *Needed more time for training management on system. Our calendar was cut short this year; this was the first year using the budgeting software.*

BONNEVILLE POWER ADMINISTRATION (BPA)

Bryan V. Crawford

Personal Background

Work history (most recent job first):

Company:	Title:
BPA	Financial Analyst—Team lead for Capital Budgeting
BPA	Budget Analyst—Internal budget development and external budget presentation to Federal Executive Branch and Congress.

Current Responsibilities:

Bryan Crawford is the Project Lead for the Capital Investment Review Team at the Bonneville Power Administration. This cross-agency team has been charged with developing a revised capital investment review process that incorporates industry best practices and leads to more efficient and effective investment analysis, review, selection, and performance measurement. Prior to this project, Bryan has led other efforts focused on financial and policy analysis and development, including corporate cash management, divestiture, and potential corporate restructuring. Bryan holds a BA and MA in Art History, and a Masters in Management from the Atkinson Graduate School of Management at Willamette University. He has 10 years experience in finance, accounting, and budget development and execution.

Company Background:

Industry: Wholesale electric generation and transmission

Product(s)/Service(s): Wholesale electric power and transmission services

Organizational structure: Agency of the Federal Government and part of the Department of Energy. BPA is the largest Power Marketing Administration, responsible for the sale and marketing of the power produced by the federal hydropower projects of the Columbia River Basin in the Pacific Northwest.

Size:

Number of employees: 2,768 (1998)

Revenue: $2.3 billion (1998)

Interview

The budgeting process

1. How long does your budget process typically last (from the time that people can create a budget to the time that it is finalized)? *BPA's budgeting process usually takes about five years from beginning to end. This is consistent with BPA and federal policies, which is to show spending level estimates five years before the year begins. So for example, BPA's FY 1998 took five years and 19 iterations to complete.*

2. How long do you plan for it to last? *About the time it currently takes. BPA has been working diligently over the past few years to streamline its process and focus on having the right level of detail developed at the right time. We are trying to put the concept of "just-in-time" budgeting in place, where budgets are developed in aggregate early, and then refined in detail as the operating year approaches. We are currently implementing a new capital investment review process that focuses on strategic planning, discounted cash-flow analysis, and performance measurement.*

3. How does your budgeting process begin? *Depending on whether we are developing rates, or within a rate period, the process begins with a review of the spending level estimates included in the rate case for the year in question, and the financial targets set in the rate case or subsequently. Once overall business line targets are set, the business lines are instructed to develop the needed level of detail. In the past, we began with a bottom-up review of costs. Now the emphasis is more on top-down targets, based on current market conditions and past financial results.*

4. How many people are involved in the process? *BPA has a small budget staff at the Agency level (numbering less than 15) that work to establish the budgeting process, consolidate results, and support Agency top management review. The business lines have their own budget staff that translate targets into budgets, monitor results, and assist in future target setting. Overall, BPA has approximately 85 people at one time or another during the fiscal year involved in budget preparation and reporting.*

5. What are some of the biggest obstacles you face during the budgeting process? *Maintaining a clear connection between strategic planning and budget development.*

6. What have you done to address these obstacles? *We have worked to involve the Budget Manager more in developing the process with Strategic Planning.*

7. How would you like your budgeting process to change in the future, e.g., more/less employee involvement, shorter/longer duration, more/less approval and review, new software, abandon budgeting, and so forth? *We would like to reduce the number of iterations, more effectively involve managers at earlier stages in the budget development, better link top-down guidance with bottom-up budget development, and create more powerful incentives linking performance with goals.*

8. How do you use or plan to use the Internet/intranet in your budgeting process? *Other than for facilitating communication on assumptions and process, we are not currently using the Internet for budget development or implementation purposes.*

9. What impact do you expect technology to have on your budget process in the future? *BPA is currently in the process of implementing an Enterprise Resource Planning system. Part of this system will be a new software package for budget development.*

Budget reporting and usage

1. What type of reports do you use to communicate the budget? *Access and Excel reports, mostly*

2. What are the most beneficial key metrics (performance indicators) in your industry? *Net income and economic value seem to be the most prevalent.*

3. How do you incorporate these metrics into your budget reports? *We attempt to show both of these statistics on a quarterly basis and use them in setting targets.*

4. How do you define significant budget variance? *We have adopted no standardized definition, but generally look to a combination of percentages and dollars.*

5. How do you address significant budget variances? *Discussions among executive managers.*

6. How are your budgets used (to assess financial results, reward performance, etc.)? *Generally one target of the agency, as well as a target for most of the business units, is based on financial results. When a pre-determined amount of targets have been met, this triggers a payment to employees.*

7. How do you foresee your budget being used in the future? *To make better business decisions.*

Budgeting software, selection, and implementation

Software usage

1. What type of software do you use for your budget process (Excel, specific budget software, etc.)? *Currently we use Access, Excel, and Word.*

2. How has the use of technology helped or hindered your budgeting process? *Technology has made each iteration's turnaround time quicker, but this in turn has allowed more time for even more iterations.*

3. What type of time savings have you realized as a result of your software usage? *As a result of the combination of factors described above, no actual time savings have resulted to date.*

4. How is your budget integrated with your actuals to calculate variances (e.g., import of budget amounts into G/L, export of G/L amounts to budget software, etc.)? *Budget amounts are uploaded into the accounting system.*

Software purchase and selection

1. How did you organize your software selection process? *We hired a consultant to incorporate Best Practices and created an internal team to ensure adoption of the selection.*

2. What challenges did you encounter during the software selection process? *Getting past the "hype" to see what the software could really deliver.*

3. What were the top factors you used to compare the different budgeting solutions? *Flexibility in adopting best practices to our specific situation and circumstances.*

4. What features (in general) did you overlook that you wish you hadn't? *The ability to quickly implement top-down guidance in the budget development process.*

CAR WASH PARTNERS, INC.

Raymond Wallace

Personal Background:

Work history (most recent job first):

Company:	Title:
Car Wash Partners, Inc.	Manager of Corporate Planning & Development

Current Responsibilities:

Due to the size of the corporation (currently ten professionals at corporate headquarters) my responsibilities include due diligence related to acquisitions (from financial statement due diligence to reviewing contracts, leases, etc. prepared by our attorneys), budgeting (preparing all budget worksheets, gathering all worksheets from each site, and through consolidation), and numerous special financial projects (from benchmarking current operations to investigating how nonrecurring transactions should be recorded in the general ledger to preparing financial presentations for the Board of Directors). Basically, I'm the right hand to the CFO in the preparation and evaluation of financial material. I do very little regarding actual accounting (which is handled by our corporate controller and three regional controllers).

Company Background:

Industry: Automotive/car wash

Product(s)/Service(s):

We are currently an aggressive operator of car washes in the United States with our operations in Texas, Minnesota, Iowa, Idaho, and Utah. We acquire car wash operations to which we feel we can make significant improvements to increase their current operating profits (the industry is primarily measured on its cash flow generation [EBITDA] and not income).

Organizational structure:

Decentralized for all locations except our Texas operations (accounting, other than payroll, is centralized at Corporate). Regional controllers (two currently; we anticipate adding one more as we acquire more locations) handle all financial aspects (except Texas, as noted). The regional financial statements are consolidated by the corporate controller in Tucson.

Size:

Number of employees: approximately 1000 hourly employees, approximately 50 exempt employees

Revenue: n/a

Interview

The budgeting process

1. How long does your budget process typically last (from the time that people can create a budget to the time that it is finalized)? *This is management's first attempt at the budgeting process. Note that management was replaced with the current team in March 1999. We anticipate that the overall process will end up taking about 2.5 months (original worksheets were sent to the corporate controllers at the end of November 1999).*

2. How long do you plan for it to last? *The budget process was planned to last approximately eight weeks: two weeks for each site to review prior year's financial information and develop assumptions for year 2000, two weeks for the finance department to review the original assumptions and return to regions for explanation/changes, one week for revisions to original assumptions, one week for the finance department second review, one week for CEO review and discussion with regional VPs, one week to finalize and submit to Board of Directors for approval.*

3. How does your budgeting process begin? *We have developed a new financial statement structure. We are currently running two different regional financial statement presentations (e.g., west coast and central had developed their own presentation) and provided to each regional controller a FY 1999 income statement by month for each location. Each regional controller then reviewed the 1999 information with the regional VPs to determine if there were any anomalies in the 1999 operations. The regional controller, regional VP, and area managers (area managers manage approximately four to five car wash or lube locations) developed expectations as to volume, COGS, labor rates, occupancy costs, etc. They then compared all revenues and expenses budgeted by dollar per car (DPC, total revenue for the month divided by the number of budgeted cars, etc.) and to FY 1999 DPC for that line item. Due to the tight margins associated with the*

business, it is difficult to have large fluctuations in revenues/expenses unless something significant occurs (e.g., new technology related to chemicals or the equipment used to wash cars). Thus, the DPC for FY 1999 and FY 2000 will be relatively consistent. Large fluctuations from budgeted DPC versus prior year DPC are investigated and corrected if necessary. Thus, to significantly improve earnings before interest taxes, depreciation, and amortization (EBITDA) and net income, there needs to be an increase in volume (but there can also be minor increases if labor is controlled better).

4. How many people are involved in the process? *Approximately 28 people (three regional VPs, CFO, CEO, Marketing VP, one Finance, three Accounting, four Area Managers, two Operations, one HR, one Information Technology, and approximately ten general managers).*

5. What are some of the biggest obstacles you face during the budgeting process? *Several obstacles exist: (1) Our accounting system is not equipped for budgeting and everything has had to be done in Microsoft Excel. This leads to significant hours reconciling information rather than reviewing the information received from the sites. We are currently looking into several different first and second tier accounting systems. (2) The human factor of not responding in a timely manner. (3) Changes made to budget must be reconciled continuously to insure integrity of the data. (4) Presentation must be consistent among all reports given to management and sites. Most of these obstacles lead to the fact that we don't have a system that will allow us to manage the flow of information easily. Thus, I've been relegated to "data gatherer" with little/no time for evaluation of the data.*

6. What have you done to address these obstacles? *Little has been done at this point (other than investigating new computer systems). Due to the current make up of Corporate and the fact that the systems are not where they need to be, we've been working hard to standardize our reporting format and using Excel's linking function to summarize data from the detail general ledger accounts to something more reasonable for CEO and board review. Note that this linking function has been a source of difficulty as well, as changes to the underlying source data (e.g., moving or adding rows/columns) have created linking problems at the summary level.*

7. How would you like your budgeting process to change in the future (e.g., more/less employee involvement, shorter/longer duration, more/less approval and review, new software, abandon budgeting, etc.)? *The first thing would be to get some sort of information system that would allow for better control of the data. We currently have*

100+ GL accounts, more than 30 locations, and we plan to add approximately 20 acquisitions a year, and management wants a monthly budget for each location, then a monthly budget for each acquisition. (For example, if we purchase three washes named Jones Washes, they are always grouped as Jones Washes and summarized and compared to other similar purchases). Then management wants monthly budgets for each region (e.g., north, south, etc.), then for all locations, then for all locations plus corporate. Management also wants monthly balance sheet and cash flow budgets for all of the above. Due to the large number of spreadsheets and locations, you can see the need for a system that would help manage the information.

I would also like to see the response from the locations much quicker as each VP, Area Manager, General Manager, and Manager should understand the current operations of each site and should have a good feel for how the wash will perform. The one downside is that the weather plays a vital role in how well each wash does, so it's tough for them to budget the weather. However, they do have past history regarding each month and how the weather affected income, so they should use that as a guide. I believe the number of individuals involved is reasonable as well as the number of reviews/approvals.

8. How do you use or plan to use the Internet/intranet in your budgeting process? *I tried to get general inflation figures as well as estimated payroll inflation figures with no luck. I believe it's out there somewhere, but with all the junk that is on the Net, I don't have time to sift through all of the "hits" I receive. I really need to figure out how to query the Net to get the information that would be helpful. We've been using e-mail exclusively in our budgeting as we've sent our Excel work papers back and forth. Thus, we receive the information relatively quickly and there is no need for data input on my side.*

9. What impact do you expect technology to have on your budget process in the future? *Technology will play a key role that will allow me to go from data gathering and summarization to the review process that I'm supposed to be doing. We will be able to gather and sort/summarize data more quickly and will be able to change how the summarizations flow much more easily. There will also be less need for reconciliation of data.*

I also believe it will allow us faster analysis, as we should be able to determine if variances are due to volume fluctuations or price/usage issues (e.g., was there a problem with our chemical mix, did the equipment malfunction and cause over/under usage of chemicals, or was it due to fact that we had 15% volume fluctuation?).

I anticipate that in the future we will have a system that will allow the regional controllers to log directly into our budget system (either through telephone lines, the Net, or some other method) and make all budget revisions on a real-time basis. I will then become a manager of the budget process and less of an information gatherer as is currently the case.

Budget reporting and usage

1. What type of reports do you use to communicate the budget? *Excel spreadsheets summarized based on key roll-up financial statement line items (e.g., wash sales, extra package sales, cost of wash sales, labor, occupancy, G&A, etc.).*

2. What are the most beneficial key metrics (performance indicators) in your industry? *Dollar Per Car (DPC) is a key measure (see previous comments) as we don't usually see large fluctuations in the DPC for sales, cost of sales, and volume fluctuations can be eliminated. Percent to Total Sales is also key, which allows management to determine if those items considered fixed or variable/fixed are areas of concern (labor is considered variable/fixed because we require a minimum number of employees and because we add bodies as volume increases, it is very easy to get to a point where we are staffed at a level that exceeds the need based on volume). Labor as a percentage of sales help determine if local managers are overutilizing labor.*

3. How do you incorporate these metrics into your budget reports? *All spreadsheets and reports presented to management include a DPC column and when we discuss financial performance with management, DPC analysis is always included.*

4. How do you define significant budget variance? *Variances greater than 5–10% from expected DPC are investigated and discussed with the area and general managers. Volume variances are investigated to determine if it was weather-related or some other issue that marketing should address.*

5. How do you address significant budget variances? *CEO and CFO get involved when significant issues arise.*

6. How are your budgets used (to assess financial results, reward performance, etc.)? *Used to evaluate/assess monthly activity. However, EBITDA is used to reward performance.*

7. How do you foresee your budget being used in the future? *Based on my limited time in this industry, my impression is that the budget will continue to be used as a monthly assessment tool and will have little*

impact in other areas (e.g., performance reward system—the employees know that if they increase cash flow, they increase the value of the overall company). However, we are currently attempting to revise the performance reward system to include budget variance consequences (may prove too difficult to implement in the short term).

Budgeting software, selection, and implementation

Software usage

1. What type of software do you use for your budget process (e.g., Excel, specific budget software, etc.)? *Excel used exclusively. Once the budget is approved, we will download (probably manually) the budget to our current accounting software.*

2. How has the use of technology helped or hindered your budgeting process? *Technology has been a great help considering the alternatives (e.g., manual computations). However, as we are in the middle of the technology revolution, we should have some budgeting system that works better than Excel. I know they exist, but we don't have them. Hopefully our system search/acquisition will greatly improve the process.*

3. What type of time savings have you realized as a result of your software usage? *We've saved significant time (considering the alternative) relying on the computation function and linking function of Excel. We have also saved significant time because the use of e-mail has made this happen in almost real time. I was able to get multiple revisions sent to me in Excel and I was able to download directly to my spreadsheet without physically touching any of the worksheets from the sites or waiting for a package delivery (this also includes the money saved in sending packages, etc.).*

4. How is your budget integrated with your actuals to calculate variances (e.g., import of budget amounts into G/L, export of G/L amounts to budget software, etc.)? *The budget information will be downloaded to our current accounting system to provide an actual versus budget report for revenues. I believe we will have to export balance sheet and cash flow information for budget comparisons.*

Software purchase and selection

1. How did you organize your software selection process? *We hired our outside accounting firm to do a study of our current operations and suggest the appropriate accounting system for our expected growth (currently 2 tier-one and 1 tier-two systems have been suggested). We also did some research on our own and have investigated other*

tier-one and tier-two systems besides the accounting firms' suggestions. A decision is to be made by March 1 and implemented by June 30 (tight deadline in order to implement system across numerous locations).

2. What challenges did you encounter during the software selection process? *I've noticed that the people from the software companies we've talked with tend to be the sales/marketing people who often will sell you the world, but can't answer many operational questions (our corporate controller had specific questions regarding functionality, and the salespeople either gave incomplete information or tried to invent an answer). Each system needs to undergo a detailed trial run before any system is purchased.*

3. What were the top factors you used to compare the different budgeting solutions? *Ease, functionality, and timeliness are very critical. The number of steps that need to be performed is also a factor.*

E! ENTERTAINMENT TELEVISION NETWORKS

Caroline Frost

Personal Background:

Work history (most recent job first):

Company:	Title:
E! Entertainment Television Networks	Assistant Controller

Current Responsibilities:

Monthly financial reporting; Supervise AP, AR, and GL accounting; Finance Systems Administrator; Financial Systems Implementations

Company Background:

Industry: Cable TV

Product(s)/Service(s): Two Cable Network Channels, E! and Style. Revenues are generated via advertising sales and subscriber fees paid via cable affiliates.

Organizational structure: The main areas include Programming, Sales, and Administration.

Size:

Number of employees: approximately 1,000

Revenue: n/a

Interview

The budgeting process

1. How long does your budget process typically last (from the time that people can create a budget to the time that it is finalized)? *The process begins around mid-September, after the August numbers are final. The final board of director's review takes place toward the end of November and the approved numbers are imported into Great Plains for reporting purposes toward the end of December.*

2. How long do you plan for it to last? *People take as long as they are given.*

3. How does your budgeting process begin? *We begin by importing actuals into the budget system and distributing hard copies of payroll worksheets to Senior VPs. We do a second pass to budget for operating income and expenses after the payroll information is returned to us inserted as totals into the expense worksheets.*

4. How many people are involved in the process? *Five people in finance participated in the budget process and approximately 35 people from the various departments were also involved during the last budget cycle.*

5. What are some of the biggest obstacles you face during the budgeting process? *Coordinating the efforts of everyone involved in the process.*

6. What have you done to address these obstacles? *We have not adequately addressed this issue. One solution would be to reduce the number of people involved. Another solution would be to reforecast more frequently. If we were to do this, everyone would retain the procedures necessary to navigate the budgeting system.*

7. How would you like your budgeting process to change in the future (e.g., more/less employee involvement, shorter/longer duration, more/less approval and review, new software, abandon budgeting, so forth)? *I would like to see monthly forecasting on a smaller scale with the result of maintaining more up-to-date information. Currently the budget is out of date in only a few months. I would like to provide a working tool for the managers as well as a more meaningful tool to evaluate future cash needs.*

8. How do you use or plan to use the Internet/intranet in your budgeting process? *Our goal is to have the web interface functioning for our next large budget cycle.*

9. What impact do you expect technology to have on your budget process in the future? *I expect the user interfaces to become friendlier and the speed to improve.*

Budget reporting and usage

1. What type of reports do you use to communicate the budget? *Our reports included January through December Income Statements and actual to budget comparison reports.*

2. What are the most beneficial key metrics (performance indicators) in your industry? *The most significant measurement of performance that our owners hold us to is EBITDA, which stands for earnings before interest, taxes, depreciation, and amortization.*

3. How do you incorporate these metrics into your budget reports? *We have summary reports that provide high-level analysis and significant comparisons.*

4. How do you define significant budget variance? *It depends on too many factors to give a single simple answer here.*

5. How do you address significant budget variances? *Each department head is responsible for budget variances in their area. Significant variances are explained quarterly to our owners and if necessary, decisions will be made to adjust performance goals.*

6. How are your budgets used (to assess financial results, reward performance, etc.)? *They are used to assess financial results and also for performance evaluation.*

7. How do you foresee your budget being used in the future? *I would like to provide a tool to department heads that will assist them in managing their departments more effectively.*

Budgeting software, selection, and implementation

Software usage

1. What type of software do you use for your budget process (Excel, specific budget software, etc.)? *FRX reports converted into Excel worksheets. Duplicate worksheets linked into a budget consolidation model.*

2. How has the use of technology helped or hindered your budgeting process? *Easy importing of actual and budget data into and out of Great Plains has helped.*

3. What type of time savings have you realized as a result of your software usage? *We have only been through the first year of the budget process following the implementation. I expect to see the time savings in the second year.*

4. How is your budget integrated with your actuals to calculate variances (e.g., import of budget amounts into G/L, export of G/L amounts to budget software, etc.)? *We currently import and export budget data easily into our accounting and reporting system. Once the budget has been approved it is imported into Great Plains. We report against it monthly using FRX.*

Software purchase and selection

1. How did you organize your software selection process? *I oversaw the selection process. A committee of users was created who sat in on demos of competing budgeting systems. A decision was made by the group on which application seemed to best satisfy our needs.*

2. Which challenges did you encounter during the software selection process? *It took a great deal of work to come up to speed on the technical issues. The various applications evaluated offered significantly different approaches to the budgeting problem. We also had to arrive at a solution that could accommodate a MAC and PC environment.*

3. What were the top factors you used to compare the different budgeting solutions? *The solution needed to be cross-platform, and preferably have a web interface option. It needed to be affordable and relatively simple to implement. We needed to be able to manage it in the finance area with minimal help from IT people.*

4. What features (in general) did you overlook that you wish you hadn't? *We did not spend a great deal of time on the web functionality. We did not appreciate the reduced functionality of the web compared to the client installations and we had to scramble to stay on schedule with the implementation. However, we understood that the web technology was new and anticipated enhancements prior to the next budget pass.*

Software implementation

1. Would you consider your software implementation successful or unsuccessful? Why? *Yes, our goal was to have a system selected and available for the budget cycle just two months from the start of the system implementation. This goal was successfully met.*

2. What factor had the most influence on the outcome of the software implementation? *We had a written implementation plan as part of the contract. It showed who was responsible for what, down to the day a task needed to be completed. Even though we did not always do things*

exactly as indicated by the plan, everyone knew what the expectations were and we adjusted to stay on schedule.

3. What were the biggest obstacles in the implementation of your software? *We struggled with the speed of the web interface. We were able to improve the speed somewhat, but in retrospect we should have created budget pages with fewer calculations. We also found the programming of the forms to be fairly complex. It is essential that one person take ownership of the system and master its complexity.*

4. How were either you or someone from your company involved in the software implementation? *I, as the Assistant Controller, was responsible for the coordination of the selection and implementation of the system but not for the actual budget. This required a significant team effort in the transition of skills from one user to another and coordinating the actual budget process. Our MIS team handled the actual system installations and database setups. They also assisted in the setup of the web interface. We hired a budget manager after the system had been installed and just before the actual budget process began. He worked with the Controller and a person in our business development department to actually complete the first budget in the new system. We also did a great deal of data validation with our existing report rollups in FRX, which required coordination with myself.*

5. What advice would you give to other companies to be successful with their budgeting software implementation? *Have someone who is knowledgeable in finance, budgeting, accounting systems, and system implementation oversee the budget implementation. An MIS person would not have the accounting skills to evaluate the workflow issues. Ideally, have the person who is going to be responsible for the budget closely involved in the selection and implementation.*

6. If you have recently implemented or purchased budgeting software, how has your budgeting process changed? *We would like to forecast more frequently. Rather than have the users go into the system and budget these forecasts it may be easier to have one person coordinate the input of these changes. No decision has been made, but the coordination of the people involved in the budget process is almost more work than just making reforecast changes directly in the finance department.*

7. If you could redo the implementation, what would you change? *We had differences in opinion among the people involved in the budget process about what the budget model should look like. For the sake of a speedy implementation, we defaulted to the model that was previously used in Excel, essentially recreating the same reports and*

rollups. While this allowed us to get something up and going in time for the first budget cycle, it really needed to be revised to work better with the web interface. I would have liked to have spoken with more people who actually implemented the web interface so as to have avoided these design issues. I would have created a specialized input format for the web users.

INFILTRATOR SYSTEMS, INC.

Cheryl Harger

Personal Background:

Work history (most recent job first):

Company:	Title:
Infiltrator Systems, Inc.	Senior Financial Analyst

Current Responsibilities:

Coordinate the sales forecast and budget process; P&L forecasting, cash flow forecasting

Company Background:

Industry: Manufacturing

Product(s)/Service(s): Plastic chambers for septic stormwater systems

Organizational structure: Privately held

Size:

Number of employees: 420

Revenue: $80 million

Interview

The budgeting process

1. How long does your budget process typically last (from the time that people can create a budget to the time that it is finalized)? *6 months*

2. How long do you plan for it to last? *4 months*

3. When does your budgeting process begin? *July*

4. How many people are involved in the process? *30*

5. What are some of the biggest obstacles you face during the budgeting process? *Getting senior management to review and provide guidance/direction as to funding new initiatives.*

6. What have you done to address these obstacles? *Incorporate department/sales presentations to senior management earlier on in budget process to encourage discussion and provide guidance to those preparing the budgets.*

7. How would you like your budgeting process to change in the future (e.g., more/less employee involvement, shorter/longer duration, more/less approval and review, new software, abandon budgeting, etc.)? *This year we plan to start a rolling budget process, updating the budget on a quarterly basis, which will roll into the final budget for 2001. We also plan to push senior management for earlier review and finalization, instead of letting it sit for two months with no action being taken.*

8. How do you use or plan to use the Internet/intranet in your budgeting process? *When all our salesmen are on the Intranet (this spring), we plan to implement a rolling sales forecast, which will then tie into the budget process as well.*

9. What impact do you expect technology to have on your budget process in the future? *We are purchasing new sales forecasting software this year and then an ERP system (to be implemented in early 2001), which should have a forecasting/budgeting module.*

Budget reporting and usage

1. What type of reports do you use to communicate the budget? *Custom reports from the Access database and Excel spreadsheets, identifying budget versus actual by department by line item.*

2. How do you incorporate these metrics into your budget reports? *We don't at this time.*

3. How do you define significant budget variance? *>10%*

4. How do you address significant budget variances? *Need to justify the variance; Why is it necessary? What is the benefit to the Company?*

5. How are your budgets used (to assess financial results, reward performance, etc.)? *Assess financial results*

6. How do you foresee your budget being used in the future? *Eventually, they will be used to reward performance.*

Budgeting software, selection, and implementation

Software usage

1. What type of software do you use for your budget process (Excel, specific budget software, etc.)? *Access database*

2. How has the use of technology helped or hindered your budgeting process? *Helped in consolidating all the departments; we used to use Excel. We can now get reports easier, too.*

3. What type of time savings have you realized as a result of your software usage? *Less time consolidating (making sure formulas are correct); also, integrity of data is more assured—less likely to accidentally change or delete a number.*

4. How is your budget integrated with your actuals to calculate variances (e.g., import of budget amounts into G/L, export of G/L amounts to budget software, etc.)? *We exported actuals from G/L into Access database and used them for comparison purposes only. Budget items have to input manually into the G/L, which is time consuming and leaves a lot of room for human error.*

MORNINGSTAR, INC.

Joseph Sutton

Personal Background:

Work history (most recent job first):

Company:	Title:
Morningstar, Inc.	Director of Finance
Price Waterhouse	Staff auditor

Current Responsibilities:

Internal reporting on product profitability, variance analysis, cash management and treasury functions, and risk management.

Company Background:

Industry: Financial information publisher on the Internet, CD-rom, and in print.

Product(s)/Service(s): www.Morningstar.com, Principia® suite of products, Morningstar FundInvestor, Morningstar StockInvestor, Morningstar ClearFuture™.

Organizational structure: c-corp

Size:

Number of employees: 490

Revenue: $52 million

Interview

The budgeting process

1. How long does your budget process typically last (from the time that people can create a budget to the time that it is finalized)? *About 3 months*

2. How long do you plan for it to last? *About 3 months*

3. How does your budgeting process begin? *A meeting with the managers who have budget responsibilities discuss broad company objectives for the next year and product plans. So I guess the product plans actually come first.*

4. How many people are involved in the process? *There are about 30 or so managers who do budgets.*

5. What are some of the biggest obstacles you face during the budgeting process? *Information flow about expectations between support areas and the products, and the executive committee and the products/ support areas. Followed closely by getting people to turn them in on time.*

6. What have you done to address these obstacles? *Meetings early in the process to set expectations helped some this year. The timeliness issue is tough. We've decided to produce information for executive committee review and just leave blanks for the departments/products that don't have their information in the system yet. That gets them moving.*

7. How would you like your budgeting process to change in the future, e.g., more/less employee involvement, shorter/longer duration, more/ less approval and review, new software, abandon budgeting, and so forth? *Shorter duration is definitely better, but people do need time to*

review information. Our new system this year will allow people to access this year's data next year when creating the new budget. I'd like the process to generate information for two years or more, with the second being more of a forecast than a budget. Less involvement in the middle of the process from the executive committee would be good, since they tend to vacillate and lead managers down the wrong path. If I can get them to stick to their schedule, it would be a miracle.

8. How do you use or plan to use the Internet/intranet in your budgeting process? *Mostly on the analysis and variance side of things. 99% of the managers are on site, so that's not a big issue for us.*

9. What impact do you expect technology to have on your budget process in the future? *I'm hoping that our newly acquired international partners will have budgets prepared in a timely fashion that are easily uploaded into our system. Since we can't even get our budgeting system to talk to our accounting system while the HR system is online as well (even though they all come from the same vendor), that goal seems remote.*

Budget reporting and usage

1. What type of reports do you use to communicate the budget? *Summary reports by product/department and by segment of the company. Then consolidate them for the company as a whole.*

2. What are the most beneficial key metrics (performance indicators) in your industry? *Page views currently. Also, registered users and end-users (for company sponsored products).*

3. How do you incorporate these metrics into your budget reports? *Haven't really yet, except to drive the revenue figures on the budget. We'll be using the statistical accounts this quarter to generate that information.*

4. How do you define significant budget variance? *20% and $25,000 (both)*

5. How do you address significant budget variances? *Discuss with manager. Summarize those discussions across the company and present to the Executive Committee.*

6. How are your budgets used (to assess financial results, reward performance, etc.)? *Only for assessing financial results. This year some people may finally be held accountable for their budgets for performance, but it's not the norm.*

7. How do you foresee your budget being used in the future? *Not too differently than it is now.*

Budgeting software, selection, and implementation

Software usage

1. What type of software do you use for your budget process? *Best-of-breed budgeting software. Some Excel is still used to format better reports.*

2. How has the use of technology helped or hindered your budgeting process? *Helped: makes roll-ups and consolidations virtually error free compared to linking spreadsheets. Hindered: not as much functionality as Excel when inputting, so managers don't like that. Also, report formats are more limited and difficult to produce.*

3. What type of time savings have you realized as a result of your software usage? *Consolidations take place very quickly. More time can be spent on analyzing.*

4. How is your budget integrated with your actuals to calculate variances (e.g., import of budget amounts into G/L, export of G/L amounts to budget software, etc.)? *This is changing. We used to use Excel for both. Now we are developing reports in the general ledger to do the comparisons online with drill-down functionality.*

Software purchase and selection

1. How did you organize your software selection process? *RFP, software vendor selection, interview, implementation.*

2. Which challenges did you encounter during the software selection process? *Vendors that over promised and under delivered, or more appropriately, determining if the VAR was good or not. Time between presentations was tough too. It's hard to remember all of the functionality.*

3. What were the top factors you used to compare the different budgeting solutions? *Ease of consolidation, security, generation of reports, drill-down capability.*

4. What features (in general) did you overlook that you wish you hadn't? *Integration from third party software that was sold as "part" of the accounting/budgeting solution. It didn't go as smoothly as indicated at the sale. The VAR was horrible as well.*

Software implementation

1. Would you consider your software implementation successful or unsuccessful? Why? *I would say it was successful since we mostly met our deadlines with getting the budgeting package up and running. It's still not talking to our G/L though.*

2. What factor had the most influence on the outcome of the software implementation? *Time to install and generating reports to extract the information.*

3. What were the biggest obstacles in the implementation of your software? *The report generation language.*

4. How were either you or someone from your company involved in the software implementation? *I provided oversight and guidance. Department members were more hands on. I conducted training for the managers in how to use the system.*

5. What advice would you give to other companies to be successful with their budgeting software implementation? *Get a complete customer list from the reseller and call customers at random. Make sure the software really is totally integrated with the accounting system.*

6. If you have recently implemented or purchased budgeting software, how has your budgeting process changed? *n/a*

7. If you could redo the implementation, what would you change? *Start it sooner and give more time for report preparation at the beginning. Also, as we predicted when signing the agreement, the report writing training took place too early in the process and was forgotten by the time it was needed.*

SALESLOGIX CORPORATION

Rachael Bertrandt and Michelle Hanson

Personal Background:

Work history (most recent job first):

Title:	Company:
(Rachael Bertrandt) Senior Accountant	Medicis Pharmaceutical Corporation
(Michelle Hanson) Supervising Senior Auditor	KPMG Peat Marwick

Current Responsibilities:

(Rachael Bertrandt) Business Analysis, Budgeting

(Michelle Hanson) Financial Reporting

Company Background:

Industry: Software Development

Product(s)/Service(s): CRM Middle Market E-Commerce Products

Organizational structure: By product line

Size:

Number of employees: 327

Revenue: $36 million

Interview

The budgeting process

1. How long does your budget process typically last (from the time that people can create a budget to the time that it is finalized)? *3 to 4 months*

2. How long do you plan for it to last? *About 3 months*

3. How does your budgeting process begin? *With a preparatory e-mail to management and executives*

4. How many people are involved in the process? *Approximately 35*

5. What are some of the biggest obstacles you face during the budgeting process? *Clear communication of company-wide objectives from the executive level.*

6. What have you done to address these obstacles? *Executive budget meetings to make strategic decisions.*

7. How would you like your budgeting process to change in the future, e.g., more/less employee involvement, shorter/longer duration, more/less approval and review, new software, abandon budgeting, and so forth? *Better communication, shorter duration.*

8. How do you use or plan to use the Internet/intranet in your budgeting process? *We currently use the intranet to allow access for the different departmental budgets.*

9. What impact do you expect technology to have on your budget process in the future? *To make consolidation and reporting easier and less time consuming.*

Budget reporting and usage

1. What type of reports do you use to communicate the budget? *Product line P&Ls, department operating expenses summaries, headcount/personnel summaries*

2. What are the most beneficial key metrics (performance indicators) in your industry? *Revenue growth, revenue and operating margins, and revenue per employee.*

3. How do you incorporate these metrics into your budget reports? *Through the software; we write them into the reports.*

4. How do you define significant budget variance? *Judgment depends on the expense function—all items with a variance greater than 10% and $50,000 are reviewed.*

5. How do you address significant budget variances? *Follow-up procedures with management and/or executives to determine the reason for the variance.*

6. How are your budgets used (to assess financial results, reward performance, etc.)? *Review monthly operating results, update forecasts, and award bonuses.*

7. How do you foresee your budget being used in the future? *(See question six.)*

Budgeting software, selection, and implementation

Software usage

1. What type of software do you use for your budget process (Excel, specific budget software, etc.)? *Best-of-breed budgeting solution.*

2. How has the use of technology helped or hindered your budgeting process? *The software has really assisted us throughout the process, particularly in consolidating our product lines and complex department structure.*

3. What type of time savings have you realized as a result of your software usage? *After a round of budget changes, consolidation takes minutes versus days.*

4. How is your budget integrated with your actuals to calculate variances (e.g., import of budget amounts into G/L, export of G/L amounts to budget software, etc.)? *The budget will be exported into the accounting system, and the actuals imported into the budgeting package. Currently this allows us many different reporting options, including a drill-down feature in our G/L software that is not available in the budgeting solution.*

Software purchase and selection

1. How did you organize your software selection process? *(1) Researched software choices via the Internet (2) Requested quotes and software information. (3) Performed a feasibility analysis and selected three or four vendors. (4) Had selection of vendors perform demos for us. (5) Chose software based on ease of use, cost-value assessment, report writer functionality, scalability, and interfacing with the general ledger system recently updated.*

2. Which challenges did you encounter during the software selection process? *Salespeople from losing software companies.*

3. What were the top factors you used to compare the different budgeting solutions? *(See question one.)*

4. What features (in general) did you overlook that you wish you hadn't? *Drill-down capabilities within the software.*

Software implementation

1. Would you consider your software implementation successful or unsuccessful? Why? *Successful, because we were able to get the software installed and deployed to the end-users within a very tight schedule of approximately two weeks.*

2. What factor had the most influence on the outcome of the software implementation? *Our highly skilled consultant from the reseller.*

3. What were the biggest obstacles in the implementation of your software? *At the time of implementation, the company consisted of one product line—by the end of the budgeting process we had three product lines, and a far more complex department structure.*

4. How were either you or someone from your company involved in the software implementation? *Michelle was instrumental in communicating the company organization, department structure, and reporting needs.*

5. What advice would you give to other companies to be successful with their budgeting software implementation? *Communication of your needs and knowing what your structure is.*

6. If you have recently implemented or purchased budgeting software, how has your budgeting process changed? *We went from using Excel spreadsheets to having a true database of budget information available.*

7. If you could redo the implementation, what would you change? *Not a lot.*

APPENDICES

In order to save you time and money in your software selection and implementation process, several useful documents from the Appendices are provided on the World Wide Web. Please visit http://wiley.com/rasmussen. The user password is Budgeting. These documents are in Word format, and you will be able to download them and adjust them as necessary.

APPENDIX A

SAMPLE CONFIDENTIALITY AND NON-DISCLOSURE AGREEMENT (SALES/DEMO PROCESS)

In connection with discussions on July 21, 1998 and thereafter, between ABC Software, Inc. of 270 S. Peck Drive, Los Angeles, CA 91212, including but not limited to all affiliates of ABC, Inc., and XYZ, LTD of 3110 Johnson Rd., Edison City, FL 33090 regarding information on themselves, their relationships and transactions, and certain of their products, the parties hereto propose to provide to each other, with either in the role as "Donor" or "Recipient" (dependent upon direction of information flow as exchanged from time to time), certain confidential and proprietary information ("Confidential Information" as further defined below) for "Evaluation" or for commercial use. In consideration of Donor's providing this information, and for other good and valuable consideration, the extent and sufficiency of which is acknowledged by Recipient hereby agrees to the terms and conditions as follow with respect to the treatment and use of such confidential information.

1. Definition:

    a. Confidential Information shall mean materials, information, data and like items which have been or which may be disclosed, whether orally, in writing or within media used in electronic data processing and programs, including but not limited to information concerning 1) collection, tabulation and analysis of data, 2) computer programming methods, designs, specifications, plans, drawings, and similar materials, 3) programs, databases, inventions (whether or not eligible for legal protection under patent, trademark, or copyright laws), 4) research and development, and 5) work in progress. Additionally so defined is all information on any or all aspects of the business of Donor and its affiliate(s), including without limitation 6) any and all financial statements, 7) business and/or marketing plans or programs, 8) pending or threatened litigation, 9) prospective or existing contractual relations, 10) customer, vendor, or affiliate lists or identification(s), and any other information of like nature, value, meaning, or significance to categories described as 1) through 10) herein. Confidential information includes the fact of disclosure or evaluation, as well as any tangible or intangible material or information-conveying aspect, whether disclosed in oral or written form or otherwise, when and as involved in any disclosure by Donor or Recipient, and whether or not any such material or aspect is specifically marked, labeled or described as "confidential." This definition shall be subject to exclusions as appear below:

b. Confidential Information does not include any information which

    i) is in the public domain at the time disclosed or communicated to Recipient; or which enters the public domain at the time disclosed or communicated to Recipient; or which enters the public domain through no act, fault, or responsibility of Recipient;

   ii) is lawfully obtained by the Recipient, with permission to disclose, from a third party who is not, to Recipient's knowledge, subject to any contractual or fiduciary duty not to disclose;

  iii) has been independently derived or formulated by the Recipient without reference to the Confidential Information given either before or after the effective date of this Agreement;

  iv) the Recipient can demonstrate was lawfully in its possession, free of any duty not to disclose, before the date of disclosure by Donor to the Recipient.

2. Duty of Confidentiality. Recipient agrees to receive the Confidential Information in confidence, to keep the same secret and confidential, to make no additional copies of same without the express written consent of Donor, and not to disclose Donor's Confidential Information to any party whatsoever, save for its officers, directors, employees, and agents as required for Evaluation hereunder or for commercial use under a coexistent Agreement, without the prior written approval of Donor. Further, Recipient shall ensure that each of its officers, directors, employees, and agents to whom Donor's Confidential Information might be disclosed under the terms of this Agreement,

shall be held to subscribe to all the terms of this Agreement and to agree to be bound by all Agreement terms and conditions.

3. Duty of Care. Recipient shall in its protection of Donor's Confidential Information from risk of unauthorized disclosure, exercise the same level of care as it does and/or would exercise to safeguard its own confidential and proprietary information, and in no event afford any less such protection and safeguarding as may be regarded as reasonable in view of the premises of this Agreement and Recipient's undertakings pursuant hereto.

4. No License. Nothing in this Agreement shall be construed as granting any license or right under any patent, trade secret, copyright, or otherwise, nor shall this Agreement impair the right of either party to contest the scope, validity, or alleged infringement of any patent, copyright, or trade secret. Nor shall the parties hereto use any part of the Confidential Information disclosed for any purpose other than furtherance of the relationship between the parties.

5. Termination of Evaluation; Termination of Commercial Agreement. If Evaluation is terminated for any reason, or if a commercial agreement under whose operation Donor's information has been divulged shall terminate, and in any event upon the reasonable request of Donor at any time, Recipient shall return or destroy, at Donor's option, all copies of Donor's Confidential Information and all notes, in documents or on media of any type, related thereto, as may be in Recipient's possession or under the Recipient's direct or indirect control. All such written or media-carried notes shall be subject to such return or destruction, regardless of the authorship of such notes. Recipient shall confirm in writing that it has retained no copies, notes, or other records of the Confidential Information in any medium whatsoever.

6. Injunctive Relief: Enforcement Costs. Recipient acknowledges that any breach of this Agreement would cause Donor irreparable harm which would be difficult if not impossible to quantify in terms of monetary damages. Recipient consents to a granting of immediate injunctive relief to Donor upon any breach of this Agreement, in addition to all other remedies available to Donor at law or in equity. Recipient waives any requirement that Donor post a bond in connection with any application for or order granting injunctive relief. Further, in event of legal process for breach or other cause, the prevailing party shall be entitled to recover its costs, including costs of suit, expenses and any Attorney's fees involved in any action to enforce the terms of this Agreement.

7. Miscellaneous.

    A. This Agreement shall be governed by the laws of the State of California. Each party irrevocably submits to the jurisdiction of the courts of the State of California for resolution of any dispute hereunder, without regard to the conflicts of law principles thereof.

    B. This Agreement may be modified only by a writing executed by both parties. The parties agree that this Agreement represents the entire agreement between the parties as to the subject hereof, and that all prior understanding, agreements, and representations related to the subject matter hereof have been incorporated into this Agreement. This Agreement rescinds and supplants any prior Agreement(s) as to the subject matter hereof.

    C. This Agreement shall become effective on date first written above, and remain in effect for the duration of the period of Evaluation or until this Agreement has been formally supplanted by any Subscriber, vendor-relationship, financial relationship or similar agreement between the parties which specifically absorbs, rescinds, or replaces this Agreement. Failing such specific absorption, rescission or replacement, this Agreement shall remain in full force and effect for the period of five (5) years following the completion of the period of Evaluation or the expiry of any consequent Subscriber or other agreement between the parties.

IN WITNESS WHEREOF, each party agrees to and accepts this Agreement and its terms, by signature of its authorized official below.

_____   _____

ABC, Inc.   XYZ, Ltd

*by:*_____   *by:* _____

Title: *Title:*

Date: *Date:*

APPENDIX B

SAMPLE RFP

Request for Proposal

Vendor: ABC Software, Inc.

XYZ Corporation

Budgeting and Planning System

CONTENTS

Instructions

Vendor Identification

Introduction

    A. Vendor Response to RFP

    B. Vendor Product Review

    C. Review of Vendor Installations

    D. Implementation Proposals

    E. Contract Development

    F. Final Selection

Budget System Busines Requirements

    Security

    Budget System Setup/Maintenance

    User Capabilities

    Budget Reporting

    Data Interface with External Systems

    Other Information

Budget System Technical Requirements

    Technical Architecture (User Interface, Middleware, RDBMS)

Vendor Information

Vendor History and Organization

Financial Status

Costs/Fee Structures

Training Process

Documentation

End-User Support

Product Enhancements

Site Visit

Vendor Experience

Consultant Qualifications and Project Organization

Standard PC Configurations, XYZ Corporation

INSTRUCTIONS

Use the enclosed file containing this document. The document is written in MS Word 2000 and the file is called <filename>.

1. Enter your answers next to each question. Be short and straight to the point wherever possible.

2. You can use attachments to include any additional relevant information you believe is important to disclose.

3. If you have any questions, contact <contact person's name, phone number, and e-mail address>.

4. Include the completed requirements document with your proposal.

Vendor Identification

Software Name	\<software name\>
Vendor Name	ABC Software, Inc.
Authorized Signature	\<contact person's signature\>
Print Name	\<name of contact person\>
Address	\<street\>, \<city\>, \<state\>, \<zip code\>, \<country\>
Telephone Number	\<vendor's phone number\>
Fax Number	\<vendor's fax number\>
E-mail Address	\<contact person's e-mail address\>
Web Address	\<vendor's Web address\>
Date	\<date of RFP completion\>

INTRODUCTION

Company XYZ currently utilizes a mainframe based budgeting system. There are approximately xxx budget users, yyy cost centers, and zzz account numbers used for budgeting purposes. The system allows the users to enter data into \<description of current system\>.

XYZ is seeking a user-friendly, robust budgeting and analysis tool to meet our present and anticipated future needs. Over the last several months the requirements in the enclosed Request for Proposal (RFP) have been developed to evaluate commercial budgeting systems. Your system has been selected as a candidate to receive this RFP.

The following is a summary of the process that will be utilized to select the successful bidder:

A. Vendor Response to RFP

Please complete your responses to the following requirements questionnaire, based on the latest version of your software that is currently installed and in use at customer sites, and submit two copies of your responses to:

<contact name>

<phone number>

<fax number>

<e-mail>

<address>

Any questions may also be directed to the person listed above.

We will rate your responses objectively and use the following key criteria:

1. Budget System Business Requirements match (50%). See Section below.

2. Budget System Technical Requirements match (15%). See Section below.

3. Vendor Information (35%). See Section below.

The responses to this RFP must be received no later than <date>.

B. Vendor Product Review

From the initial evaluation of the vendor responses, XYZ will select no more than three vendors who will be invited to conduct a product demonstration. Demonstrations will be conducted in early <month>; each company will be given up to four hours to conduct the demonstration. The primary emphasis of the demonstration should be for the vendor to introduce their company and demonstrate the capabilities of their product. The vendor's ability to communicate succinctly will be an important consideration in the selection process.

C. Review of Vendor Installations

An important factor in the evaluation process will be the review of one or more installations of your software. Each vendor will be requested to provide a contact at several sites that are most comparable to XYZ's environment, and are already using your product. We will be looking to discuss with the contact how the software is being used, the effectiveness of the installation, and the relative success of the implementation process.

D. Implementation Proposals

Subsequent to product demonstrations and reference evaluation, XYZ will solicit implementation proposals from the finalists and from other independent implementation vendors. The cost and quality of the implementation support will be critical factors in vendor selection.

E. Contract Development

XYZ reserves the right to reject any and all proposals and alternatives. XYZ intends to negotiate and enter into a contract with the selected vendor. Negotiations must be conducted between the selected vendor firm and XYZ. The content of the RFP and successful vendor proposals will become an integral part of all contracts, but either may be altered by the final negotiated provisions of the contract.

If in the opinion of XYZ, a contract, for any reason, cannot be negotiated with the selected vendor firm, XYZ may so notify the vendor. XYZ, within its discretion, may select other vendors from the proposals submitted or reject all proposals and/or may re-issue the RFP.

F. Final Selection

Final selection of a vendor and product will be decided based on the outcome of the above mentioned process. The selection will be made by <date>, and all parties that have made it to this point of the RFP process will be notified of the decision during the week of <date>.

BUDGET SYSTEM BUSINESS REQUIREMENTS

Security

1. Does the system offer the ability to schedule unattended backup at pre-defined times?
2. Does the system facilitate data recovery with an ability to recover the entire data set or specific data set as required?
3. Does the system offer a detailed on-line transaction log including time, date, system user, changes made?
4. Does the system offer access by individual modules/screen levels/field levels?
5. Does the designation of Budget System Administrator (BSA) allow access to all cost centers?
6. Does BSA only control access of budget system by use of User IDs?
7. Do users only have access to the cost center budgets as designated by BSA?
8. Is there multi-level security access to system?

9. Can BSA allow/restrict access to system at a Manager level, then at a Director level, then at the Vice President level?

10. Can BSA control access to system to the three levels mentioned above for read, write, update, and delete capabilities?

11. Does BSA control the ability for users to access multiple versions of budgets?

12. What controls are in place to prevent one version from overwriting another version?

13. Do budget users have the ability to add/change/delete entry forms?

14. Budget users should not have the capability to access taxes, benefits, and other overhead screens controlled by BSA.

15. Is there an audit trail to trace the source of all transactions at both terminal and user ID level?

16. Ability to close budgets and prevent revisions with proper security.

Budget System Setup/Maintenance

1. Can the administrator monitor and administer the system remotely?

2. Does the system offer audit trail of reporting structure changes (e.g., acquisitions/dispositions, etc.) showing the date of change, effective date of the change, and the user's ID?

3. Is an intuitive mapping tool included that allows the administrator or users to quickly define or redefine the account formats and reporting structure?

4. Can relationships be defined by dragging and dropping the linkages between accounts?

5. Can the system have multiple charts of accounts?

6. Can one to one, one to many, many to one relationships be used when defining the account relationships?

7. Can BSA update/maintain various secured tables, centrally controlled variables, user access, and so forth?

8. Can unlimited number of data entry screens be defined?

9. Can Chart of Accounts (cost center, natural account, sub-account, line of business, etc.) be imported from another system?

10. What maintenance is required when new accounts, departments,

Lines of Business, and so on are added (i.e., are such changes made at the individual report level or centrally done with automated update to all reports)?

11. Can BSA design forms for various types of expenses such as Salaries, Travel, Consulting, Capital Expense, Outside Services, Advertising, and so forth? (Forms for general expenses should also be available.)

12. Does budget system have the capability of calculating payroll taxes, benefits, and other overhead costs automatically, which can be controlled by the BSA?

13. Is there the ability to maintain organizational structure and reporting requirements (i.e., Designate cost centers reporting to different VPs)?

14. What are the budget system's multi-company capabilities?

15. How many simultaneously produced budgets from the organization can be maintained in your system for ultimate roll-up and how would past budgets be accessed?

16. Can natural accounts be split into multiple categories? (for example, ability to designate natural accounts into four categories: Controllable Personnel Service; Controllable Other; Uncontrollable Personnel Service; Uncontrollable Other)

17. Does the system have the capability to allocate based on statistical data, and if so, can the statistical data be imported into the system?

18. Can the BSA send notes to the end-users?

19. How is salary planning accomplished in the system?

20. How do the completed budget submissions get distributed and collected from the users?

21. Does the budget system allow for sophisticated management of consolidation data submission workflows?

22. Does the budget system allow at least $<n>$ segments for each natural account to comply with our current system?

23. Capable of storing $<n>$ years of data?

24. Capable of handling minimum of $<n>$ concurrent users?

25. Does system have automated system of checks and balances at both the input and output level?

26. Assign budget exchange rates to conversion codes.

User Capabilities

1. Web capabilities (please describe)

2. Does the system offer a restatement tool to allow the administrator to make changes centrally?

3. Does the system offer detailed audit of the changes made between various budget submissions (e.g., variance by detailed account)?

4. Does the system offer audit trails of the various budget submissions showing the date of submission and the version number?

5. Does the system allow the user to send/commit specific "chunks" of data (i.e., allow incremental submission of data)?

6. Is there a sophisticated audit trail to track the adjustments of data? (Changes should be flagged so that the local entities are quickly aware of any topside adjustments and vice versa.)

7. Is on-line help with a search engine available to allow users to search for specific help topics?

8. Does the system offer context-sensitive help screens?

9. Can the system interface with <general ledger>, text files (e.g., other G/L packages) or spreadsheet (e.g., Excel, Lotus)?

10. Can a budget be created from both bottom-up and top-down approach?

11. Based on user-defined drivers/parameters, can a new budget be automatically generated whenever there are changes to these drivers?

12. How do the budget users enter data for employees' salaries, benefits, and controllable expenses?

13. From a non-technical user's point of view, how is the system oriented to minimize data entry (e.g., a way to spread a number evenly each month throughout the year) and how is it generally easy to use?

14. Are there specific screens for different types of expenses (i.e., employee form)?

15. Do budget users have the ability to add forms or alter forms set up by BSA?

16. Will budget users have access to multiple versions of the budget?

17. How can versions be compared to one another?

18. Can the budget users create what-if analyses for their cost centers?

19. Do users have the ability to perform current year forecasting?

20. Can users attach notes to budget line items?

21. How does the system provide capital budgeting?

22. Are there batch processes that need to run on a periodic basis, or is this a real-time system?

23. What level of detail is captured during budget modifications for audit trail purposes?

24. Does system provide drill-down capability for end-users, and if so, how does this work?

25. Does the system maintain flags for budgetary restrictions (e.g., an expense is not allowed for a specific department).

26. Does the system allow budgeting at a summary level with expenditures/revenue at more detailed level.

27. Does it have the ability to enter a) a monthly budget, b) a quarterly budget, c) an annual budget?

28. Does it have the ability to budget in multiple currencies?

29. Does it have the ability to revalue the budget based on changes in exchange rates?

30. When a transaction is entered into the system it must be able to be checked against a business rule and provide the option to do one of the following (user security level will determine the choices available):

   - reject the transaction
   - accept the transaction, but deliver a warning to the user
   - accept the transaction and generate a report of the items entered which are non-compliant with the business rules
   - permit override

Budget Reporting

1. Are charting and graphing of figures available?

2. Can users perform on-line analytical processing in local currency and USD, slicing-and-dicing, and drill-down reporting?

3. Does the system allow users to attach memo/commentary for specific data?

4. Is trending analysis available?

5. Is comprehensive ratio analysis available?

6. Is drill-down analysis available?

7. Is Detect and Alert/Exception analysis available?

8. Is Rank and Sort analysis available?

9. Is Top–Bottom results analysis available?

10. Is print preview available?

11. Is batch printing available?

12. Is the system mail-enabled and Internet-ready to enable delivery of the reports by e-mail and to allow access to live reports via the intranet?

13. Do users have the flexibility to route the reports to different local or network printers?

14. Are users able to generate ad-hoc reports without the assistance of IT resources?

15. Does the system offer audit trail reports of journal entries made by headquarters and similar ability for the local entities?

16. Can the system validate that the balance sheet is balanced?

17. Can the system validate beginning balances for Retained Earnings to prior quarter's/month's final numbers?

18. Can the system validate that designated accounts are eliminated upon consolidation?

19. Can the system validate flow-through of Net Income to the Equity section?

20. Is data balancing enforced with automated validation and reconciliation routines?

21. Can the same foreign exchange rate translation and rounding methodology be applied to all modules?

22. Can topside adjustments be managed automatically?

23. Can the system handle the head office allocation process?

24. Can consolidated results be permanently stored or simply output in different report formats?

25. Is a standard Windows graphical user interface (GUI) used to facilitate consolidation tree creation?

26. Are custom, ad-hoc consolidation trees available?

27. Is consolidation processed in real time, and does it reflect the subsidiaries' most current results and exchange rates?

28. Is currency translation processed in real time?

29. Do all modules use one common set of currency tables?

30. Are an unlimited number of currency tables allowed?

31. Can multiple exchange rate tables be applied against one set of data, creating multiple sets?

32. How are unlimited date-stamped versions of the currency tables allowed?

33. How are European common currency (Euro) conversion issues handled?

34. What types of reports are standard with the budget system?

35. Does the system have secure, personalized report views?

36. Can general ledgers with different charts of accounts be consolidated, i.e., are there conversion translation table capabilities?

37. Is there automated elimination of intercompany balances and zeroing out of intercompany average balances?

38. Can descriptions to automated and manual eliminations be added?

39. Can the budget be reported by each of the following account segments: Cost Center, Natural Account, Line of Business, Function, and Operation?

40. Can the budget users produce cost center and consolidated cost center reports at their local printer?

41. Can the budget users produce exception reports (i.e., all variances greater than 10%)?

42. Does the system have rule-based report exception highlighting?

43. What does your system provide in the way of automatic report printing and distribution of user budget reports?

44. Can budget users create their own reports which would present the information in their own format?

45. What is the average amount of time required to write a production report?

46. How does BSA create reports to meet various reporting needs (ad-hoc reporting)?

47. What report writer(s) are included in this budget system?

48. Does the system have mathematical and report design flexibilities and capabilities similar to Excel?

49. Is there a direct interface with Excel (plug-in) for spreadsheet-based report writing?

50. Does the system have offsite or Internet access for data input and report output?

51. Does the system have high volume/batch speed printing capabilities?

52. Can software handle multi-level company consolidations, minimum <n> levels?

53. Is the creation of new reports user-friendly?

54. Can reports be produced using data such as units (headcount/employee type), rates (taxes), and dollars (total salary)?

55. Does the system interact directly with Microsoft Office to allow users to produce graphs, charts, and high quality reports without re-keying data?

56. What functionality does the system have for dealing with standard cost tables?

57. Does the system have the ability to predict/project balance sheet based on income statement?

58. Does the system have Web capabilities (please describe)?

59. Does the system have Web access to navigable report libraries and report viewing?

60. Can the system provide various report templates (e.g., budget to actual, one budget ledger compared to a different budget ledger, actual to actual) for current year, prior years (up to five), and projected years?

61. Does the system have the ability to perform statistical analysis on all budget reports?

62. Does the system have the ability to revalue the budget based on changes in exchange rate?

63. Does it allow users to develop "what if" scenarios (e.g., a working budget) without affecting the actual budget (e.g., changes in exchange rates)?

64. Does the system have the ability to report across years on the budget/actual activity taking place for a project?

65. How does the system track cost center, natural account, line of business, and operation?

66. How are roll-ups performed on the items mentioned in question 65?

67. XYZ Corporation consists of six groups with multiple departments within each group. How does your system support multi-dimensional

structures which require several detail lines rolling up to various levels, along with the need to drill down to the lowest level of support detail? Full multi-dimensional and drill-down support?

68. The are currently multiple reports that are produced by our existing budget system that are used throughout the organization which any new system must be able to produce. Can your budget system produce the following?

- **Budget Detail Report by Company by Natural Account by Month.** This report details all budget transactions relating to a natural account by company.

- **Budget Detail Report by Company by Department by Cost Center by Natural Account by Month.** This report details all budget transactions by natural account by month.

- **Budget Detail Report by Company by Cost Center by Natural Account by Month.** This report is the same as the report above, except that the cost centers are listed by Department (VP line area).

- **Cost Center Analysis Report by Department by Natural Account comparing current year Projected to next year Budget.** It also includes the current year budget and YTD actual. This report summarizes all transactions for an annual total by natural account.

- **Natural Account Analysis Report by Cost Center comparing current year Projected Forecast to next year Budget.** It also includes the current year Budget and YTD Actual. This report summarizes the transactions and lists all cost center totals for each natural account.

- **Forecast Report by Cost Center by Month.** This includes the actual expense for the months designated and budget data for the remaining months. It also includes any budget adjustments entered by the budget preparers.

- **FTE Report by Cost Center by Department by Month.** This report summarizes FTEs by Part-Time, Full-Time, and Temporary.

- **There is also a report summary based on user ID.** The user would request the Cost Center Analysis Report, the Budget Detail by Month Report, and the Forecast Report from his/her workstation through the budget system. When these reports are requested, in addition to the individual reports, a summary report is provided for all cost centers selected by the user.

Data Interface with External Systems

1. Can the system import/export non-financial data?

2. Can pieces of the budget be imported/exported?

3. Does the system have the ability to import actual data to replace budget data on a monthly basis to produce forecast reporting?

4. Input from general ledgers will be in dollars. Can system convert to thousands with smart rounding?

5. Does the system have the ability to give users a "spreadsheet" draft or upload/download to and from spreadsheets?

6. Can system handle automated uploads from multi-source general ledger systems?

7. XYZ Corporation requires data input/export capability in interfacing with the various software applications listed below. What sort of interface capability would be used to pass data between your system and XYZ's applications? Please address each separately.

   a) <General ledger software>—version x.x for AS400; download actuals to budget system. Upload budget to the general ledger.

   b) <HR/Payroll software>—version x.x for AS400; download actuals to the budget system to perform projections.

   c) <Sales order entry software>—NT Server, Sybase database; download actuals to the budget system.

   d) <Project software>—NT Server, SQL database; download aggregate actuals to the budget system.

   e) <Spreadsheet software>—version x.x on workstations; both upload and download capability.

Other Information

1. Can the system house all monthly, quarterly, and budget data?

2. What three features distinguish the software product from its competitors? Who are the software's competitors?

3. What are the major enhancements in upcoming releases of the new software?

4. What is the upgrade plan (within the next 12–24 months, indicating significant features of these upgrades)?

BUDGET SYSTEM TECHNICAL REQUIREMENTS

Technical Architecture (User interface, middleware, RDBMS)

1. Does the system use server-based technology?

2. Is the system scalable to support entities of varying sizes at reasonable cost?

3. Is the system providing a low hardware intensive solution for the smaller entities?

4. Does the system provide a distributed solution for the entities that are not on the WAN/intranet?

5. Does the system ensure proper data replication between the local systems and the central system?

6. Key attributes of the architecture must include the following. Portability across multiple computer platforms; the platform must contain no device-dependent code; ANSI standard tools and languages should be used and proprietary extensions avoided.

   - The Windows 2000 interface to the budget system database management system (DBMS) must be developed in commercially available application development tools such as Microsoft Visual Basic.

   - All connections to system must be via industry-standard telecommunications protocol such as TCP/IP, and preferably Windows NT Server compliant.

   - The System shall be supported by a commercially available ANSI-, SQL-, and ODBC-compliant Database Management System (DBMS), preferably Microsoft SQL Server.

   - The system must have an open, standards-based set of application program interfaces (APIs).

7. It is highly desirable that the application is "Cluster Aware," that is, that the application supports Microsoft clustering technology.

8. The system must strictly adhere to open systems standards such as COM, DDE, ODBC.

9. It must have Microsoft Office integration.

10. It must have integration of industry standard Crystal report writer.

11. Does the system have Intranet/Internet-enabled application (which modules/functionality)?

12. Extensive System Technical Documentation must be provided.

13. Detail the system's change control/version management process.

14. Please provide the optimal hardware configuration to support our needs.

15. How are software modifications handled with regard to upgrades to future versions?

16. Is the source code available?

17. Is there international support?

18. Can your system be set up to provide shared and simultaneous user access with up to <n> user workstations?

VENDOR INFORMATION

Vendor History and Organization

Briefly describe your company, its history, and its mission as it relates to the product under evaluation.

- How is your company organized?

  Public/Private (if public, traded under what name and symbol?)

  Parent and subsidiary relationships

  Functionally (Sales, Marketing, Customer Service, etc.)

- Detail by function how many people support the product under review, (Technical Support Level 1, Level 2, Level 3, Development, R&D, etc.)

- Do you have résumés of key support personnel available?

- Years in operation:

- Head office location:

- Number of offices worldwide:

- Number of staff:

- Total number of clients:

- Number of installations Worldwide by Continent:

  Europe:

US:

Asia:

Africa:

Australia:

- Implementations in <xyz> Industry:
- Total number on latest version:
- Total number of clients in any version:
- Date of original release:
- Date of latest release:
- Number of complete installations in last 18 months:
- Number of product upgrades in last 18 months:
- Number of planned installations in next 18 months:
- Company Product and Services Focus:

Financial Status

- Please provide financial statements for the last three years.
- What is your financial rating?
- What is your pure dollar investment into R&D on the product under evaluation?

Costs/Fee Structures

Detail all costs associated with implementing the product in question (excluding hardware):

- Software licensing
- Training
- Implementation support
- End-user support
- Source Code
- Relational Database Management System/Operating System (RDBMS/OS)
- Other

TRAINING PROCESS

- Do you provide training using internal resources?
- Do you conduct training at customer sites?
- Do you conduct training at various locations worldwide (i.e., have multiple sites outside North America)?
- What is the availability of self-guided training (e.g., CD-ROM or Internet-based training)?
- What other options are available to train end-users and budget administrators?
- What is the average time investment to adequately train:

- End-Users?

- Super-Users?

- Budget system administrators?

- Technical support staff?

DOCUMENTATION

What documentation is provided with the package, i.e., on-line hard copy, CD-ROM, Internet enabled?

END-USER SUPPORT

- Do you provide on-site support?
- Do you provide hot-line support 24 hours a day, 7 days a week?
- Do you provide international support (i.e., have support center(s) outside of North America)?
- Do you provide an 800 number for customer support?
- What are your hours of operation in Eastern Standard Time (EST)?
- What is your support policy?
- What is your response time standard for telephone assistance?
- How many prior releases do you officially continue to support?
- What process do you employ for urgent software bugs?
- What process do you employ for urgent requests?

- How do you incorporate the Internet into your support process?
- How are Frequently Asked Questions (FAQs) maintained for end-users to browse?
- What are the credentials of your implementation and support staff, i.e., what experience (business/technical), education, and other credentials do they possess?
- What other services do you provide (user group conferences, facilitated chat rooms, newsletters, etc.)

PRODUCT ENHANCEMENTS

- How often do you issue software releases?
- When was the latest version of your product released?
- What is the average cost associated with migrating to a new release?
- How do clients provide input to your R&D process to help determine the evolution of the product?

SITE VISIT

Are you open to a site visit by a team from XYZ including Finance, Internal Audit, and Information Technology to review your various business processes?

VENDOR EXPERIENCE

- Please provide a sample listing by industry of companies that are currently using your product.

Industry	Company
ABC	XYZ

- Please provide three customer references who have more than <n> budget users *live* on your product.

Company	Contact	Phone
XYZ	John Doe	123-456-7890

- How long was each implementation?
- How much support (in hours) did your company provide in these implementations?

- What percentage of these hours were billable versus the percentage included with the purchase of your product?
- Please provide references from other <industry> companies that are using the product we are considering.

CONSULTANT QUALIFICATIONS AND PROJECT ORGANIZATION

1. Organization of project team:
2. Qualifications of each consultant on project team:
3. List some of the companies for which you have done implementation for over the last five years:
4. Methodology (used for information gathering, installation, modifications, testing, etc.):

STANDARD PC CONFIGURATIONS, XYZ CORPORATION

For new purchases

Pentium II, 400Mhz

64mb RAM

12gb Hard Drive

14/32X CD-ROM Drive

STB 4mb Video

Windows 2000

MS Office 2000

3Com 10/100 TX Network Card

Typically installed at present

Pentium 166

32mb RAM

2gb Hard Drive

Windows 98

MS Office 97

Token Ring Network Card

APPENDIX C

SOFTWARE CANDIDATE EVALUATION AND RATING SHEET

COMPANY NAME: _____

EVALUATOR NAME: _____ DATE: _____

COMPLIED WITH INSTRUCTIONS? ___ YES ___ NO (explain on reverse)   MAXIMUM   TOTAL
SELECT FOR INTERVIEW?   ___ YES ___ NO   POINTS: SCORE:

Company qualifications. Related work last three years, pertinence of experience, related work with our industry, financial stability, and capability of company—comments:

_____
                                                              10 points
_____

Consulting qualifications. Experience, organization of team, expertise and breadth of experience, availability during <date> and <date>, location of nearest office—comments:

_____
                                                              10 points
_____

Project approach. Thorough, detailed, well-organized proposal; adequate implementation schedule; effective acceptance testing plan; understanding of scope of work and our company's needs; approach to training; quality and quantity of documentation—comments:

_____
                                                              10 points
_____

Quality of product. System architecture, flexibility of product, expected performance level, and response time estimates—comments:

_____
                                                              12 points
_____

Features. Response to key requirements, additional features offered, custom design flexibility, printing and other publishing features, Web readiness, system security elements—comments:

_____
                                                              12 points
_____

Convenience of use. Data input screens, on-screen help and warning messages, "user-friendly" features—comments:

_____
                                                              12 points
_____

Fit with current hardware and software. Cost of additional hardware, need for modifications, network interface, networking features—comments:

_____
                                                              12 points
_____

Maintenance and technical support. Types of support, available hours, problem resolution—comments:
_____
                                                               7 points
_____

Additional benefits. Other extraordinary or unique qualifications—comments:
_____
                                                               5 points
_____

Reasonableness of fees. Payment schedule, agreement terms—comments:
_____
                                                              10 points
_____

TOTAL SCORE: _____

APPENDIX D

SAMPLE LICENSE AGREEMENT

LICENSE AGREEMENT FOR ABC BUDGETING SOFTWARE

The License Agreement and Commercial Terms and Conditions herein cover the licensing of the ABC Budgeting Software (herein described as "BS"), associated technical support, and any optional classroom training that the Licensee receives from the Licensor (herein referred to as ABC, Inc.). The Licensee, also referred to as Purchaser in this document, is XYZ Corporation of <City>, <State>.

Licensee:

    a. is granted a non-exclusive license to use BS only as set forth in this License.

    b. may not rent or lease the software but may transfer the software and accompanying materials providing the recipient agrees to the terms of this agreement, and the recipient re-registers the software with ABC, Inc.

    c. acknowledges that BS, which includes, without limitation, any form of BS software, user manuals thereto, copies, modifications, enhancements, revisions, or updates thereof, and magnetic media, as defined herein ("BS") and underlying ideas, algorithms, concepts, procedures, processes, principles, and methods of operation, is confidential and contains trade secrets, and Licensee shall use its best efforts to maintain confidentiality. Licensee agrees that this obligation shall survive termination of this License.

    d. ABC, Inc. grants Licensee the unlimited right to use the software at the number of sites set forth in this contract. Licensee may access the software from a hard disk, over a network, or by any other method Licensee chooses.

    e. may not decompile BS from object code to source code or cross-compile or otherwise adapt or modify BS, and may not reverse-engineer BS in any manner.

    f. may not use, copy, modify, or transfer BS or user manuals or any copies except as expressly provided in this license.

Copyright

Licensee acknowledges that all intellectual property rights in BS are owned by ABC, Inc. Without limiting the generality of the preceding, BS and user manuals are copyrighted and may not be copied except as specifically allowed by this License for back-up purposes and to load BS into the computer as part of executing BS. All other copies of BS and related user manuals are in violation of this License. The copyright protection claim also includes all forms and matters of copyrightable material and information now allowed by statutory or common law or hereinafter granted, including, without limitation, material generated from the software programs which are displayed on the screen, such as icons, screen displays, etc. ABC, Inc. indemnifies and holds the Licensee harmless from all claims, losses, damages, etc. arising out of copyright infringement claims by third parties.

Restriction on Use and Disclosure

ABC, Inc. is supplying the Licensee, directly or indirectly, software to be used by the Licensee for financial consolidation and reporting. The Licensee agrees not to duplicate such materials, except as permitted in this License; provided that such restrictions shall not apply with respect to any portion of such materials: (i) which corresponds in substance to that developed by the Licensee and in the Licensee's possession prior to the Licensee's receipt of same from ABC, Inc., (ii) which at the time of disclosure thereof by ABC, Inc. to the Licensee is, or thereafter becomes through no act or failure to act on the Licensee's part, part of the public domain by publication or otherwise, or (iii) which corresponds in substance to that furnished to the Licensee by others as a matter of right without restriction on disclosure; and provided further that the occurrence of (i), (ii), or (iii) above shall not be construed as granting any rights, either express or implied, under ABC, Inc.'s copyrights which relate to the materials furnished to the Licensee. ABC, Inc. materials provided under this Agreement shall not be deemed to be within the foregoing exceptions merely because such materials are embraced by more general materials in the public domain or in the Licensee's possession. In addition, any combination of features shall not be deemed to be within the foregoing exceptions merely because individual features are in the public domain or in the Licensee's possession, but only if the combination itself and its principle of use are in the public domain or in the Licensee's possession. It is expressly understood and agreed that the Licensee shall not disclose any commercial/business information that ABC, Inc. may furnish to the Licensee in writing or otherwise. ABC, Inc. makes no warranties, representations, or guarantees with respect to information supplied hereunder, the use thereof, or the results obtained therefrom.

Disclaimer and Limitation of Liability

ABC, Inc. does not warrant that BS will meet your requirements or that the operation of BS will be uninterrupted or error free. ABC, Inc. shall not be liable to the Licensee or to any third party for any direct, indirect, incidental, special, or consequential damages (including business interruption, loss of anticipated profits, loss of good will, or other economic or commercial loss), or for personal injury (including death) resulting from any cause whatsoever arising out of the Licensee's use of or reliance on such deliverables and services, and regardless of the form of action, whether in contract or tort, including breach of any warranty, even if ABC, Inc. has been advised of the possibility of such damages. BS is licensed in perpetuity "as is" and without any warranty of merchantability or fitness for a particular purpose. Furthermore, neither ABC, Inc., nor any of its employees, subcontractors, consultants, or other assigns, make any warranty, expressed or implied; or assume any liability or responsibility for any use, or the results of such use, of any information, product, process, or other service provided with this software.

Ownership

ABC, Inc. is, and shall remain, the sole and exclusive owner of the magnetic media, BS, any copies of BS, and the user manuals. ABC, Inc. has all proprietary rights in BS and user manuals, including but not limited to all processes, ideas, and data supplied by ABC, Inc. to Licensee. Any back-up copies made by Licensee shall be the sole and exclusive property of ABC, Inc.

Hiring of Employees

While this Agreement is in force, and for a period of six months after the termination of this Agreement for any reason, neither party will employ or offer employment to any person employed by or acting on behalf of the other party, without the prior written permission of the other party.

Termination

Immediate Termination:

Either party may terminate this Agreement forthwith if the other party:

a) assigns its rights or obligations under the Agreement otherwise than stated in this Agreement;

b) enters into a composition with its creditors; is declared bankrupt; goes into liquidation; or a receiver, or a receiver and manager, or statutory receiver is appointed in respect of it.

Termination by Either Party on Notice:

If one party defaults in the performance of any of its obligations under this Agreement and: the default is capable of being remedied, and, within ten (10) working days of notice by the non-defaulting party specifying the default, is not remedied; or the default is not capable of being remedied, the non-defaulting party may immediately terminate, or temporarily suspend the operation of this Agreement, at its sole discretion.

Termination by the Purchaser:

In addition to any other remedy, the Purchaser may terminate this Agreement upon written notice if the services do not meet the agreed acceptance criteria in this Agreement. If the Purchaser gives notice to the ABC, Inc. to terminate this Agreement, the Purchaser may, in addition to terminating this Agreement and any other specific rights:

a) recover any sums paid to ABC, Inc. for consulting services which have not been performed;

b) request, ABC, Inc., at its own expense, to return all property belonging to the Purchaser;

c) pursue any additional or alternative remedies provided by law.

Waiver

No delay, neglect, or forbearance by either party in enforcing against the other any provision of this Agreement will be a waiver, or in any way prejudice any right, of that party.

Notices

Any notice given pursuant to this Agreement will be sufficiently given if it is in writing and delivered, or sent by prepaid post or facsimile to the other party at the address as shown:
The Purchaser's contact name and address:
See Attachment 1 of this document.
ABC, Inc.'s contact name and address:
Johnny B. Good, Fountain Drive, Suite 200, Beverly Hills, CA 90210

Entire Agreement

This License Agreement constitutes the entire understanding between ABC, Inc. and the Licensee and supersedes any previous communications, representations, or agreements by either party, whether oral or written. The terms and conditions contained herein take precedence over the Licensee's additional or different terms and conditions that may be contained in any acknowledgment form, manifest, or other document forwarded by the Licensee to ABC, Inc. to which notice of objection is hereby given. No change of any of the terms or conditions herein shall be valid or binding on either party unless in writing and signed by an authorized representative of each party. If any of the provisions hereof are invalid under any applicable statute or rule of law, such provisions are, to that extent, deemed omitted, but these terms and conditions shall remain otherwise in effect. There are no understandings, agreements, representations, or warranties, expressed or implied, that are not specified herein respecting the subject matter hereof. The agents, employees, distributors, and dealers of ABC, Inc. are not authorized to modify this Agreement nor to make statements, representations, or terms binding on ABC, Inc. Accordingly, any statements, representations, or terms not made or given directly and expressly by ABC, Inc., whether oral or written, are not binding on ABC, Inc.

General

If any of the provisions or portions thereof of this License are invalid or unenforceable under any applicable statute or rule or law, they are to that extent to be deemed omitted. It is agreed that the laws of the State of California shall govern without reference to the place of execution or performance, and the parties agree to submit to the courts of the State of California. Licensee acknowledges that Licensee has read this license, understands it, and agrees to be bound by its terms and conditions. Licensee also agrees that its use of BS acknowledges that Licensee agrees to the terms and conditions of this License. Licensee further agrees that the License is a complete and exclusive statement of the agreement between Licensee and XYZ, Inc., and that it supersedes all proposals or prior agreements, oral or written, and any and all other communications relating to the subject matter of this license.

APPENDIX E

SAMPLE SUPPORT PLAN/AGREEMENT

ECONOMY SUPPORT PLAN

(for customers who need two hours or less support per month)

- One Registered contact on your staff
- Prioritized in-coming call
- Two Hours included per month* (balance cannot be accumulated)
- Same-day response guaranteed
- $175 per Month

NORMAL SUPPORT PLAN

- Two Registered contacts on your staff
- Prioritized in-coming call
- Three Hours guaranteed response time
- Limited to five hours per month*
- $400 per Month

PREMIER SUPPORT PLAN

- Five Registered contacts on your staff
- Two Assigned Support Engineers assigned to your account
- Unlimited use
- Two Hours guaranteed response time
- Access to the Online Consultant (www)
- A Consultant on site by the next day
- $1,500 per Month

DAY BY DAY - ACCOUNT ATTENTION PLAN

On five working days notification, a Senior Support Engineer is assigned to your account for special attention to you during days of heavy workloads. For example, you can reserve three days when receiving all monthly reporting files from subsidiaries at the end of your budgeting process.

Immediate Response Time!

1 day	$500
3 days	$1,250
1 week	$2,000

CASE-BY-CASE SUPPORT PLAN

On a per call/case basis, the charge will be $50 for the first 15 minutes and $35 for each additional 15-minute interval.

24-BY-7

Special Support Plan: "Premier 24/7" may be purchased for varying time periods.

Price: On request.

All services may be purchased for a limited period of time, based on your workloads, monthly reporting, and so forth.

If time limit is exceeded, calls will be invoiced in 15-minute intervals, at an hourly rate of $140.

APPENDIX F

SAMPLE CONSULTING AGREEMENT

CLIENT NAME _____

CLIENT ADDRESS _____

CITY, STATE, ZIP CODE_____

This Consulting AGREEMENT (the "Agreement") is entered into by and between CLIENT and CONSULTANT. The effective date of this agreement is the same date as the software agreement contract is signed.

Whereas the Client wishes to obtain the consulting services of Consultant to assist Client in connection with the design and implementation of budget model and Consultant has negotiated the terms of such an Agreement with Client and has agreed to the terms as set forth hereafter.

Now therefore, the parties hereby agree as follows:

1. *Term of Agreement:*

    The Client hereby hires Consultant and Consultant accepts such contract work for a term for as long as professional services are requested by Client, terminating when the budget model project is completed, according to project plan, unless sooner terminated as hereinafter provided.

2. *Survival of Agreement:*

    This Agreement shall not be terminated by a restructuring of the company or of the Consultant. If either of the parties restructures but remain in business, the contract shall survive.

3. *Legal Representation:*

    Each party acknowledges that they were advised that they were entitled to separate counsel and they have either employed such counsel or voluntarily waived their right to consult with counsel.

4. *Notices:*

    All notices and other communications provided for or permitted hereunder shall be in writing and shall be made by hand delivery, first class mail, telex or telecopier, addressed as follows:

    «address here»

    All such notices and communications shall be deemed to have been duly given when delivered by hand, if personally delivered; three (3) business days after deposit in any United States Post Office in the continental United States, postage prepaid, if mailed; when answered back, if telexed; and when receipt is acknowledged, if telecopied.

5. *Attorney's Fees:*

In the event that a dispute arises with respect to this Agreement, the party prevailing in such dispute shall be entitled to recover all expenses, including, without limitation, reasonable attorneys' fees and expenses, incurred in ascertaining such party's rights or in preparing to enforce, or in enforcing, such party's rights under this Agreement, whether or not it was necessary for such party to institute suit.

6. *Complete Agreement of the Parties:*

This is the complete Agreement of the parties and it supersedes any agreement that has been made prior to this Agreement.

7. *Assignment:*

This Agreement is of a personal nature and may not be assigned.

8. *Binding:*

This Agreement shall be binding both of the parties hereto.

9. *Number and Gender:*

Whenever the singular number is used in this Agreement and when required by the context, the same shall include the plural. The masculine gender shall include the feminine and neuter genders, and the word "person" shall include a corporation, firm, partnership, or other form of association.

10. *Governing Law:*

The parties hereby expressly acknowledge and agree that this Agreement is entered into in the State of <state> and, to the extent permitted by law, this Agreement shall be construed, and enforced in accordance with the laws of the State of <state>.

11. *Failure to Object Is Not a Waiver:*

The failure of a party to object to, or to take affirmative action with respect to, any conduct of the other which is in violation of the terms of this Agreement shall not be construed as a waiver of the violation or breach or of any future violation, breach, or wrongful conduct until 180 days since the wrongful act or omission to act has passed.

12. *Severability:*

If any term of this Agreement is held by a court of competent jurisdiction to be invalid, void, or unenforceable, the remainder of the provisions of this Agreement shall remain in full force and effect and shall in no way be affected, impaired, or invalidated.

13. *Further Assistance:*

From time to time each party shall execute and deliver such further instruments and shall take such other action as any other party may reasonably request in order to discharge and perform their obligations and agreements hereunder and to give effect to the intentions expressed in this Agreement.

14. *Incorporation by Reference:*

All exhibits referred to in this Agreement are incorporated herein in their entirety by such reference.

15. *Cross References:*

All cross-references in this Agreement, unless specifically directed to another agreement or document, refer to provisions in this Agreement, and shall not be deemed to be references to any overall transaction or to any other agreements or documents.

16. *Miscellaneous Provisions:*

The various headings and numbers herein and the grouping of provisions of this Agreement into separate divisions are for the purpose of convenience only and shall not be considered a part hereof. The language in all parts of this Agreement shall in all cases be construed in accordance to its fair meaning as if prepared by all parties to the Agreement and not strictly for or against any of the parties.

17. *Work to Be Performed:*

As requested by you, Consultant will develop a budget model using Vendor software. This budget model will be based upon the existing spreadsheet model system used by Client (Attachment X) and/or additional design specifications agreed upon by Client and Consultant. The budget model created by Consultant must be capable of meeting the specifications agreed upon by Client and Consultant, listed in Attachment X.

18. *Performance of Duties:*

Consultant agrees to perform at all times faithfully, industriously, and to the best of their ability, experience, and talents all of the duties that may reasonably be assigned to them hereunder, and shall devote such time to the performance of such duties as may be necessary.

19. *Fees and Expenses:*

The fee for the services provided by Consultant to Client will be $X/hour (not to exceed $X for all services provided). This service cost does not include any time for work performed that is not identified in Attachment X. Additionally, this cost does not include travel, lodging, meals, or incidentals. These will be billed at actual and/or per diem rates.

20. *Independent Contractor:*

In performing services and duties hereunder, Consultant and any person acting on Consultant's behalf shall do so as independent contractors and are not, and are not to be deemed, employees or agents of Client or any other person acting on behalf of Client. Consultant shall be responsible for meeting any legal requirements imposed on Consultant or any person acting on his behalf as a result of this Agreement, including but not limited to the filing of income tax returns and the payment of taxes; and Consultant agrees to indemnify Client for the failure to do so, if Client is required to make any such payment otherwise due by Consultant or any such person acting on Consultant's behalf.

21. *Remedy for Breach:*

Consultant acknowledges that the services to be rendered by Consultant hereunder are of a special, unique, and extraordinary character which gives this Agreement a peculiar value to Client, the loss of which cannot be reasonably or adequately compensated in damages in an action at law, and that a breach by Consultant of this Agreement shall cause Client irreparable injury. Therefore, Consultant expressly acknowledges that this Agreement may be enforced against him by injunction and other equitable remedies, without bond. Such relief shall not be exclusive, but shall be in addition to any other rights or remedies Client may have for such breach.

22. *Causes for Termination:*

This Agreement shall terminate immediately upon the occurrence of any one of the following events:

a. The expiration of the term hereof;

b. The written agreement of the parties;

c. The occurrence of circumstances that make it impossible for the business of Client to be continued;

d. The occurrence of circumstances that make it impossible for the business of Consultant to be continued;

e. Consultant's breach of his duties hereunder, unless waived by Client or incurred by Consultant within 30 days after Client's having given written notice thereof to Consultant.

23. *Compensation upon Termination*

Unless otherwise mutually agreed in writing by the parties, the termination of this Agreement due to any cause other than that specified in Paragraph 22.d shall not relieve Client of its obligation to make any payment of money or any delivery of shares or securities which would have been required, or could have been required by Consultant, pursuant to Paragraph 19, if this Agreement had not been so terminated.

IN WITNESS WHEREOF, the parties have executed this Agreement on the date above.

Signature:

_____   _____

_____   _____

(Printed Name)	**(Printed Name)**
For Client	For Consultant

APPENDIX G

SAMPLE IMPLEMENTATION PROJECT PLAN

ID	Task Name	Duration
1	Budget Model Implementation	49 days
2		
3	**Team Selection**	5 days
4	Select personnel from client organization	5 days
5	Interview and select consultants	5 days
6		
7	**Planning**	8 days
8	Initial Planning	2 days
9	Agree upon project start and end dates	1 day
10	Review maximum hours and/or dollars set for project	1 day
11	Agree upon project status updates, team meetings, etc.	1 day
12	Define roles of client and consultant	1 day
13	Establish who will be responsible for what	1 day
14	Determine budget model approval process	1 day
15	Establish contact personnel for client and consultants	1 day
16		
17	Outline scope and complexity of model	6 days
18	Software and systems	1 day
19	Finalize list of all software and modules to be installed	1 day
20	Distribute list of software to IT department	1 day
21	Map integration of systems and installed software	1 day
22	Budgeting and reporting	5 days
23	Determine level of detail required for budgeting and reporting	1 day
24	Discuss budgeting dimensions (accounts, depts., etc.)	1 day
25	Discuss reporting dimensions (accounts, depts., etc.)	1 day
26	Budget model design discussion	3 days
27	Discuss account segment mapping	3 days
28	Discuss budget model functionality	3 days
29	Discuss design of budget reports	3 days
30	Actual/budget data integration	1 day
31	Determine where budget and G/L data will reside	1 day
32	Determine how amounts will transfer between systems	1 day
33	Users	1 day
34	Determine users and user security	1 day
35	Discuss amount of training required for users	1 day
36		
37	Sign-off on project specifications and deliverables	0 days
38		
39	**Installation**	8 days
40	Confirm that hardware is ready	0 days
41	Confirm that software is available	0 days
42	Confirm that appropriate service packs are available	0 days
43	Confirm system integration of third-party products	0 days
44	Verify that workstations have required software and drivers	0 days

ID	Task Name	Duration
45	Determine optimal hardware configuration	0 days
46	Verify that database and server startup parameters are correct	0 days
47	Install software and database on server	1 day
48	Install software on workstations	1 day
49	Verify that all users can logon and access system	1 day
50		
51	Training	34 days
52	Finalize list of people to be trained	0 days
53	Schedule training classes	0 days
54	Reserve training facilities	0 days
55	Obtain list of resources (e.g., projector, PCs, etc.) for training	0 days
56		
57	Super-user training	2 days
58	Train users to be administrators of system	2 days
59	Discuss mapping of account segments	2 days
60	Discuss roll-up structures	2 days
61	Review budget model design	2 days
62	Plan end-user training, testing groups	0 days
63		
64	End-user training	1 day
65	Review access to system, how to change passwords, etc.	1 day
66	Provide time-line of budget cycle	1 day
67	Explain budget model and design	1 day
68	Review differences between new and former budget models	1 day
69	Teach users how to input, store, and modify information	1 day
70	Identify contact person during budget cycle	1 day
71		
72	Model Design	43 days
73	Reserve proper work facilities available for consultant	0 days
74		
75	Preliminary model design	12 days
76	Finalize account segment mapping	2 days
77	Finalize roll-up structure	2 days
78	Finalize reporting and budgeting dimensions	2 days
79	Finalize input forms to be used	2 days
80	Finalize formatting (e.g., precision, fonts, colors, etc.)	2 days
81	Import necessary tables from G/L system	1 day
82	Import sample data to test budget forms and reports	1 day
83	Design input forms	3 days
84	Review input forms and obtain feedback	1 day
85	Design budget reports	2 days
86	Review budget reports and obtain feedback	1 day
87	Review preliminary model and obtain feedback	1 day
88	Incorporate feedback into model	1 day

ID	Task Name	Duration
89	Finalize all preliminary specifications	0 days
90		
91	**Final model design**	**19 days**
92	Verify that all preliminary feedback has been incorporated	0 days
93	Import data that will be used in production environment	1 day
94	Audit import data for accuracy	1 day
95	Design final input forms	5 days
96	Design final reports	2 days
97	**Test model for desired functionality**	**2 days**
98	Verify that model functions as intended	2 days
99	Verify that amounts are calculated correctly	2 days
100	Check for standard formatting	2 days
101	Verify that agreed-upon model specifications have been met	0 days
102	Approve model for preliminary testing	0 days
103		
104	**Discuss feedback from preliminary testing**	**3 days**
105	Determine changes needed	3 days
106	Estimate time required to make needed changes	3 days
107	Make and test modifications and changes	3 days
108	Approve model for final testing	0 days
109		
110	**Discuss feedback from final testing**	**1 day**
111	Assess severity of comments from final testing	1 day
112	Incorporate feedback from final testing	1 day
113	Determine if changes need to be made to the model	1 day
114	If changes are made, revise timeline and schedule re-testing	1 day
115	Approve final model	0 days
116		
117	Verify that all required approvals have been obtained	0 days
118	Train end-users	0 days
119	Model ready for production use	0 days
120		
121	**Testing**	**29 days**
122	Select reference groups	0 days
123	Establish testing duration	0 days
124	Select testing data	0 days
125		
126	**Preliminary testing**	**3 days**
127	Test user access and security	3 days
128	Test budget forms for proper functionality	3 days
129	Test that users can modify and edit amounts	3 days
130	Test summary accounts for proper consolidation	3 days
131	Test roll-up structure for proper consolidation	3 days
132	Test budget reports	3 days

Milestones (Week 4): ◆ W04/3, ◆ W04/3

ID	Task Name	Duration
1	**Budget Model Implementation**	**49 days**
2		
3	**Team Selection**	**5 days**
4	Select personnel from client organization	5 days
5	Interview and select consultants	5 days
6		
7	**Planning**	**8 days**
8	**Initial Planning**	**2 days**
9	Agree upon project start and end dates	1 day
10	Review maximum hours and/or dollars set for project	1 day
11	Agree upon project status updates, team meetings, etc.	1 day
12	**Define roles of client and consultant**	**1 day**
13	Establish who will be responsible for what	1 day
14	Determine budget model approval process	1 day
15	Establish contact personnel for client and consultants	1 day
16		
17	**Outline scope and complexity of model**	**6 days**
18	**Software and systems**	**1 day**
19	Finalize list of all software and modules to be installed	1 day
20	Distribute list of software to IT department	1 day
21	Map integration of systems and installed software	1 day
22	**Budgeting and reporting**	**5 days**
23	Determine level of detail required for budgeting and reporting	1 day
24	Discuss budgeting dimensions (accounts, depts., etc.)	1 day
25	Discuss reporting dimensions (accounts, depts., etc.)	1 day
26	**Budget model design discussion**	**3 days**
27	Discuss account segment mapping	3 days
28	Discuss budget model functionality	3 days
29	Discuss design of budget reports	3 days
30	**Actual/budget data integration**	**1 day**
31	Determine where budget and G/L data will reside	1 day
32	Determine how amounts will transfer between systems	1 day
33	**Users**	**1 day**
34	Determine users and user security	1 day
35	Discuss amount of training required for users	1 day
36		
37	Sign-off on project specifications and deliverables	0 days
38		
39	**Installation**	**8 days**
40	Confirm that hardware is ready	0 days
41	Confirm that software is available	0 days
42	Confirm that appropriate service packs are available	0 days
43	Confirm system integration of third-party products	0 days
44	Verify that workstations have required software and drivers	0 days

Week 6 / Week 7 / Week 8 / Week 9 / Week 10 (S M T W T F S)

Appendix G - Sample Implementation Project Plan

ID	Task Name	Duration
45	Determine optimal hardware configuration	0 days
46	Verify that database and server startup parameters are correct	0 days
47	Install software and database on server	1 day
48	Install software on workstations	1 day
49	Verify that all users can logon and access system	1 day
50		
51	Training	34 days
52	Finalize list of people to be trained	0 days
53	Schedule training classes	0 days
54	Reserve training facilities	0 days
55	Obtain list of resources (e.g., projector, PCs, etc.) for training	0 days
56		
57	Super-user training	2 days
58	Train users to be administrators of system	2 days
59	Discuss mapping of account segments	2 days
60	Discuss roll-up structures	2 days
61	Review budget model design	2 days
62	Plan end-user training, testing groups	0 days
63		
64	End-user training	1 day
65	Review access to system, how to change passwords, etc.	1 day
66	Provide time-line of budget cycle	1 day
67	Explain budget model and design	1 day
68	Review differences between new and former budget models	1 day
69	Teach users how to input, store, and modify information	1 day
70	Identify contact person during budget cycle	1 day
71		
72	Model Design	43 days
73	Reserve proper work facilities available for consultant	0 days
74		
75	Preliminary model design	12 days
76	Finalize account segment mapping	2 days
77	Finalize roll-up structure	2 days
78	Finalize reporting and budgeting dimensions	2 days
79	Finalize input forms to be used	2 days
80	Finalize formatting (e.g., precision, fonts, colors, etc.)	2 days
81	Import necessary tables from G/L system	1 day
82	Import sample data to test budget forms and reports	1 day
83	Design input forms	3 days
84	Review input forms and obtain feedback	1 day
85	Design budget reports	2 days
86	Review budget reports and obtain feedback	1 day
87	Review preliminary model and obtain feedback	1 day
88	Incorporate feedback into model	1 day

Appendix G - Sample Implementation Project Plan

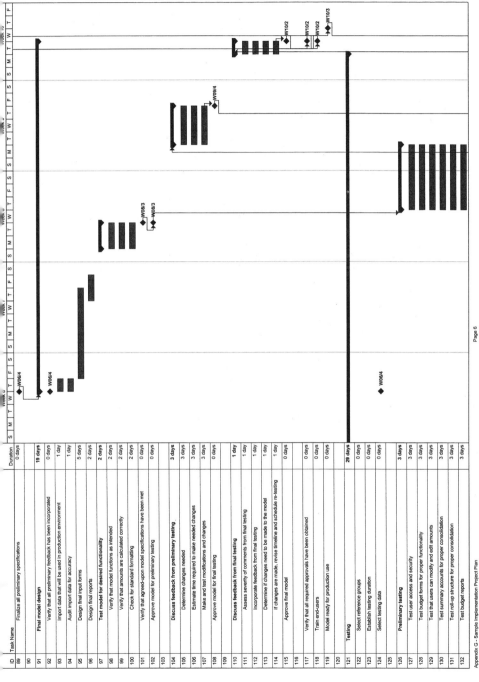

ID	Task Name	Duration
89	Finalize all preliminary specifications	0 days
90		
91	**Final model design**	**19 days**
92	Verify that all preliminary feedback has been incorporated	0 days
93	Import data that will be used in production environment	1 day
94	Audit import data for accuracy	1 day
95	Design final input forms	5 days
96	Design final reports	2 days
97	**Test model for desired functionality**	**2 days**
98	Verify that model functions as intended	2 days
99	Verify that amounts are calculated correctly	2 days
100	Check for standard formatting	2 days
101	Verify that agreed-upon model specifications have been met	0 days
102	Approve model for preliminary testing	0 days
103		
104	**Discuss feedback from preliminary testing**	**3 days**
105	Determine changes needed	3 days
106	Estimate time required to make needed changes	3 days
107	Make and test modifications and changes	3 days
108	Approve model for final testing	0 days
109		
110	**Discuss feedback from final testing**	**1 day**
111	Assess severity of comments from final testing	1 day
112	Incorporate feedback from final testing	1 day
113	Determine if changes need to be made to the model	1 day
114	If changes are made, revise timeline and schedule re-testing	1 day
115	Approve final model	0 days
116		
117	Verify that all required approvals have been obtained	0 days
118	Train end-users	0 days
119	Model ready for production use	0 days
120		
121	**Testing**	**29 days**
122	Select reference groups	0 days
123	Establish testing duration	0 days
124	Select testing data	0 days
125		
126	**Preliminary testing**	**3 days**
127	Test user access and security	3 days
128	Test budget forms for proper functionality	3 days
129	Test that users can modify and edit amounts	3 days
130	Test summary accounts for proper consolidation	3 days
131	Test roll-up structure for proper consolidation	3 days
132	Test budget reports	3 days

Appendix G - Sample Implementation Project Plan

Page 6

Appendix G - Sample Implementation Project Plan

ID	Task Name	Duration
133	Test system performance	3 days
134	Test for user-friendliness	3 days
135	Collect and discuss feedback	3 days
136	Determine revisions to make to model	0 days
137		
138	**Final testing**	**2 days**
139	Test changes and modifications made from preliminary testing	2 days
140	Test that model can be used in production environment	2 days
141	Test system performance	2 days
142	Test user access and security	2 days
143	Test budget forms for proper functionality	2 days
144	Test summary accounts for proper consolidation	2 days
145	Test roll-up structure for proper consolidation	2 days
146	Test that users can modify and edit amounts	2 days
147	Test budget reports	2 days
148	Collect and discuss feedback	2 days
149	Assess whether model can go live	0 days
150		
151	**Going Live**	**1 day**
152	Make sure that all approvals have been obtained	1 day
153	Establish start and end dates for budget entry	1 day
154	Verify that all known problems have been resolved	1 day
155	Verify that all users can access system	1 day
156	Inform users of contact person(s) for problems	1 day
157	Inform IT of date users will begin accessing system	1 day
158	Begin using budget model	0 days

Project: Implementation Plan
Date: Fri 05/19/00

Task

Split

Progress

Milestone

Summary

Rolled-Up Task

Rolled-Up Split

Rolled-Up Milestone ◇

Rolled-Up Progress

External Tasks

Project Summary

Page 8

Appendix G - Sample Implementation Project Plan

APPENDIX H

SOFTWARE AND VENDOR LIST WITH WEB ADDRESSES

Vendor	Product	Address
Adaytum Software	Adaytum Planning	Web: www.adaytum.com 2051 Killebrew Drive, Suite 400 Bloomington, MN 55425-1820 Ph: 612-858-8585 Fax: 612-858-8881
Advance Planning Solutions, Inc.	Advance	Web: www.advancemodels.com 383 Fourth Street, Suite 201 Oakland, CA 94607 Ph: 510-433-1777 Fax: 510-433-1770
Best Software	Best! Imperativ Planning and Analysis	Web: www.bestsoftware.com 11413 Isaac Newton Square Reston, VA 20190 Ph: 800-368-2405 Fax: 800-793-2329
Cognos Corporation	LEX2000	Web: www.lex2000.com 67 South Bedford Street Burlington, MA 01803 Ph: 770-908-9757 Fax: 770-980-1356
Comshare	Comshare BudgetPlus	Web: www.comshare.com 555 Briarwood Circle Ann Arbor, MI 48108 Ph: 734-994-4800 Fax: 734-994-5895
EPS Software	Budget 2000	Web: www.epssoftware.com 2 Robert Speck Parkway Suite 600 Mississauga, Ontario Canada L4Z IH8 Ph: 905-279-8711 Fax: 905-279-2232

Vendor	Product	Address
Helmsman Group, Inc.	Helmsman	Web: www.helmsmangroup.com 666 Helmsman Group, Suite 1236 Plainsboro, NJ 08536 Ph: 609-275-9416 Fax: 609-275-6512
Hyperion Solutions Corporation	Hyperion Pillar	Web: www.hyperion.com 1344 Crossman Avenue Sunnyvale, CA 94089 Ph: 800-286-8000 Fax: 800-882-5596
InAlysys, Inc.	Personal Analyst	Web: www.inalysys.com 2900 Bristol Street, Suite J208 Costa Mesa, CA 92626 Ph: 714-668-2600 Fax: 714-668-2604
KCI Computing, Inc.	Control	Web: www.kcicorp.com 2221 Rosecrans Avenue, Suite 136 El Segundo, CA 90245 Ph: 310-643-0222 Fax: 310-643-6222
Longview Solutions, Inc.	Khalix	Web: www.longview.com 65 Allstate Parkway, Suite 200 Markham, Ontario L3R 9XI Ph: 610-889-9380 Fax: 610-889-2422
MIS AG	MIS Alea	Web: www.mis-ag.com 325 Columbia Turnpike Florham Park, NJ 07932 Ph: 973-765-0405 Fax: 973-765-0305

Vendor	Product	Address
Oracle	Oracle Financial Analyzer	Web: www.oracle.com 500 Oracle Parkway Redwood Shores, CA 94065 Ph: 800-ORACLEI Fax: 650-506-7200
Planet Corporation	Budget Maestro	Web: www.planetcorp.com 233 Cochituate Road Framingham, MA 01701 Ph: 508-820-4812 Fax: 508-820-1219
Powerplan Corp.	Powerplan	Web: www.planningandlogic.com 2130 Main Street, #245 Huntington Beach, CA 92648 Ph: 714-969-5353 Fax: 714-969-0933
Solver, Inc.	Enterprise Reporting	Web: www.solverusa.com 270 N. Canon Dr., #1166 Beverly Hills, CA 90210 Ph: 310-247-2222 Fax: 310-246-5199
SRC Software	SRC Advisor Series	Web: www.srcsoftware.com 2120 SW Jefferson Street Portland, OR 97201 Ph: 800-544-3477 Fax: 503-223-7922
Super Budget, Inc.	Super Budget	Web: www.superbudget.com Boston Fish Pier West I 212 Northern Avenue Boston, MA 02210 Ph: 888-972-6367 Fax: 617-753-7350

Vendor	Product	Address
Timeline, Inc.	Timeline Budgeting	Web: www.timeline.com 3055 112th Avenue NE, Suite 106 Bellevue, WA 98004 Ph: 425-822-3140 Fax: 425-822-1120
Walker Interactive Systems	Walker Horizon Financial Consolidation	Web: www.walker.com 303 Second Street, North 3 San Francisco, CA 94107 Ph: 800-330-9664 Fax: 415-243-1532

GLOSSARY OF BUDGETING TERMS

accounts payable   Amounts owed by a business for purchases received and accepted.

accounts receivable   Amounts owed to a business by customers for goods and services received and accepted.

accrual accounting   An accounting basis in which revenue is recorded when earned and costs and balance sheet changes are recorded when commitments are made. Large, one-time expenses can also be averaged over the year or a portion thereof.

accrued expense   A cost recorded as an expense that represents future actual expenditure.

accumulated depreciation   The total depreciation of a fixed asset from its purchase to the present time.

administrative budget   A formal and comprehensive financial plan through which management may control day-to-day business affairs and activities.

allocated cost   Cost of one type that is assigned or charged to costs of other types.

allotment   Part of an appropriation which may be encumbered or expended during an allotment period, which is usually less than one fiscal year. Bimonthly and quarterly allotment periods are most common.

amortization   Prorating the cost of an asset, liability, or expenditure over a specified period of time.

analysis of variances   Analysis and investigation of causes for variances between standard costs and actual costs. A variance is considered favorable if actual costs are less than standard costs. It is unfavorable if actual costs exceed standard costs.

annual budget   A budget prepared for a calendar or fiscal year.

asset   Anything owned that has monetary value.

backlog   Orders that have been received but not yet delivered. Also called sales backlog or orders backlog.

balance sheet   A financial statement showing the assets, liabilities, and equity of a business as of a certain date.

balanced budget   A budget in which total expenditures equal total revenue. An entity has a budget surplus if expenditures are less than tax revenues. It has a budget deficit if expenditures are greater than tax revenues.

book value   The current accounting worth of a business or a balance sheet item. For a fixed asset, it equals cost minus accumulated depreciation. For a business, it is the same as equity, net worth, or shareholders' equity.

break-even analysis   Analysis that determines the break-even sales, which is the level of sales where total costs equal total revenues.

break-even chart   The chart where sales revenue, variable costs, and fixed costs are plotted on the vertical axis while volume, x, is plotted on the horizontal axis. The break-even point is the point where the total sales revenue line intersects the total cost line.

budget   A quantitative plan of activities and programs expressed in terms of the assets, equities, revenues, and expenses which will be involved in carrying out the plans, or in other quantitative terms such as units of product or service. The budget expresses the organizational goals in terms of specific financial and operating objectives.

budget control   Budgetary actions carried out according to a budget plan. Through the use of a budget as a standard, an organization ensures that managers are implementing its plans and objectives and their activities are appraised by comparing their actual performance against budgeted performance. Budgets are used as a basis for rewarding or punishing them, or perhaps for modifying future budgets and plans.

budget variance   1. Any difference between a budgeted figure and an actual figure; 2. Flexible budget variance. This is the difference between actual factory overhead costs and standard (flexible budget) costs, multiplied by the standard units of activity allowed for actual production. The budget variance is used in the two-way analysis of factory overhead. It includes the fixed and variable spending variances and the variable overhead efficiency variance, which are used in the three-way analysis.

budget fund   Annual budgets of estimated revenues and expenditures prepared for most governmental funds. The approved budgets of such funds are recorded in budgetary accounts in the accounting system to provide control over revenues and expenditures.

budgeting models   Mathematical models that generate a profit-planning budget. The models help planners and budget analysts answer a variety of what-if questions. The resultant calculations provide a basis for choice among alternatives under conditions of uncertainty.

burden rate   The percentage rate at which a cost burden is added to particular other costs. The most common burden rates are the various overhead rates.

capital   The investment in a business, ordinarily equal to equity plus debt.

capital budget   A budget or plan of proposed acquisitions and replacements of long-term assets and their financing. A capital budget is developed by using a variety of capital budgeting techniques, such as the payback method, the net present value (NPV), or the internal rate of return (IRR) method.

capital budgeting   The process of making long-term planning decisions: (1) Selecting new facilities or expanding existing facilities. Examples include investments in long-term assets such as property, plant and equipment, and resource commitments in the form of new product development, market research, refunding of long-term debt, and introduction of a computer. (2) Replacing existing facilities with new facilities. Examples include replacing a manual bookkeeping system with a computerized system and replacing an inefficient lathe with one that is numerically controlled.

capital expenditure Purchase of buildings, equipment, tools, and the like, that will be accounted for as fixed assets and depreciated over a multiyear period.

capital expenditure budget A budget plan prepared for individual capital expenditure projects. The time span depends upon the project. Capital expenditures to be budgeted include replacement, acquisition, or construction of plants and major equipment.

capital rationing The problem of selecting the mix of acceptable projects that provides the highest overall net present value (NPV), where a company has a limit on the budget for capital spending. The profitability index is used widely in ranking projects competing for limited funds.

cash accounting An accounting basis in which revenue, expense, and balance sheet items are recorded when cash is paid or received.

cash budget A budget for cash planning and control, presenting expected cash inflow and outflow for a designated time period. The cash budget helps management keep cash balances in reasonable relationship to its needs. It aids in avoiding idle cash and possible cash shortages.

cash flow The increase or decrease in the cash of a business over a particular period of time.

cash flow forecasting Forecasts of cash flow, including cash collections from customers, investment income, and cash disbursements.

causal forecasting model A forecasting model which relates the variable to be forecast to a number of other variables that can be observed.

continuous budget An annual budget which continues to the earliest one month or period and adds the most recent one month or period, so that a twelve-month or other periodic forecast is always available.

contribution margin A percentage measure of profitability, equal to revenue minus variable or direct costs, divided by revenue. (The term is sometimes used for only the dollar amount of revenue minus variable or direct costs, although the latter is more often called contribution).

contribution margin analysis Also called Cost-Volume-Profit (CVP) analysis that deals with how profits and costs change with a change in volume. More specifically, it looks at the effects on profits of changes in such factors as variable costs, fixed costs, selling prices, volume, and mix of products sold. By studying the relationships of costs, sales, and net income, management is better able to cope with many planning decisions.

contribution (margin) income statement An income statement that organizes the cost by behavior. It shows the relationship of variable costs and fixed costs, regardless of the functions with which a given cost item is associated.

contribution margin (CM) ratio The contribution margin (CM) as a percentage of sales.

contribution margin (CM) variance The difference between actual contribution margin per unit and the budgeted contribution margin per unit, multiplied by the actual number of units sold. If the actual CM is greater than the budgeted CM per unit, a variance is favorable. Otherwise, it is unfavorable. CM variance = (actual CM per unit − budgeted CM per unit) × actual sales.

control concept A concept that ensures that actions are carried out or implemented according to a plan or goal.

corporate planning model   An integrated business planning model in which marketing and production models are linked to the financial model. Corporate planning models are the basic tools for risk analysis and what-if experiments.

correlation   The degree of relationship between business and economic variables such as cost and volume. Correlation analysis evaluates cause/effect relationships. It looks consistently at how the value of one variable changes when the value of the other is changed. A prediction can be made based on the relationship uncovered. An example is the effect of advertising on sales.

cost allocation   The process of assigning or charging one type of cost to other costs.

cost behavior patterns   The way a cost will react or respond to changes in the level of activity. Costs may be viewed as variable, fixed, or mixed. A mixed cost is one that contains both variable and fixed elements. For planning, control, and decision purposes, mixed costs need to be separated into their variable and fixed components, using such methods as the high-low method and the least-squares method. An application of the variable-fixed breakdown is a break-even and contribution margin analysis.

cost-benefit analysis   An analysis to determine whether the favorable results of an alternative are sufficient to justify the cost of taking that alternative. This analysis is widely used in connection with capital expenditure projects.

cost burden   The amount of cost added to a particular cost as the result of allocating another type of cost to it.

cost control   The steps taken by management to assure that the cost objectives set down in the planning stage are attained and to assure that all segments of the organization function in a manner consistent with its policies. For effective cost control, most organizations use standard cost systems in which the actual costs are compared to standard costs for performance evaluation and the deviations are investigated for remedial actions. Cost control is also concerned with feedback that might change any or all future plans, the production method, or both.

cost effective   The most cost effective program would be the one with the lowest cost-benefit ratio among various programs competing for a given amount of funds.

cost of goods sold (COGS)   The direct costs of producing revenue, burdened by closely associated indirect costs. Also, beginning inventory plus purchases minus ending inventory. Often called cost of sales or cost of revenue.

cost pool   A grouping of costs for the purpose of allocation to, or identification with particular cost centers, products, or services. Common cost pools are various overhead costs, general and administrative costs, and corporate costs.

cost-volume formula   A cost function in the form of

$$Y = A + Bx$$

Where $Y =$ the semivariable (or mixed) costs to be broken up

$A = 5$ the fixed cost component

$B = 5$ the variable rate per unit of x

The formula is used for cost prediction and flexible budgeting purposes.

cost-volume-profit analysis   *See* Contribution Margin Analysis

current assets   Cash and those assets that will be converted into cash within a year.

current liabilities   Debts and payments that are due within a year.

current ratio   The ratio of current assets to current liabilities.

days inventory   The amount of inventory relative to the cost of goods sold, expressed in "days" typically as 365 times inventory divided by annual cost of goods sold.

days payables   The amount of payables relative to total material purchased, expressed in "days" typically as 365 times accounts payable divided by annual material purchases.

days receivables   The amount of accounts receivable relative to revenue, expressed in "days" typically as 365 times accounts receivable divided by annual revenue.

decision support system (DSS)   A branch of the broadly defined Management Information System (MIS). It is an information system that provides answers to problems and that integrates the decision-maker into the system as a component. The system utilizes such quantitative techniques as regression and financial planning modeling. DSS software furnishes support to the accountant in the decision-making process.

delphi method   A qualitative forecasting method that seeks to use the judgement of experts systematically in arriving at a forecast of what future events will be or when they may occur. It brings together a group of experts who have access to each other's opinions in an environment where no majority opinion is disclosed.

depreciation   The gradual decline in value of an asset because of use or age; the expense arising therefrom.

direct cost   Cost directly associated with production of specific revenue.

direct labor budget   A schedule for expected labor cost. Expected labor cost is dependent upon expected production volume (production budget). Labor requirements are based on production volume multiplied by direct labor hours per unit. Direct labor hours needed for production are then multiplied by direct labor hours per unit. Direct labor hours needed for production are then multiplied by direct labor cost per hour to derive budgeted direct labor costs.

direct materials budget   A budget that shows how much material will be required for production and how much material must be bought to meet this production requirement. The purchase depends on both expected usage of materials and inventory levels.

disbursement   An amount of cash paid out.

discounted cash flow (DCF) techniques   Methods of selecting and ranking investment proposals, such as the net present value (NPV) and internal rate of return (IRR) methods where time value of money is taken into account.

efficiency variance   Difference between inputs (materials and labor) that were actually used and inputs that should have been used (i.e., standard quantity of inputs allowed for actual production), multiplied by the standard price per unit.

equity   The accounting value of a business, equal to assets minus liabilities. Commonly used interchangeably with book value, net asset value, net worth, and shareholders' equity.

factory overhead budget   A schedule of all expected manufacturing costs except for direct material and direct labor. Factory overhead items include indirect material, indirect labor, factory rent, and factory insurance. Factory overhead may be variable, fixed, or short-run forecasting.

financial budget   A budget that embraces the impacts of the financial decisions of the firm. It is a plan including a budgeted balance sheet, which shows the effects of planned operations and capital investments on assets, liabilities, and equities. It also includes a cash budget, which forecasts the flow of cash and other funds in the business.

financial projection   An essential element of planning that is the basis for budgeting activities and estimating future financing needs of a firm. Financial projections (forecasts) begin with forecasting sales and their related expenses.

financial statement   An accounting document showing the financial status of a business or the results of business activity.

finished goods inventory   The portion of inventory that consists of goods and products ready for sale.

fiscal year (FY)   The twelve-month period for which financial results are prepared and reported. It may be different, by company choice, from the calendar year.

fixed assets   Assets which will extend beyond the current accounting period: machinery, land, buildings, and the like.

fixed cost   A cost that does not vary with revenue over a relevant range of revenue amount.

fixed overhead variance   The difference between actual fixed overhead incurred and fixed overhead applied to production.

flash report   A report that provides the highlights of key information promptly to the responsible non-financial manager. An example is an exception report, such as performance reports, that highlight favorable or unfavorable variances. A flash report allows managers to take a corrective action for an unfavorable variance.

flexible (variable) budget   A budget based on different levels of activity. It is an extremely useful tool for comparing the actual cost incurred to the cost allowable for the activity level achieved. It is dynamic in nature rather than static.

forecast   1. A projection or an estimate of future sales, revenue, earnings, or costs; 2. A projection of future financial position and operating results of an organization.

fringe benefits   Payments by a company for things of value to, and for the use of, employees, such as insurance and vacations.

general and administrative expense (G&A)   Cost necessary to operate a business but not associated directly with the production of revenue, such as the cost of accounting.

goodness-of-fit   A degree to which a model fits the observed data. In a regression analysis, the goodness-of-fit is measured by the coefficient of determination (R-squared).

gross margin   A measure of profitability equal to revenue minus cost of goods sold divided by revenue. (The term is sometimes used for only the dollar amount of revenue minus costs of goods sold, although the latter is more often called gross profit).

indirect cost   Cost not directly related or assignable to the production of specific revenue, products, or services.

internal rate of return (IRR)   The rate earned on a proposal. It is the rate of interest that equates the initial investment (I) with the present value (PV) of future cash flows. That is, at IRR

I = PV, or NPV (net present value) = 0.

investment center   A responsibility center within an organization that has control over revenue, cost, and investment funds. It is a profit center whose performance is evaluated on the basis of the return earned on invested capital.

judgmental (qualitative) forecast   A forecasting method that brings together, in an organized way, personal judgments about the process being analyzed.

labor efficient variance   The difference between the amount of labor time that should have been used and the labor that was actually used, multiplied by the standard rate.

labor rate (price) variance   Any deviation from standard in the average hourly rate paid to workers, multiplied by the hours worked.

labor variance   The difference between the actual costs of direct labor and the standard costs of direct labor. Labor variance is divided into labor rate variance and labor efficiency variance.

long-range budget   Projections that cover more than one fiscal year. It is also called strategic budgeting. The five-year budget plan is the most commonly used.

management by exception   A management concept or policy by which management devotes its time to investigating only those situations in which actual results differ significantly from planned results. The idea is that management should spend its valuable time concentrating on more important items (such as shaping of the company's future strategic course).

management control system   A system under which managers assure that resources are obtained and used effectively and efficiently in the accomplishment of the organization's goals.

management information system (MIS)   A computer-based or manual system which transforms data into information useful in the support of decision making.

margin   A percentage measure of profitability relative to revenue. (Also sometimes used as the dollar amount of revenue minus selected costs.)

markup   A measure of profitability equal to revenue minus costs (typically, direct cost or purchase cost) divided by that same cost. (The term is sometimes used for the dollar amount of revenue minus cost.)

master (comprehensive) budget   A plan of activities expressed in monetary terms of the assets, equities, revenues, and costs which will be involved in carrying out the plans. Simply put, a master budget is a set of projected or planned financial statements.

materials price variance   The difference between what is paid for a given quantity of materials and what should have been paid, multiplied by actual quantity of materials used.

materials quantity (usage) variance   The difference between the actual quantity of materials used in production and the standard quantity of materials allowed for actual production, multiplied by the standard price per unit.

materials variance   The difference between the actual costs of materials and the standard costs of materials. Material variance is divided into materials price variance and materials quantity variance.

moving average   For a time series, an average that is updated as new information is received. With the moving average, the manager employs the most recent observations to calculate an average, which is used as the forecast for the next period.

naïve forecast   Forecasts obtained with a minimal amount of effort and data manipulation, based solely on the most recent information available. One such naïve method would be to use the most recent datum available as the future forecast.

net present value (NPV)   The difference between the present value (PV) of all cash inflows generated by the project and the amount of the initial value (I).

net present value method   A method widely used for evaluating investment projects. Under the net present value method, the present value (PV) of all cash inflows from the project is compared to the initial investment (I).

operational (operating) budget   A budget that embraces the impacts of operating decisions. It contains forecasts of sales, net income, the cost of goods sold, selling and administrative expenses, and other expenses.

overhead   Indirect costs that are often used to describe indirect cost in a particular function or activity, closely associated with production of revenue but not assignable to a particular product or service. Typical classes of overhead are manufacturing labor overhead, manufacturing material overhead, engineering overhead, and service overhead.

overhead pool   A cost pool for a particular type of overhead.

overhead rate   The percentage rate at which a particular overhead cost is added to particular direct cost, calculated by dividing the applicable overhead cost by the direct cost.

payback period   The length of time required to recover the initial amount of a capital investment.

percentage of completion   A method of accounting, used for large and long contracts, that recognizes revenue during the course of the contract in accordance with the proportion of work that has been completed, or cost that has been incurred.

period cost   Cost expensed during the same period in which it is incurred.

pro forma balance sheet   A Budgeted Balance Sheet.

pro forma income statement   A Budgeted Income Statement.

production budget   A schedule for expected units to be produced. It sets forth the units expected to be manufactured to satisfy budgeted sales and inventory requirements. Expected production volume is determined by adding desired ending inventory to planned sales and then subtracting beginning inventory.

profit center   The unit in an organization that is responsible for revenues earned and costs incurred. The manager of a profit center has control over revenues and costs, as well as attempts to maximize profit.

profit planning   A process of developing a profit plan which outlines the planned sales revenues and expenses and the net income or loss for a time period. Profit planning requires preparation of a master budget and various analyses for risk and "what-if" scenarios. Tools for profit planning include the cost-volume-profit (CVP) analysis and budgeting.

profit variance   A difference between actual profit and budgeted profit. Profit, whether it is gross profit in absorption costing or contribution margin in direct costing, is affected by sales price, sales volume, and costs.

profit-volume chart   A chart that determines how profits vary with changes in volume. Profits are plotted on the vertical axis while units of output are shown on the horizontal axis.

profitability index The ratio of the total present value (PV) of future cash inflows to the initial investment (I).

projected (budgeted) balance sheet A schedule for expected assets, liabilities, and stockholders' equity. It projects a company's financial position at the end of the budgeting year. A budgeted balance sheet discloses unfavorable financial conditions that management may want to avoid, serves as a final check on the mathematical accuracy of all other budgets, and highlights future resources and obligations.

projected (budgeted) income statement A summary of various component projections of revenues and expenses for the budget period. It indicates the expected net income for the period.

quantitative forecasting A technique that can be applied when information about the past is available, if that information can be quantified, and if the pattern included in past information can be assumed to continue into the future.

raw materials inventory The portion of inventory that consists of purchased material that will be used to make revenue-producing products, and the purchase cost of that material.

residual A synonym for error. It is calculated by subtracting the forecast value from the actual value to give a residual or error value for each forecast period.

responsibility accounting The collection, summarization, and reporting of financial information about various decision centers (responsibility centers) throughout an organization.

responsibility center A unit in the organization which has control over costs, revenues, or investment funds. Responsibility centers are classified as cost centers, revenues centers, profit centers, and investment centers.

return on assets Profit divided by assets, a measure of the percentage of the value of its assets that is earned by the business.

return on capital Profit divided by capital, a measure of the percentage of total investment earned by the business.

return on equity Profit divided by equity, a measure of the percentage of the owners' investment earned by the business.

return on investment For an entire business, synonymous with return on capital. For a given capital investment within a business, the ratio of the profit or cash flow that will result to the amount of the investment.

risk analysis The process of measuring and analyzing the risks associated with financial and investment decisions. Risk refers to the variability of expected returns (earnings or cash flows).

sales budget An operating plan for a period expressed in terms of sales volume and selling prices for each class of product or service. Preparation of a sales budget is the starting point in budgeting, because sales volume influences nearly all other items.

sales forecasting A projection or prediction of future sales. It is the foundation for the quantification of the entire business plan and the master budget. Sales forecasts serve as a basis for capacity planning, budgeting, production and inventory planning, manpower planning, and purchasing planning.

sales price variance   The difference between the actual number of units sold and the budgeted number, multiplied by the budgeted selling price per unit. It is also called sales quantity variance.

simulation   An attempt to represent a real life system via a model to determine how a change in one or more variable affects the rest of the system. It is also called "what-if" analysis.

simulation model   A "what-if" model that attempts to simulate the effects of alternative management policies and assumptions about the firm's external environment. It is basically a tool for management's laboratory.

standard cost of sales   Calculated, anticipated cost of a product, used as expense when sale of that product is recorded on the P&L.

standard cost system   A system by which production activities are recorded at standard costs and variances from actual costs are isolated.

standard direct cost   Production or operating costs that are carefully pre-determined. A standard cost is a target that should be attained.

standard hours allowed   The standard time that should have been used to manufacture actual units of output during a period. It is obtained by multiplying actual units of production by the standard labor time.

standard labor rate   The standard rate for direct labor that includes not only base wages earned but also an allowance for fringe benefits and other labor-related costs.

standard materials price   The standard price per unit for direct materials. It reflects the final, delivered cost of the materials, net of any discounts taken.

standard quantity allowed   The standard amount of materials that should have been used to manufacture units of output during a period. It is obtained by multiplying actual units of production by the standard material quantity per unit.

static (fixed) budget   A budget based on one level of activity (e.g., one particular volume of sales or production).

strategic planning   The implementation of an organization's objectives. Strategic planning decisions will have long-term impacts on the organization while operational decisions are day-to-day in nature.

variable cost   Cost that varies with revenue.

variable overhead efficiency variance   The difference in actual and budgeted variable overhead costs that are incurred due to inefficient use of indirect materials and indirect labor.

variable overhead spending variance   The difference in actual and budgeted overhead costs that result from price changes in indirect materials and indirect labor and insufficient control of costs of specific overhead items.

variance   The difference of revenues, costs, and profit from the planned amounts. One of the most important phases of responsibility accounting is establishing standards in costs, revenues, and profit and establishing performance by comparing actual amounts with the standard amounts. The differences are calculated for each responsibility center, analyzed, and unfavorable variances are investigated for possible remedial action.

working capital   Current assets minus current liabilities.

work in progress inventory   The portion of inventory that consists of partially completed products, and the associated burdened labor and material costs.

zero-based budgeting (ZBB)   A planning and budgeting tool that uses cost/benefit analysis of projects and functions to improve resource allocation in an organization. Traditional budgeting tends to concentrate on the incremental changes from the previous year. It assumes that the previous year's activities and programs are essential and must be continued. Under zero-base budgeting, however, cost and benefit estimates are built up from scratch (from the zero level) and must be justified.

INDEX

A

actuals. *See* Actual amounts
actual amounts (actuals), used in
 testing, 170
Adaytum Planning, 105
Adaytum Software, 105
alerts, 95, 107
allocations, 86, 95, 107
American Furniture Company, 177–81
American Pharmaceutical Association,
 181–84
Analysis
 qualitative, 19
 quantitative, 18
analytical features, 83–84, 96–97
application service providers (ASP),
 98–99, 143–48
 selection criteria, 146–47
 when to consider, 145–46
ASCII, 66, 74
ASP. *See* application service providers
assumptions, 80, 86

B

Balanced Scorecard, 97
benchmarking, 94
Best! Imperativ Planning &
 Analysis, 104
Best-of-breed budgeting software,
 69–77, 79–101, 103–7
 Buyers guide, 103–7
 combining with the use of
 Excel,112–13
 compared to Excel, 110–11
 evaluation of, 133
Big Five consulting companies, 132
Big Five firms. *See* Implementation,
 using a Big Five firm
Blue Cross of Northeastern Pennsylva-
 nia, 184–87
Bonneville Power Administration,
 187–90
Bottom-up budgeting. *See* Budgeting &
 planning processes, bottom-up
Budget Maestro, 106

285